Harnessing Lin〈 　 　 　 　...
to Improve Education

RETHINKING EDUCATION

VOLUME 5

Series Editors:

Dr Marie Martin

Dr Gerry Gaden

Dr Judith Harford

PETER LANG

Oxford · Bern · Berlin · Bruxelles · Frankfurt am Main · New York · Wien

Androula Yiakoumetti (ed.)

Harnessing Linguistic Variation to Improve Education

PETER LANG

Oxford · Bern · Berlin · Bruxelles · Frankfurt am Main · New York · Wien

Bibliographic information published by Die Deutsche Nationalbibliothek.
Die Deutsche Nationalbibliothek lists this publication in the Deutsche
Nationalbibliografie; detailed bibliographic data is available on the Internet
at http://dnb.d-nb.de.

A catalogue record for this book is available from the British Library.

Library of Congress Cataloging-in-Publication Data:

Harnessing linguistic variation to improve education / Androula
Yiakoumetti.
    p. cm. -- (Rethinking education; 5)
  Includes bibliographical references and index.
  ISBN 978-3-0343-0726-0 (alk. paper)
  1. Language and languages--Variation. 2. Linguistic change. 3.
Linguistic minorities. 4. Multilingualism. 5. Multicultural education.
6. Education, Bilingual. 7. Language and education. I. Yiakoumetti,
Androula, 1976-
  P120.V37H37 2012
  306.44'6--dc23

                              2012011043

ISSN 1662-9949
ISBN 978-3-0343-0726-0

© Peter Lang AG, International Academic Publishers, Bern 2012
Hochfeldstrasse 32, CH-3012 Bern, Switzerland
info@peterlang.com, www.peterlang.com, www.peterlang.net

Printed in Germany

Contents

ANDROULA YIAKOUMETTI

1 Rethinking Linguistic Diversity in Education

This volume celebrates linguistic diversity. It brings together work carried out in diverse geographic and linguistic contexts including Africa, Asia, Australia, Canada, the Caribbean, Europe and the United States and highlights the efforts undertaken in these contexts to incorporate linguistic diversity into education and to harness it for learners' benefit.

Research clearly demonstrates that incorporating linguistic diversity into education can lead to social, cultural, pedagogical, cognitive and linguistic advancement. In spite of this evidence, many educational contexts around the world are characterized by an unwillingness to commit to change and a stance that argues for exclusive use of a prescribed standard variety in the classroom. It is not unusual for such settings to indirectly discourage inclusion of varieties other than the prescribed standard, to ignore the existence of these varieties, or even to ban them from the classroom. Naturally, limiting the resources that learners from diverse linguistic backgrounds are allowed to use in the classroom tends to mitigate their experience of a meaningful education.

The volume challenges the largely anachronistic ideology that promotes exclusive use of an educational monolingual standard variety and advocates the use of aboriginal/indigenous languages, minority languages, nonstandard varieties (i.e. regional, ethnic, and social varieties) and contact languages (i.e. pidgins and creoles) in formal education. Permitting the use of such varieties is a critical step towards equal linguistic rights (Skutnabb-Kangas and Phillipson, 2008).

Together, the chapters of the volume serve as a forum for exploring the implications of linguistic diversity for education. Historical and current practices for including linguistic diversity in education are addressed by considering specific bidialectal, bilingual and multilingual educational initiatives. In spite of the many geographical and linguistic settings addressed in this volume, there is a unifying theme: linguistic diversity exists worldwide but it is very rarely utilized optimally for students' benefit. When it is used, either in the form of isolated research studies or governmental initiatives, findings systematically point to the many benefits gained by linguistically-diverse students.

Thirty-five years ago, Fishman (1977) asserted that a sociolinguistic perspective on linguistic diversity in education was welcome and, fifteen years ago, Cummins (1997) warned that issues related to linguistic diversity were still at the margins of educational reform in many countries. Sadly, this marginalization is still present today and the need for a sociolinguistic perspective is still pressing. This is especially so as our world becomes more globalized and an increasing number of communities around the world face the impending loss of their linguistic varieties (Romaine, 2006). This volume goes beyond an exploration of the advantages and disadvantages of a linguistically-diverse education. The contributors unanimously make the case in favour of the benefits derived from a linguistically-diverse education.

In line with previous research, many of the contributors highlight the key role of language educators, the importance of teacher training, and the need for creating educational programmes which are informed by the specific linguistic landscapes in which they are to be employed. Some also emphasize the importance of language attitudes and the benefits derived when parents and other community members are involved in students' language education. Such involvement provides assurance that educational institutions and the wider community are in constant dialogue, listening and informing each other. Also, it ensures that any language initiative which promotes linguistic diversity and is implemented in either the school or the wider community does not remain isolated because each setting can scaffold the other.

The following issues are addressed with special reference to educational contexts:

1. indigenous mother tongues in post-colonial nations,
2. non-native Englishes,
3. minority languages,
4. social, ethnic, and regional varieties, and
5. contact languages.

Stephen May's chapter (Chapter 2) takes a prominent position in the volume as it serves as a direct call for rethinking the way in which linguistic diversity in education is approached. While this call primarily conveys an important message, it also represents a lucid rationale for the publication of this volume within the series *Rethinking Education*. May warns us that education faces a rapid and significant retrenchment of multiculturalism. Two reasons are given for this retrenchment: the pluralist dilemma and nation-state organization. He asserts that nation-states worldwide seek to reassert notions of commonality at the expense of the institutional recognition of cultural and linguistic diversity. He explains that most nation-states aspire to cultural and linguistic homogeneity and that only very few formal multilingual nation-states exist. May critically analyses current educational approaches towards linguistically-diverse students and explains that much multicultural policy recognizes the right to be different and to be respected for it but, crucially, policies do not necessarily favour maintenance of a distinct language and culture. Looking at current approaches in minority language education, May concludes that much is left to be desired. Whilst acknowledging that education alone cannot change entrenched societal attitudes, May emphasizes that education can 'be in the vanguard of reconceptualizing a more plurilingual state'.

May's chapter rings alarm bells as it portrays a rather gloomy picture for minority-language students. Globalization and transnationalism are, no doubt, enhancing linguistic diversity in schools yet current monolingual-education approaches only serve to disadvantage minority-language speakers. It is for this reason that education should be reconsidered such that it promotes plurilingual approaches. May's concerns and suggestions are followed by a chapter which also deals with transnational settings. In essence, the authors of Chapter 3 put into practice May's suggestions and recommend an innovative pedagogical approach (translanguaging) in an effort to demonstrate the benefits that minority-language students can gain from an education which has at its heart a dynamic conceptualization of bilingualism/multilingualism.

Ofelia García, Nelson Flores and Heather Homonoff Woodley (Chapter 3) focus on transglossia which is the many language practices of different transnational groups in functional interrelationship. They argue that, traditionally, bilingualism has falsely been described using monoglossic classification, terminology and principles, and they emphasize its dynamism. Their proposed pedagogy for transglossia and dynamic bilingualism, the pedagogy of translanguaging, builds on the strengths of language-minority students who are emergent bilinguals. Drawing on the practices of teachers, the authors investigate the ways in which a translanguaging pedagogy supports the English instruction of Spanish-speaking adolescents who recently immigrated to the United States. García, Flores and Woodley argue that translanguaging supports the contextualization of key words and concepts, the development of metalinguistic awareness, and the creation of affective bonds between students and teachers. Crucially, the authors also argue that translanguaging is possible across the continuum of bilingualism and thus does not require an idealized bilingual teacher with balanced competence in two languages.

Suresh Canagarajah, Madhav Kafle and Yumi Matsumoto (Chapter 4) also work within transnational frameworks and the role of the English language. They review various approaches for teaching World Englishes and suggest that students' attitudes towards local varieties of English should receive special attention as a copious literature demonstrates that students' attitudes remain negative. They go on to highlight the need to empower non-native teachers of English, many of whom also demonstrate a preference for native standard varieties. The authors conclude that language awareness should be promoted among students such that they become competent in negotiating the diverse English varieties that they will encounter in their everyday life in transnational settings.

Continuing with the exploration of the role of English, Sandra Lee McKay's chapter (Chapter 5) complements that of Canagarajah, Kafle and Matsumoto in that it adds empirical findings from work carried out in Asia and Africa. Specifically, McKay explores the role of English as an international language by focussing on two English language education policies: one in South Africa and one in Japan. She explains that, although warranted, multilingualism is not promoted in those contexts due to attitudes regarding English. South Africa looks inwards, advocating the use of English for economic advancement and inter-ethnic relations. Japan looks outwards, advocating the use of English because it is concerned with its international role as a nation. McKay's explanations accord well with the assertions of May (Chapter 2). Both authors emphasize that, although many settings are ripe for multilingualism, there is insufficient support for embracing the linguistic and cultural heritage of minority-language speakers. McKay concludes by suggesting that pedagogies of English as an international language must affirm the value of multilingualism if English is to spread in a manner which preserves linguistic and cultural diversity. She says that this affirmation can be achieved by utilizing the local linguistic landscape when devising curricula and by presenting a realistic account of the value of English learning.

Linda Tsung (Chapter 6) provides a valuable re-iteration of McKay's conclusions albeit in the entirely dissimilar context of the Chinese Yunnan province. She asserts that only with appropriate multilingual education for ethnic minorities can the Han majority prosper and develop harmoniously together with the ethnic minority communities. Multilingual education in the context of this chapter refers to schooling in which students' minority-language mother tongues are used alongside standard Chinese (Putonghua). Tsung discusses a number of challenges faced by multilingual education (such as the poor availability and quality of appropriate textbooks and a shortage of teachers) and echoes McKay in suggesting that future minority language policy needs to integrate national policies and local needs.

Peter Garrett, Josep M. Cots, David Lasagabaster and Enric Llurda (Chapter 7) explore the self-reported attitudes of tertiary-level students towards linguistic diversity and minority-language maintenance by focussing on three diverse bilingual contexts: the Basque Autonomous Community, Catalonia and Wales. Specifically, the authors compare the attitudes of students with reference to the promotion of the minority language (i.e. Basque, Catalan and Welsh) on the one hand and the drive towards internationalization on the other. Of course, these (very often opposing) forces (i.e. promotion of minority languages versus internationalization) are also of concern to other contributors (e.g. May and McKay). Quantitative analysis of students' questionnaires focussed on the effects of the sociolinguistic context, sex, the degree type the students pursued, and knowledge of minority language. In general, students' attitudes reflected the reality of their respective wider university sociolinguistic contexts and were in accordance with attitudinal patterns recorded in previous studies. The authors draw optimism from the results as students are in favour of learning minority languages. These findings are especially welcome as they demonstrate a positive attitude towards linguistic diversity and maintenance of minority languages.

Nkonko M. Kamwangamalu (Chapter 8) revisits the much talked-about debate around the issue of the medium of instruction in Africa by drawing on insights from language economics, game theory, the tragedy of the commons, and language ecology. He discusses two ideologies with which African countries have been battling: the ideology of decolonization which favours the use of minoritized African languages as media of instruction and the ideology of development which favours instruction in the languages of former colonial powers. The author questions the predominance of these two extreme ideologies and calls for new policies which assign to indigenous African languages some of the advantages that are currently associated only with colonial languages. Kamwangamalu's chapter voices concerns which are also dealt with in chapters which follow it: chapters 10, 11 and 12, for instance, also directly or indirectly address the perennial issue of which languages should be used as media of instruction in linguistically-diverse communities.

Chapters 9 and 10 focus on dialectally-diverse students and education. Jessica Ball and Barbara May Hanford Bernhardt (Chapter 9) review research conducted primarily on First Nation English dialects in Canada and relate it to research carried out in other dialectally-diverse communities worldwide in an effort to emphasize the need for more investigation. They assert that new pedagogical approaches and assessments are needed for the understanding and support of dialectal students' learning experiences and highlight the importance of language-attitude change and teacher training. They also warn that nonstandard-speaking students are too often misdiagnosed as having language impairment. Ball and Bernhardt make a convincing case that, to produce successful students, there is a need for teachers and speech-language specialists to identify students' true language deficits such that these deficits can be appropriately targeted and subsequently alleviated.

Ian G. Malcolm and Adriano Truscott (Chapter 10) argue that the oppositional relationship between Standard Australian English and Aboriginal English (whereby the latter is subordinate to the former) inevitably invokes 'shame' in education. By focussing on three diverse schools (i.e. fringe metropolitan, fringe rural, and rural/remote), the authors investigate an excellent initiative of two-way bidialectal education which has been implemented in Western Australia. Findings revealed that factors such as time, retention of teaching staff, and community engagement are important for the success of such education. In all three schools, there was evidence of positive steps towards repertoire building. Drawing on empirical data, this chapter helps highlight the great benefits that can be gained from an education which embraces dialectal diversity and aims to enhance all children's linguistic and cultural experience.

The penultimate chapter of the volume sets out clear evidence for the benefits of incorporating linguistic variation into education. Jeff Siegel's chapter (Chapter 11) comes as an answer to all those (policy makers, teachers, parents, and students) who may have concerns about the benefits of incorporating students' familiar and very often undervalued linguistic varieties into education. Siegel provides a thorough review of teaching approaches which, to varying degrees, employ expanded pidgins or creoles to help expanded pidgin- or creole-speaking students acquire literacy and proficiency in the standard language of the educational system. He discusses instrumental approaches, English-as-a-second-language approaches, accommodation approaches, and awareness approaches by drawing on a variety of geographical and linguistic settings. He concludes that such approaches bring about many educational benefits such as increases in students' motivation, self-esteem, cognitive development, and acquisition of the valued standard language.

I conclude the volume by revisiting some of the key purported dangers of nonstandard dialectal varieties as they are said to primarily manifest themselves in formal education and in the workplace. Some of the issues with which I deal include dialect speakers' inferiority to standard speakers, dialectal interference in writing, prohibition of the dialect from formal education, and the employability of dialect speakers. The reason for choosing these specific issues is that there is still a wide discrepancy between research findings and widespread public opinion. I assert that, when designing successful education policies, research should be consulted appropriately and unjustified attitudes towards linguistic variation should be put aside, such that linguistically-diverse students can reap the benefits of multidialectism/ multilingualism. This chapter brings the volume to an end and provides a re-iterative tone, as it calls for a rethinking of educational policies, just as May did in the first substantive chapter (Chapter 2).

An important common thread deserves special note: all contributors make the case that an education which incorporates linguistic diversity can be only beneficial. Across the diverse linguistic and educational settings that are covered, it is agreed that incorporating linguistic diversity into education requires a great deal of effort on the part of governments, communities, policy makers, educators, and learners. The consensus is that research which addresses linguistic diversity via education needs to continue until we see nonstandard varieties, minority languages, and indigenous mother tongues enjoying a new vitality. Education has the ability to bring about such change and also holds the key to maintaining it. It is thus time to rethink education as pedagogical initiatives based on linguistic equality have obvious advantages for students, educators, and the wider community in general. It is hoped that this volume will help to pave the way towards more appropriate pedagogical policies and approaches and will encourage the development of new curricula and learning materials that harness linguistic diversity.

References

Cummins, J. (1997). Cultural and Linguistic Diversity in Education: A Mainstream Issue?, *Educational Review*, 49 (2), 105–114.

Fishman, J.A. (1977). 'Standard' versus 'Dialect' in Bilingual Education: An Old Problem in a New Context, *The Modern Language Journal*, 61 (7), 315–325.

Romaine, S. (2006). Planning for the Survival of Linguistic Diversity, *Language Policy*, 5 (4), 441–473.

Skutnabb-Kangas, T. and Phillipson, R. (2008). A Human Rights Perspective on Language Ecology. In A. Creese, P. Martin and N.H. Hornberger (eds), *Encyclopedia of Language and Education 2nd edition: Volume 9 Ecology of Language*, 3–14. New York: Springer.

STEPHEN MAY

2 Educational Approaches to Minorities: Context, Contest and Opportunities

Introduction

Just over a decade ago, the prospects of acknowledging ethnic, cultural and linguistic diversity more directly and positively within education seemed within grasp. At that time, multicultural and bilingual educational approaches were increasingly commonplace in modern liberal democracies (May, 1999, 2002; Banks and Banks, 2004). Similarly, multiculturalism appeared to be gaining widespread acceptance as a public policy response to the burgeoning diversity of state populations in an era of globalization and increasing transmigration (Kymlicka, 1998, 2001, 2007). Both developments built upon a history of nearly fifty years of advocacy of multicultural and bilingual education, and wider state policies of inclusion for minority groups, which had its genesis in the US Civil Rights movement but had extended to other western countries, including Canada, Britain, Australia and New Zealand. Even critics of multiculturalism conceded its impact on public policy, particularly within education – a wearied resignation most notably captured in Nathan Glazer's (1998) phrase, 'we are all multiculturalists now'. Multiculturalism, at least in Glazer's view, had finally 'won' because the issue of greater public representation for minority groups was increasingly commonplace in discussions of democracy and representation in the civic realm – including, centrally, within schools (see, for example, Goldberg, 1994; Taylor, 1994; Kymlicka, 1995).

How times have changed. Over the last decade, and particularly post 9/11, we have seen a rapid and significant retrenchment of multiculturalism as public policy, particularly within education. In the United States, a

burgeoning standards and testing movement, spearheaded by (2001) No
Child Left Behind, has replaced earlier attention to racial and ethnic diversity (May and Sleeter, 2010). Decades of affirmative action and related civil
rights advances for African Americans have been dismantled, most notably
in relation to access to higher education (Kellough, 2006). The related
provision of bilingual education, particularly for Latino/a Americans, has
also been severely circumscribed, and in some US states actually proscribed,
by legislation promoting a monolingual English language philosophy as
a prerequisite for US citizenship (Crawford, 2008; May, 2012: Ch. 6).
Meanwhile, across Europe, multiculturalism as public policy is in apparent full retreat, as European states increasingly assert that minority groups
'integrate' or accept dominant social, cultural linguistic and (especially)
religious mores as the price of ongoing citizenship (Modood, 2007). Again,
education has been a key focus, with bilingual and multicultural education
programmes facing significant retrenchment across Europe as a result.

How can this widespread retrenchment of multicultural and bilingual
education be explained, particularly after a near fifty-year period within
which significant advances had seemingly been achieved? In what follows,
I argue that two key underlying reasons for the apparent ease with which
such multicultural / bilingual education initiatives have been dismantled
rest with what Brian Bullivant (1981) has described as the *pluralist dilemma*
and a related ideology of nation-state organization which presupposes the
subsumption of distinct minority languages and cultures, and associated
public monolingualism. Let me look briefly at each of these in turn.

The pluralist dilemma

The pluralist dilemma involves the often-difficult balancing act between
maintaining cohesion on the one hand and recognizing pluralism on the
other within modern nation-states. As Bullivant observes, it is 'the problem
of reconciling the diverse political claims of constituent groups and individuals in a pluralist society *with the claims of the nation-state as a whole*'

(1981: x; my emphasis); what he elsewhere describes as the competing aims of 'civism' and 'pluralism'. In an earlier analysis, Schermerhorn has described these countervailing social and cultural forces as *centripetal* and *centrifugal* tendencies. As he observes:

> Centripetal tendencies refer both to cultural trends such as acceptance of common values, styles of life etc., as well as structural features like increased participation in a common set of groups, associations, and institutions ... Conversely, centrifugal tendencies among subordinate groups are those that foster separation from the dominant group or from societal bonds in one way or another. Culturally this most frequently means retention and presentation of the group's distinctive tradition in spheres like language, religion, recreation etc. (1970: 81)

How then can the tensions arising from the pluralist dilemma best be resolved in the social and political arena? Drawing on political theory, two contrasting approaches have been adopted in response to this central question, which Gordon (1978, 1981) has described as 'liberal pluralism' and 'corporate pluralism'. Liberal pluralism, exemplified in the seminal contribution of John Rawls (1971), is characterized by the absence, even prohibition, of any national or ethnic minority group[1] possessing separate standing before the law or government. Its central tenets can be traced back to the French Revolution and Rousseau's conception of the modern polity as comprising three inseparable features: freedom (non-domination), the

---

1 Drawing on Will Kymlicka's (1995) seminal work, national and ethnic minority groups can be distinguished as follows. National minorities are those groups that have always been associated historically with a particular territory, but have been subject to colonization, conquest, or confederation and, consequently, now have only minority status within a particular nation-state. These groups include, for example, the Welsh in Britain, Catalans and Basques in Spain, Bretons in France, Québécois in Canada, and some Latino groups (such as Puerto Ricans) in the US, to name but a few. National minorities also include the world's indigenous peoples who have been subject to the same historical processes, but often at much greater cost. Ethnic minorities, in contrast, have migrated from their country of origin to a new host nation-state, or in the case of refugees have been the subject of forced relocation. For further discussion of the implications of this distinction for language rights, see May (2012).

absence of differentiated roles, and a very tight common purpose. On this view, the margin for recognizing ethnic, cultural and linguistic differences within the modern nation-state is very small (Taylor, 1994). In contrast, corporate pluralism or multiculturalism, as it is now more commonly described, involves the recognition of minority groups as legally constituted entities, on the basis of which, and depending on their size and influence, economic, social and political awards are allocated.

It is clear, however, that for most commentators the merits of liberal pluralism significantly outweigh those of a group-rights or multiculturalist approach. In effect, the answer to the pluralist dilemma has been consistently to favor civism over pluralism. On this basis, the 'claims of the nation-state as a whole' – emphasizing the apparently inextricable interconnections between social cohesion and national homogeneity – have invariably won the day over more pluralist conceptions of the nation-state where ethnic, linguistic and cultural differences *between different groups* are accorded some degree of formal recognition. As such, formal differentiation within the nation-state on the grounds of minority group association is rejected as inimical to the individualistic and meritocratic tenets of liberal democracy. Where countenanced at all, alternative ethnic, cultural or linguistic affiliations should be restricted solely to the private domain since the formal recognition of such alternative collective identities is viewed as undermining personal and political autonomy, and fostering social and political fragmentation. As the political philosopher, Will Kymlicka observes, 'the near-universal response by liberals has been one of active hostility to minority rights ... schemes which single out minority cultures for special measures ... appear irremediably unjust, a disguise for creating or maintaining ... ethnic privilege' (1989: 4). Any deviation from the strict principles of universal political citizenship and individual rights is seen as the first step down the road to apartheid. Or so it seems. The resulting liberal consensus is well illustrated by Brian Bullivant himself:

> Certain common institutions essential for the well-being and smooth functioning
> of the nation-state as *a whole* must be maintained: common language, common
> political system, common economic market system and so on. Cultural pluralism
> can operate at the level of the *private*, rather than public, concerns such as use of

ethnic [sic] language in the home ... But, the idea that maintaining these aspects of ethnic life and encouraging the maintenance of ethnic groups almost in the sense of ethnic enclaves will assist their ability to cope with the political realities of the nation-state is manifestly absurd. (1981: 232; emphases in original)

These emphases explain why multicultural and bilingual education initiatives now face such significant retrenchment. In short, nation-states around the world are currently seeking to reassert notions of commonality and civism *at the specific expense* of the institutional recognition of cultural and linguistic diversity, aka multiculturalism. The latter is constructed, pejoratively, as a threat to the state, as unnecessarily destabilizing and undermining of social cohesion. As a consequence, the hard-fought advances for minority groups to cultural and linguistic rights and recognition are now at serious risk.

Nation-state organization and the role of language

In addressing the question of why this apparent consensus on the pluralist dilemma is so strongly in favor of cohesion at the expense of pluralism, we also need to examine the origins of modern nation-states themselves, and the public role of language(s) within them.

Modern nation-state organization is actually a relatively recent historical phenomenon, deriving from the rise of political nationalism in Europe from the middle of the last millennium onwards. In particular, the French Revolution of 1789 and its aftermath are often credited with establishing the archetypal modern nation-state – a form of political organization not countenanced before, a polity represented and *unified* by a culturally and linguistically homogeneous civic realm (see Bauman and Briggs, 2003; May, 2012: Ch. 2 for further discussion). Previous forms of political organization had not required this degree of linguistic uniformity. For example, empires were quite happy for the most part to leave unmolested the plethora of cultures and languages subsumed within them – as long as taxes were paid, all was well. But in the politics of European nationalism – which, of course, was also to spread subsequently throughout the world – the idea of a single, common 'national' language (sometimes, albeit rarely, a number of national languages) quickly became the leitmotif of modern social and political organization.

How was this accomplished? Principally via the political machinery of these newly emergent European states, with mass education often playing a central role. As Gellner (1983) has outlined, the nationalist principle of 'one state, one culture, one language' saw the state, via its education system, increasingly identified with a specific language and culture – invariably, that of the majority ethnic group. The process of selecting and establishing a common national language as part of this wider process usually involved two key aspects: *legitimation* and *institutionalization* (Nelde, Strubell and Williams, 1996; May, 2012). Legitimation is understood to mean here the formal recognition accorded to the language by the nation-state – usually, by the constitutional and/or legislative benediction of official status. Accordingly, 'la langue officielle a partie liée avec l'État' (Bourdieu, 1982: 27) – the legitimate (or standard) language becomes an arm of the state. Institutionalization, perhaps the more important dimension, refers to the process by which the language comes to be accepted, or 'taken for granted' in a wide range of social, cultural and linguistic domains or contexts, both formal and informal. Both elements achieve a central requirement of the modern nation-state – that all its citizens adopt a common (usually singular) language and culture for use in the civic or public realm.

This establishment of chosen 'national' languages, however, usually also occurred alongside an often-punitive process of 'minoritizing' or 'dialectalizing' potentially competing language varieties within these same nation-states. These latter language varieties were, in effect, *positioned* by these newly formed states as languages of lesser political worth and value. Consequently, national languages came to be associated with modernity and progress, while their less fortunate counterparts were associated (conveniently) with tradition and obsolescence. More often than not, the latter were also specifically constructed as *obstacles* to the political project of nation-building – as threats to the 'unity' of the state. The inevitable consequence of this political imperative is the establishment of an ethnically exclusive and culturally and linguistically homogeneous nation-state – a realm from which minority languages and cultures are effectively banished. Indeed, this is the 'ideal' model to which most nation-states (and nationalist movements) still aspire – albeit in the face of a far more complex and contested multiethnic and multilingual reality (McGroarty, 2002, 2006; May, 2012). As Nancy Dorian summarizes it: 'it is the concept of the nation-state coupled with its official standard language ... that has in modern times posed the keenest threat to both the identities and the languages of small [minority] communities' (1998: 18). Florian Coulmas observes, even more succinctly, that 'the nation-state as it has evolved since the French Revolution is the natural enemy of minorities' (1998: 67).

Not surprisingly, perhaps, the result of the pre-eminence of this organizational principle of cultural and linguistic homogeneity is that there are only a very few *formal* multilingual nation-states in the world today – India and Switzerland being two notable examples. Where English is the dominant language, the prospects of formal multilingualism become even more remote, not least because of the additional position of English as the current world language or lingua mundi (Crystal, 2003; McCrum, 2011). In this respect, even nation-states such as Canada and Australia, which have adopted overtly multilingual policies in recent times, still continue to struggle to bring that multilingualism *effectively* into the public domain.

Situating educational approaches to diversity

Highlighting the pluralist dilemma and the principles of nation-state organization upon which it is predicated allows us to *situate* current educational trends towards culturally and linguistically diverse students within a more critical, diachronic and societal framework of analysis. In short, the adoption of particular educational approaches towards these students is inevitably framed within wider sociohistorical and sociopolitical influences that must be examined alongside the curricular and pedagogical specifics of the approaches in question. This allows us also to address directly another central, highly vexing, question – why the relative educational efficacy of various approaches for such students seems to have so little influence on educational decision-making processes. We see this clearly, for example, in the current moves to dismantle, or ignore, bilingual education approaches in many nation-states around the world, despite their well-attested educational effectiveness for culturally and linguistically diverse students (May, 2008, 2010). In contrast, assimilationist/monolingual educational approaches – despite an equally clearly established history of failing to educate such students successfully (Nieto and Bode, 2007; May and Sleeter, 2010) – continue to be the educational approach of choice. As Stacy Churchill observed of this a quarter of a century ago, an observation that still holds true today:

> Policy-making about the education of minorities must cope with an overriding fact: *almost every jurisdiction in the industrialized world is failing adequately to meet the educational needs of a significant number of members of linguistic and cultural minorities* ... (1986: 8; emphasis in original)

International measures of comparative academic achievement, such as the International Association for the Evaluation of Educational Achievement (IEA), Progress in International Reading and Literacy Study (PIRLS) and, perhaps most influentially, the OECD Program for International Student Assessment (PISA), have since regularly highlighted and confirmed this general pattern of differential achievement for culturally and linguistic minority groups, both within and across nation-states. In the end then, we can only explain this apparent conundrum via a wider sociopolitical, rather than solely educational, analysis.

In what follows, I employ Churchill's (1986) framework to this end, which, despite its longevity, still stands as one of the most comprehensive and informed accounts of its kind. Churchill outlines the six principal policy responses to the educational and language needs of minority groups within the OECD. While he suggests that the differences between the various stages are not always clear-cut, he attempts the following ranking (in ascending order) by the degree to which such policies recognize and incorporate their respective (minority) cultures and languages.

- *Stage 1 (Learning Deficit)*: where the educational disadvantages faced by minority groups are associated specifically and pejoratively with the use of the minority language. Accordingly, rapid transition to the majority language is advocated, the minority language is actively discouraged, and schooling occurs in and through 'submersion' in the majority language.
- *Stage 2 (Socially-Linked Learning Deficit)*: sometimes but not always arrived at concurrently with Stage 1, this stage associates a minority group's educational disadvantage with family status. Additional/ supplementary programmes are thus promoted which emphasize *adjustment* to the majority society.
- *Stage 3 (Learning Deficit from Social/Cultural Differences)*: most commonly associated with multicultural education, this stage assumes minority educational disadvantage arises from the inability of the majority society – particularly the education system – to recognize, accept and view positively the minority culture. However, a multicultural approach does not usually include a commensurate recognition of the minority language.
- *Stage 4 (Learning Deficit from Mother Tongue Deprivation)*: while still linked to the notion of deficit, the need for support of the minority language is accepted, at least as a transitional measure. Accordingly, transitional bilingual education programmes, which use a minority language in the initial years of schooling to facilitate the eventual transition to a majority language, are emphasized.
- *Stage 5 (Private Use Language Maintenance)*: recognizes the right of minorities groups to maintain and develop their languages and cultures in private life to ensure these are not supplanted by the dominant culture and language. Maintenance bilingual education programmes, which teach through a minority language over the course of schooling, are the most usual policy response here.
- *Stage 6 (Language Equality)*: the granting of full official status to a minority language within the nation-state. This would include separate language provision in a range of public institutions, including schools, and widespread recognition and use in a range of social, institutional and language domains.

Educating for the majority

Stage 1 represents assimilation in its starkest form. For reasons already well rehearsed, it has historically been the predominant approach adopted by modern nation-states, and the mass education systems to which they gave rise. Such 'unitary language policies' (Grant, 1997) ignore or actively suppress minority languages and cultures, and view the latter as both a threat to the social mobility of the minority individual, and to the majoritarian controlled institutions of the nation-state.

These policies had their heyday in the nineteenth century – at the peak of the nationalist nation-building project discussed earlier – and included numerous European and 'new world' examples. However, we still see examples of this astringent approach in contemporary times, including the proscription since 1997 of Tibetan in Chinese-controlled Tibet and the longstanding repression of the Kurdish language within Turkey. In the latter context, Kurdish-medium schools remain actively proscribed by the Turkish state, and Kurdish children do not even have the right to study Kurdish as a subject in school (Skutnabb-Kangas and Fernandes, 2008). Suffice it to say, that the examples of both Tibet and Turkey serve to reinforce Eli Kedourie's well-worn observation concerning the central link between education and state nationalism: 'On nationalist theory ... the purpose of education is not to transmit knowledge, traditional wisdom, and the ways devised by a society for attending to the common concerns; its purpose rather is wholly political, to bend the will of the young to the will of the nation' (1960: 83–84).

Of course, not all assimilationist policies are so overtly oppressive, and in recent years examples such as these have been limited for the most part to non-democratic, non-western and/or newly formed states. But the same aims can be achieved as effectively, if not more so, by stealth – a process that Skutnabb-Kangas (2000) has described as 'covert linguicide'. These policies are much more apparent in contemporary western democratic nation-states where 'submersion' or 'sink or swim' forms of language education – that is, requiring minority language speakers to be educated in the dominant language, come what may – continue to be widely promoted and practised.

One reason for this ongoing support of assimilationist education, aside from the apparent imperative of maintaining a common language and culture, is the still-popular conception that the 'family background' of ethnic minority students may be an obstacle to their educational and wider social mobility. This approach equates with Stage 2 of Churchill's typology and need not detain us long here since it is, in effect, no more than a modified form of assimilation. Language education policies that fall within this category may best be described as *compensatory*; that is, they aim to compensate for the supposed inadequacies of the minority student's 'family background' in order to address, and mitigate, the ongoing relative 'underachievement' of many ethnic minority students within schools.

The variables regarded as most salient with respect to family background vary but may include the immediate family environment, child-rearing practices, and/or the cultural and linguistic repertoires employed within the family (see Shields, Bishop and Mazawi, 2005; Valencia, 1997, 2010 for useful critical reviews). Whatever variables are focused upon, however, the starting premise is invariably one of cultural and linguistic 'deficit' in relation to majority group cultural and linguistic 'norms'. It follows from this view that the principal function of educational programmes is to facilitate and/or expedite the minority student's *adjustment* to 'mainstream' schooling and the cultural and linguistic mores of the dominant group, which such schooling invariably reflects. One of the most prominent examples of such programmes, launched in 1965 and still in use today, is the Head Start preschool programme in the US, aimed primarily at poor, black and Latino inner-city children. The more recent Sure Start programme (launched in 1998) is its British equivalent.

Stage 3 includes within it those policies and programmes that come under the rubric of 'multicultural education', broadly defined. As discussed at the start of this chapter, multicultural education has its origins in the late 1960s/early 1970s, when it arose as a specific policy response to the claims of minority groups, predominantly migrant groups, for greater recognition within education of their ethnic, cultural, religious and linguistic diversity. The (1978) Galbally Report, which introduced multiculturalism as public policy into Australia, clearly reflects this emphasis when it states: 'We are convinced that migrants have the right to maintain their cultural and racial [sic] identity and that it is clearly in the best interests of our nation that they should be encouraged and assisted to do so if they wish' (cited in Kane, 1997: 550).

The example of Australia highlights that multicultural education is most common and most prominent in those western nation-states that have regarded themselves historically as 'immigration societies' (Moodley, 1999) or 'polyethnic societies' (Kymlicka, 1995, 2001). In addition to Australia, these are most notably, the US, Canada and, to a lesser extent, Britain and New Zealand. Multicultural education continues to be widely practised in these nation-states at local and state level, while multiculturalism has actually come to be adopted as official public policy in both Australia (Hill and Allan, 2004; Clyne, 1998, 2005) and Canada (Kamboureli, 1998; Kymlicka, 1998; Joshee and Johnson, 2007).

Unlike the two preceding stages, multicultural education recognizes that the disadvantages faced by cultural and linguistic minorities are as much a systemic problem as they are a personal and/or familial one. In other words, we see in multicultural education the first glimmer of recognition concerning the historical role that education has played in the *institutionalized* devaluation and marginalization of minorities within the nation-state. In response, multicultural education offers the concept of 'cultural pluralism', by which the cultural values and practices of minorities come to be specifically recognized and included in the school curriculum. The central aim of this approach is to provide minority students with a positive conception of their social and cultural background in order, in turn, to foster their greater educational success.

The publication in Britain of the Swann Report (DES, 1985) exemplified this belief in the ability of cultural pluralism to effect educational change for minority students. However, the Swann Report was also to exemplify another central claim of multicultural education, namely the suggestion that cultural pluralism could in and of itself effect a more multicultural and, by implication, less discriminatory society. In this view, multicultural education would be instrumental in achieving 'positive attitudes towards the multicultural nature of society, free from ... inaccurate myths and stereotypes about other ethnic groups' (ibid: 321).

These rather grandiose claims on behalf of multicultural education have also been made widely elsewhere, most notably in the US, Canada and Australia. For example, when Canada adopted multiculturalism as official policy in 1971, the then Prime Minister, Pierre Trudeau, asserted that 'such a policy should help break down discriminatory attitudes and cultural jealousies' (cited in Berry, 1998: 84). But with the passage of time, these claims have come to be regarded by critics as largely illusory. Without wishing to rehearse the already voluminous literature on the merits and demerits of multicultural education, it is worth pointing out briefly two key criticisms that are directly relevant to our concerns here. The first has to do with multicultural education's overemphasis on *lifestyles* at the expense of life *chances*; in other words, that multicultural education overstates the significance of cultural recognition and understates, and at times disavows, the impact of structural discrimination (be it racial, cultural, religious or linguistic) on minority students' lives. Such an approach may in fact serve simply to *reinforce* the current cultural and linguistic hegemonies that multicultural education is concerned, at least ostensibly, to redress (Kalantzis and Cope, 1999; May, 1999).

Accordingly, since the 1990s, more critical advocates of multicultural education have consciously distanced themselves from this early focus on a superficial culturalism at the expense of broader material and structural concerns, advocating instead for a more 'critical multiculturalism' (see McLaren, 1995, 1997; Kincheloe and Steinberg, 1997; May, 1999; May and Sleeter, 2010). In so doing, they have acknowledged that the logic of much previous multiculturalist rhetoric failed 'to see the power-grounded relationships among identity construction, cultural representations and struggles over resources' (Kincheloe and Steinberg, 1997: 17). Rather, it engaged 'in its celebration of difference when the most important issues to those who fall outside the white, male and middle class norm often involve powerlessness, violence and poverty' (ibid). In contrast, critical multiculturalism 'takes as its starting point a notion of culture as a terrain of conflict and struggle over representation ... that may not cease until there is a change in the social conditions that provoke it' (Mohan, 1995: 385).

Unlike previous multiculturalist accounts, this more critical approach specifically highlights the ongoing effects of racism, along with its complex interconnections with other forms of discrimination and related inequalities (class, gender, sexuality etc.). What critical multiculturalism has not done, or at least not yet, is extend this analysis to include a critical reappraisal of the link between language, identity and education; something it has left to the advocates of bilingual education (see below). Thus, a second key criticism of multicultural education, including critical multiculturalism, is its ongoing unwillingness to engage directly with questions of *linguistic* discrimination, and the continued maintenance of particular linguistic hegemonies within both education and the wider nation-state.

Even where language ostensibly forms a part of multicultural educational policy, as in Australia for example, minority language support does not usually extend much further in practice than the recognition of private minority language maintenance, usually outside the state education system. This assertion might seem strange to some, given that Australia is well known for its significant attempts at language status planning in favor of minority languages, most notably via the National Policy on Languages (NPL), developed by Joseph Lo Bianco in the 1980s (Lo Bianco, 1987). However, the NPL's broad concern with ethnic identity, language rights, and language diversity as a social, cultural and economic resource – an admirable exception to much of what has been discussed previously – was quickly eclipsed by a more economically rationalist approach to language within Australia in the early 1990s, which once again peripheralized the issue of minority languages, except as potential 'trading' languages (see, for example, Dawkins, 1992). The almost sole preoccupation of language education policy since 1997 on improving literacy in English has further retrenched the role and visibility of minority languages in Australia (Lo Bianco, 2004, 2008). Meanwhile, and not surprisingly perhaps, all significant activities conducted in the public domain within Australia remain resolutely monolingual, while minority language use remains limited to a few restricted (low status) domains. Suffice it to say, this situation, as with much multiculturalist policy, does little to foster the status and use of minority languages in the longer term. In the end, the essence of the multicultural model is the recognition of the right to be different and to be respected for it, not necessarily to maintain a distinct language and culture.

In contrast, Stage 4 of Churchill's typology does recognize the importance of the link between language, identity and learning – albeit, as we shall see, in an almost solely instrumental way. The promotion of transitional bilingual programmes is characteristic of this stage. Such programmes use a minority first language in the early stages of schooling so as to facilitate the transition of the minority language speaker to the majority language. In so doing, these programmes acknowledge the now-widespread linguistic research consensus that instruction in one's first language is both linguistically and educationally beneficial, and the strongest basis for subsequent second language learning (May, 2008, 2010a; García, 2009; Baker, 2011). In this sense, it is a significant advance on the preceding approaches to minority language education. But in other more fundamental respects, transitional bilingualism is little different from its predecessors. Like the latter, transitional bilingual programmes continue to hold to a 'subtractive' view of individual and societal bilingualism. In assuming that the first (minority) language will eventually be replaced by a second (majority) language, bilingualism is not in itself regarded as necessarily beneficial, either to the individual or to society as a whole. This in turn suggests that the eventual atrophy of minority languages remains a central objective of transitional bilingualism. The (1968) Bilingual Education Act in the US exemplifies the key characteristics of this broad policy approach.

Churchill argues that Stages 1–4 all posit that minority groups should seek the same social, cultural and linguistic outcomes as those of the dominant or majority group within the nation-state. In other words, the instrumental objectives of education, as defined by the dominant group, should be the same for *all* other groups within the nation-state. The premise is thus the incorporation of minority groups into the hegemonic civic culture of the nation-state, with minimal accommodation to minority languages and cultures. This in turn is a result of the principles of nation-state organization, discussed earlier. Churchill proceeds to argue that it is only at Stages 5 and 6 that objectives and outcomes also come to incorporate the cultural and linguistic values of minority groups and, by so doing, begin to question the value of a monocultural and monolingual society. Both these stages assume that minority groups can (and should) maintain their language and culture over time, whereas Stages 1 through 4 clearly take the opposite approach. However, significant differences still remain between these latter two policy approaches.

Educating for the minority

Stage 5 recognizes the importance of maintaining minority languages and cultures, at least in the private domain. In order for this to be achieved, however, it also recognizes that some measure of *active* protection is required for the minority language if it is not to be supplanted by the dominant (usually, national) language. A maintenance approach to bilingual education is thus the most usual policy response here. In contrast to the 'subtractive' view of bilingualism held in transitional bilingual programmes, a maintenance approach regards bilingualism as an 'additive' or 'enriching' phenomenon for the individual. However, as its name suggests, the wider cultural and linguistic benefits of maintaining a minority language are also regarded as central, both for minority groups themselves and for their subsequent contribution to the nation-state. Accordingly, maintenance bilingual education is characterized by 'minority language immersion' programmes where school instruction is largely or solely in the minority language. This ensures that the minority language is maintained and fostered, given that the majority language is usually dominant in most other social and institutional domains anyway. Examples of successful maintenance bilingual programmes are numerous. They can be found in North America (French and heritage language immersion programmes in Canada, and some Spanish language education programmes in the US); in Europe (including Welsh, Basque, and Catalan language programmes) and among a wide variety of indigenous groups (including Sámi in Norway and Sweden, Māori in New Zealand, Inuit in Canada, and Native Americans in North, Central and South America).

Stage 5 thus emphasizes the importance of first languages as a key component of minority language maintenance of a wider educational success for minority students. However, changes to the formal linguistic uniformity of the nation-state are not usually countenanced at this level. The latter in fact is only addressed at Stage 6, the 'language equality' stage of Churchill's typology. At this stage, formal multilingual policies are adopted which require the dominant group to accommodate minority groups and their language(s) in all shared domains (at least in theory); a process which has been described elsewhere as *mutual accommodation* (May, 1994; Nieto and Bode, 2007). A prerequisite for this more plurilingual view of the nation-state is the formal legitimation and institutionalization of minority languages within both the state and civil society. As we have seen, examples of this approach remain relatively rare, although this should not surprise us. After all, Stage 6 challenges directly the principle of a common language and culture that underlies nation-state formation, and the longstanding derogation of other (minority) languages and cultures attendant upon it.

The territorial language principle

Where it does occur, the granting of some form of language equality at the level of the nation-state is usually based on one of two organizing principles. The first is the 'territorial language principle', which grants language rights that are limited to a particular territory in order to ensure the maintenance of a particular language in that area (see Williams, 2008 for a useful overview). The most prominent examples of this principle can be found in Québec, as well as in Belgium and Switzerland. Taking the last as an example, the Swiss confederation is officially multilingual in German, French, Italian, and Romansh and its territorial multilingualism is achieved via regional cantons in which one or more of these languages is officially recognized. The obvious consequence of this is that many Swiss do not actually become multilingual (Grin, 1999). There are also significant infrastructural differences between the four official languages. The majority of the Swiss population speak German (63.6 per cent), although there are some cantons where it does not constitute the dominant language. French is spoken by 19.2 per cent of the population, Italian by 7.6 per cent, with the latter being dominant in only one canton (Ticino). Three cantons are bilingual (in French and German) and one is trilingual (German, Romansh and Italian). Meanwhile, Romansh is spoken by only 0.6 per cent of the population, approximately 50,000 speakers, and does not constitute a majority language in any Swiss canton, making it clearly the most vulnerable of the four official languages. The consequent difficulties of status and use for Romansh led to an overhaul of Swiss language policy to provide more support for that language (Grin, 1999, 2003). However, these attempts to further support Romansh also have to contend with the growing presence of English as an additional language in Switzerland, and related calls, most notably by the Swiss National Science Foundation, for it to be made a fifth official language (Davidson, 2010).

The example of Switzerland highlights that official language status and supporting linguistic rights at regional level may still not protect the ongoing use of a language, such as Romansh, with now relatively few speakers. Nonetheless official bi/multilingualism based on the territorial language principle clearly does address and, crucially, *redress* the subsumption of other language varieties in the civic realm or public domain. As such, it provides a clear, attested alternative to the still-dominant monolingual nation-state model.

The personality language principle

The second approach to establishing formal language equality is predicated on the 'personality language principle', which attaches language rights to individuals, irrespective of their geographical position. This provides greater flexibility than the territorial language principle in the apportionment of group-based language rights, although it also has its strictures. The most notable of these is the criterion 'where numbers warrant' – that is, language rights may be granted only when there are deemed to be a *sufficient* number of particular language speakers to warrant active language protection and the related use of such languages in the public domain. Canada adopts the personality language principle, where numbers warrant, in relation to French speakers outside of Québec, via the (1982) Canadian Charter of Rights and Freedoms. A similar approach is adopted in Finland with respect to first language Swedish speakers living there. Swedish speakers can use their language in the public domain in those local municipalities where there are a sufficient number of Swedish speakers (currently, at least eight percent) for these municipalities to be deemed officially bilingual.

With over 200 language varieties spoken across thirty states and five Union territories, India though provides perhaps the best example of this principle in operation. On the one hand, we have seen in India the long-standing promotion of English, and more recently Hindi, as the state's elite, pan-Indian, languages. On the other hand, there are eighteen languages recognized in India as 'principal medium languages', which, in addition to English and Hindi, include sixteen official state languages. The division of India's states along largely linguistic grounds means that local linguistic communities have control over their public schools and other educational institutions. This, in turn, ensures that the primary language of the area is used as a medium of instruction in state schools (see Schiffman, 1996; Daswani, 2001). Indeed, dominant regional language schools account for 88 per cent of all elementary schools in India (Khubchandani, 2008). But not only that, the Constitution of India (Article 350A) directs every state, and every local authority within that state, to provide 'adequate' educational facilities for instruction in the first language of linguistic minorities, at least at elementary school level. As a result, over eighty minority languages are employed as media of instruction in elementary schools throughout India.

The potential to follow the Indian model in the educational provision of minority languages was also evident, at least initially, in post-apartheid South Africa. The then-new 1996 constitution established formal multilingualism, with the existing two official languages (English and Afrikaans) complemented by a further nine African languages. South African Sign Language was subsequently added as a twelfth official language. At the time, it seemed that a wide-ranging bi/multilingual educational approach would result (Heugh, Siegrühn, and Plüddermann, 1995).

Subsequent developments, however, have proved far less promising. Curriculum revisions over the last fifteen years have focused almost exclusively on English literacy, ignoring the wider multilingual aims of South Africa's language policy (Barkhuizen and Gough, 1996; Alexander, 2000; Heugh, 2000). There has also been a related trend towards the early transition from African languages to English as medium of instruction in South African schools, delimiting the possibility of more effective maintenance bi/ multilingual education options (Heugh, 2002, 2008). Thus, even in overtly multilingual environments, and within a political context at least ostensibly supportive of such multilingualism, the challenge of effectively implementing more plural language education policies still remains formidable.

Minority group responses to language education policies

If we return directly to Churchill's analysis for a moment, while also bearing in mind that any typology is likely to understate significant inter- and intragroup differences, we can also now attempt a broad parallel categorization of minority group responses to minority language education policy (see Churchill, 1986: 48–49):

- *Level 1, the recognition phase*: the minority group seeks to obtain initial recognition of its distinct educational needs and, in many cases, of its very existence as a distinct cultural and/or linguistic group within the nation-state.
- *Level 2, the start up and extension phase*: having obtained some recognition from educational authorities, the minority group seeks to obtain the creation of minority language educational services or, where these already exist, their further legitimation, extension and improvement. At this stage, either transitional or maintenance bilingual education aims can be pursued. As discussed previously, transitional bilingual education aims to expedite successful transference from the minority to the majority language by employing

the minority language in the early years of primary schooling. This acts as a bridge for the child to transfer their first language skills to the replacing language and, while educationally sound, remains essentially assimilative in intent. In contrast, maintenance bilingual education aims 'to the maximum extent possible [to] involve use of the minority language as a means of instruction [in order] to resist assimilation pressures outside the school environment' (Churchill, 1986: 49).

- *Level 3, the consolidation and adaptation phase*: If Level 2 is principally concerned with increasing the quantity of minority language programmes, this level is concerned with enhancing their quality. In transitional terms, the emphasis may be placed on greater, more effective social and economic integration of the minority group within the nation-state. In group maintenance terms, emphasis might be placed not only on fostering the minority language as a medium of instruction but also on employing the minority culture as a specific source and context of instruction.
- *Level 4, the multilingual coexistence phase*: At this level, distinct minority educational rights are legally and practically enshrined. In this regard, a considerable degree of autonomy is usually accorded to minority groups in relation to the actual control, organization and delivery of minority language education.

The consequences of Level 4 for minority groups bear further discussion here. The granting of a measure of educational control at this level clearly holds considerable symbolic purchase for the minority group concerned. However, three other benefits have also been recognized as a consequence of this process.

- While no causal link can be demonstrated, there appears to be a high correlation between greater minority participation in the governance of education and higher levels of academic success by minority students within that system. As Jim Cummins observed twenty-five years ago, 'widespread school failure does not occur in minority groups that are positively oriented towards both their own and the dominant culture, that do not perceive themselves as inferior to the dominant group, and that are not alienated from their own cultural values' (1986: 22). This conclusion still holds today as subsequent educational research consistently attests (see Cummins 2000; Corson, 2000; Nieto and Bode, 2007).

- The greater the participation in educational decision-making by minority group members, the more likely there is to be a match between minority aspirations and subsequent educational provision (see May, 1994; Corson, 2000; Hinton and Hale, 2001; Skutnabb-Kangas, Phillipson, Mohanty and Panda, 2009; Menken and García, 2010).

- Direct involvement in the governance of minority education strengthens community links among the members of the minority group themselves. Such involvement may also ameliorate the negative historical experiences of education held by many within the minority community as a result of the assimilationist emphases of nation-state organization. Examples of this with respect to community-based indigenous education efforts, for example, can be found in May and Aikman (2003); Hornberger (2011); McCarty (2011).

Bridging the gap between policy and practice

In this chapter, I have chosen Churchill's typology as a useful heuristic device for analysing policy responses to minority language and education. Like any typology, however, it is important to acknowledge its limitations. Perhaps the most important limitation is the inevitable gap that occurs between policy and practice (see Schiffman, 1996). These discrepancies, which are conceded by Churchill, occur both among and within nation-states and among and within particular minority groups. In relation to different policy approaches, for example, only the very old bilingual or multilingual states (Belgium, Finland and Switzerland) appear to have reached Stage 6. Sweden is at Stage 5, at least in relation to its Finnish-speaking minority (see Skutnabb-Kangas, 2000). In Canada, Article 23 of the (1982) Canadian Charter of Rights and Freedoms enshrines the right of English and French speakers, who represent 90 per cent of the country's population, to an education in their first language 'where numbers warrant', while the (1968) Bilingual Education Act ostensibly allows for a Stage 4 approach for Latino (and other) minorities in the US.

But even here, all is not as it seems. We have already seen that the official multilingualism of Switzerland does not necessarily result in individual multilingualism. Similarly, the actual implementation of a stated language education policy within schools and school systems may be far less frequent than such policy pronouncements suggest. Thus in Canada the actual exercise of minority language rights, including the right to minority language education, varies widely from province to province, ranging from Stage 6 to Stage 2 for Francophones outside of Québec. This is a product, in turn, of the federal nature of the Canadian system and the considerable administrative autonomy granted to individual provinces, particularly with respect to education (Burnaby, 2008). An even more marked disparity between policy and practice can be seen in the US. Here it is probably safe to say that despite the (1968) Bilingual Education Act, most Latino children continued to be educated in schools that were still at Stages 1 and 2, promoting the merits of an English language submersion approach. This tendency was further entrenched by (2001) No Child Left Behind, which replaced the Bilingual Act and focused solely on the acquisition of English. This has also been allied/strengthened significantly over the last fifteen years in the US by the rise of the 'English Only' movement and its trenchant opposition to, and successful dismantling of, many existing bilingual education programmes (see May, 2012: Ch. 6). In similar vein, the Indian Constitution, as we have seen, explicitly allows for, and even actively facilitates, the promotion of minority language immersion education. However, there remain strong countervailing pressures in India to learn Hindi and, particularly, English via submersion educational approaches (see Vaish, 2008).

The differences between the delivery of minority language education to different minority groups within the same nation-state can also be quite marked. For example, in New Zealand, the indigenous Māori are moving towards Stage 5 with respect to language and education policy. However, the approach to other (ethnic) minorities in New Zealand, such as Pasifika groups (those from the Pacific Islands who have since settled in New Zealand), is considerably less well advanced (Benton, 1996; May, 2010b). A similar pattern pertains in Wales, where the Welsh-speaking national minority is now well served by Welsh language education, particularly since Welsh devolution in 1999, but where migrant ethnic groups, and the languages they speak, still are not (Williams and De Lima, 2006; Mann, 2007).

Canada's approach of 'multiculturalism within a bilingual framework' also illustrates well the discrepancies evident between the various types of language education available to different minority groups. Bearing in mind the caveat of provincial variation outlined earlier, Article 23 of the (1982) Canadian Charter of Rights and Freedoms nonetheless protects the rights of English and French speakers to an education in their first language 'where numbers warrant'. However, the linguistic and educational rights of Canada's indigenous peoples are far less clearly endorsed. This is demonstrated poignantly by their initial exclusion from consideration in the Royal Commission on Bilingualism and Biculturalism (1963–71). The findings of this Commission, known as the Laurendeau-Dunton Commission, led to the adoption of English and French as co-official languages in 1969, and significantly influenced the policy of 'multiculturalism within a bilingual framework' two years later (Burnaby, 2008; see also Maurais, 1996). This discrepancy is even more evident in Australia where, despite also having an official policy of multiculturalism, its ongoing educational and wider social and political treatment of Aboriginal peoples and Torres Strait Islanders leaves much to be desired (Buchan and Heath, 2006; Robbins, 2010).

Responses to minority language education approaches from within particular minority groups are also extremely varied, as one might expect. In the 1980s, Britain broadly adopted a Stage 3 multicultural approach to education, as exemplified in the Swann Report (DES, 1985), although again actual school practice at the time seldom reflected this, tending towards more assimilative models. However, the responses from within minority groups to even this limited form of multiculturalism ranged from enthusiastic endorsement (Verma, 1989) to outright rejection (Stone, 1981).

Likewise, in the US some of the most vocal critics of multicultural and bilingual education initiatives are themselves from ethnic minority groups (Rodriguez, 1993; D'Souza, 1995).

That said, the current variations in approach, and in their delivery, need not be seen as insurmountable. With regard to issues of delivery, discrepancies between policy formulations and actual practice are increasingly being addressed by the concerted political efforts of minority groups themselves. Recent overviews of these grass-roots, or 'bottom-up' initiatives can be found in Skutnabb-Kangas et al. (2009), Menken and García (2010), Hornberger (2011), and McCarty (2011).

With regard to variety of educational approach, there is no necessary problem, in my view, with differing policy approaches being directed at different minority groups. Indeed, as I have argued at length elsewhere (see May, 2012), variations of approach should exist between, for example, national and ethnic minority groups. Thus, while the ideal might be that nation-states provide a Stage 5 (Private Use Language Maintenance) minority education policy approach for *all* minority groups, only national minorities (including indigenous peoples) could be reasonably expected to be entitled to a Stage 6 (Language Equality) policy approach. Likewise, all minorities might expect the right to mobilize to at least Level 3 (Consolidation and Adaptation Phase) in terms of their own language and education requirements. However, again, only national minorities could legitimately claim a right to the Level 4 (Multilingual Coexistence Phase).

Conclusion

In this chapter, I have argued that the varied educational approaches adopted towards cultural and linguistically minority students can only be understood in relation to the wider context of nation-state organization and the challenges this presents for managing the so-called 'pluralist dilemma'. This also helps to explain why more plurilingual approaches, despite their greater educational effectiveness, are still regularly ignored and, where they are adopted, still face considerable, often trenchant, opposition – particularly, in this post 9/11 era. A key reason for this is that such programmes effectively endorse and promote societal bilingualism. As such, they also necessarily contest existing language hierarchies, particularly the pre-eminence of the state sanctioned language, and those who speak it as a first language. A wider reason is that they present a more pluralistic understanding of the nation-state; again contesting the preserve of the dominant group to define nationhood, and associated notions of citizenship, in their own image (and language).

And yet, we also know that nation-states, subject to the wider influences of globalization and transnationalism, are becoming inexorably more culturally and linguistically diverse, as are their schools. We also know that education plays a key role in shaping conceptions of nationhood and related attitudes to language and diversity. That said, it must be stressed that education, alone, cannot change society. As Stacy Churchill concludes in his own study:

> In some cases, the educational response to minorities is in advance of public opinion to a certain extent, but the politicized nature of relations between ethnolinguistic groups and their surrounding societies sets strict limits on how far educational systems can go in responding to minority needs. The root issue is how far societies outside the education system are willing to modify their views of the roles of linguistic and cultural minorities within their countries. Educational systems cannot respond to minority needs unless societies are [also] prepared to respond to those needs. (1986: 163)

However, if education has been used historically as a key bulwark of the monolingual nation-state, it can also surely be in the vanguard of reconceptualizing a more plurilingual state – one that recognizes, values, and includes the languages and cultures of minority groups within education and the wider society. As James Tollefson argues: 'the struggle to adopt minority languages within dominant institutions such as education ... constitute efforts to legitimize the minority group itself and to alter its relationship to the state. Thus while language planning reflects relationships of power, it can also be used to transform them' (1991: 202).

Similarly, Mary McGroarty argues: 'advocates for positive language and education policies must constantly articulate the value of bilingualism [and multilingualism], and ... be able to do so in varied terms that respond to a protean environment of public discussion' (2006: 5–6).

Much still needs to be done in accomplishing these aims; the ongoing social and political pre-eminence of monolingual educational approaches, despite their disastrous consequences for minority students, and the related relative scarcity of plurilingual approaches, to education suggest as much. Indeed, this is all the more reason why we must continue to argue for plurilingual approaches to education. They provide an opportunity for extending greater *ethnolinguistic democracy* (Fishman, 1995; May, 2012) to minority groups within nation-states. They better reflect the increasingly multilingual reality of our classrooms, and the societies in which we live. And, crucially, they better equip bi/multilingual students to make their way successfully in the world. And not before time. The stakes are high but the potential rewards of a more just, inclusive, and pluralist conception of education – and, crucially, the nation-state model of which it forms a part – are even more so.

References

Allan, R. and Hill, B. (2004). Multicultural education in Australia: historical development and current status. In J. Banks and C. Banks (eds) (2004). *Handbook of research on multicultural education, 2nd edn*. San Francisco, CA: Jossey Bass.

Alexander, N. (2000). Language policy and planning in South Africa: some insights. In R. Phillipson (ed.), *Rights to Language. Equity, power and education*, pp. 170–173. Mahwah, NJ: Lawrence Erlbaum.

Baker, C. (2011). *Foundations of Bilingual Education and Bilingualism, 5th edn*. Bristol: Multilingual Matters.

Banks, J. and Banks, C. (eds) (2004). *Handbook of research on multicultural education, 2nd edn*. San Francisco, CA: Jossey Bass.

Barkhuizen, G. and Gough, D. (1996). Language curriculum development in South Africa: what place for English? *TESOL Quarterly* 30, 453–472.

Bauman, R., and Briggs, C. (2003). *Voices of Modernity: language ideologies and the politics of inequality*. Cambridge: Cambridge University Press.

Benton, R. (1996). Language policy in New Zealand: defining the ineffable. In M. Herriman and B. Burnaby (eds), *Language Policies in English-Dominant Countries*, pp. 62–98. Clevedon: Multilingual Matters.

Berry, J. (1998). Official multiculturalism. In J. Edwards (ed.), *Language in Canada*, pp. 84–101. Cambridge: Cambridge University Press.

Bourdieu, P. (1982). *Ce Que Parler Veut Dire: l'économie des échanges linguistiques*. Paris: Arthème Fayard.

Buchan, B. and Heath, M. (2006). Savagery and civilization: from terra nullius to the 'tide of history'. *Ethnicities* 6, 1, 5–26.

Bullivant, B. (1981). *The Pluralist Dilemma in Education: six case studies*. Sydney: Allen and Unwin.

Burnaby, B. (2008). Language policy and education in Canada. In S. May and N. Hornberger (eds), *Encyclopedia of Language and Education, 2nd edn, Vol. 1: Language Policy and Political Issues in Education*, pp. 331–341. New York: Springer.

Churchill, S. (1986). *The Education of Linguistic and Cultural Minorities in the OECD Countries*. Clevedon: Multilingual Matters.

Clyne, M. (1998). Managing language diversity and second language programmes in Australia. In S. Wright and H. Kelly-Holmes (eds), *Managing Language Diversity*, pp. 4–29. Clevedon: Multilingual Matters.

Clyne, M. (2005). *Australia's Language Potential*. Sydney, Australia: University of New South Wales Press.

Coulmas, F. (1998). Language rights: interests of states, language groups and the individual. *Language Sciences* 20, 63–72.

Crawford, J. (2008). *Advocating for English Learners: selected essays*. Clevedon: Multilingual Matters.

Crystal, D. (2003). *English as a Global Language. 2nd edn*. Cambridge: Cambridge University Press.

Corson, D. (2000). *Language, Diversity and Education*. Mahwah, NJ: Lawrence Erlbaum.

Cummins, J. (1986). Empowering minority students: a framework for intervention. *Harvard Educational Review* 56, 18–36.

Cummins, J. (2000). *Language, Power and Pedagogy: bilingual children in the crossfire*. Clevedon: Multilingual Matters.

Daswani, C. (ed.) (2001). *Language Education in Multilingual India*. New Delhi: UNESCO.

Davidson, K. (2010). Language and identity in Switzerland. A proposal for federal status for English as a Swiss language. *English Today* 26, 1, 15–17.

Dawkins, J. (1992). *Australia's Language: The Australian language and literacy policy.* Canberra, Australia: Australian Government Publishing Service.

DES (Department of Education and Science). (1985). *Education for All: report of the committee of inquiry into the education of children from ethnic minority groups* (The Swann Report). London: HMSO.

Dorian, N. (1998). Western language ideologies and small-language prospects. In L. Grenoble and L. Whaley (eds), *Endangered Languages: language loss and community response*, pp. 3–21. Cambridge: Cambridge University Press.

D'Souza, D. (1995). *The End of Racism: principles for a multiracial society.* New York: Free Press.

Fishman, J. (1995). On the limits of ethnolinguistic democracy. In T. Skutnabb-Kangas and R. Phillipson (eds), *Linguistic Human Rights: overcoming linguistic discrimination*, pp. 49–61. Berlin: Mouton de Gruyter.

García, O. (2009). *Bilingual Education in the 21st Century: a global perspective.* Malden, MA.: Blackwell.

Gellner, E. (1983). *Nations and Nationalism: new perspectives on the past.* Oxford: Basil Blackwell.

Glazer, N. (1998). *We are All Multiculturalists Now.* Cambridge MA: Harvard University Press.

Goldberg, D. (1994). Introduction: Multicultural conditions. In D. Goldberg (ed.), *Multiculturalism: a critical reader*, pp. 1–41. Oxford: Basil Blackwell.

Gordon, M. (1978). *Human Nature, Class and Ethnicity.* New York: Oxford University Press.

Gordon, M. (1981). Models of pluralism: the new American dilemma. *Annals of the American Academy of Political and Social Science* 454, 178–188.

Grant, N. (1997). Democracy and cultural pluralism: towards the 21st century. In R. Watts and J. Smolicz (eds), *Cultural Democracy and Ethnic Pluralism: multicultural and multilingual policies in education*, pp. 25–50. Frankfurt: Peter Lang.

Grin, F. (1999). *Language Policy in Multilingual Switzerland: overview and recent developments.* Flensburg, Germany: European Centre for Minority Issues.

Grin, F. (2003). *Language Policy Evaluation and the European Charter for Regional or Minority Languages.* Basingstoke: Palgrave Macmillan.

Heugh, K. (2000). Giving good weight to multilingualism in South Africa. In R. Phillipson (ed.), *Rights to Language. Equity, power and education*, pp. 234–238. Mahwah, NJ: Lawrence Erlbaum.

Heugh, K. (2002). The case against bilingual and multicultural education in South Africa: laying bare the myths. *Perspectives in Education* 20, 1, 171–196.

Heugh, K. (2008). Language policy in Southern Africa. In S. May and N. Hornberger (eds), *Encyclopedia of Language and Education, 2nd edn, Vol. 1: Language Policy and Political Issues in Education*, pp. 355–367. New York: Springer.

Heugh, K., Siegrühn, A. and Plüddermann, P. (eds) (1995). *Multilingual Education for South Africa*. Johannesburg: Heinemann.

Hinton, L. and Hale, K. (eds) (2001). *The Green Book of Language Revitalization in Practice*. San Diego, CA: Academic Press.

Hornberger, N. (ed.) (2011). *Can Schools Save Indigenous Languages? Policy and Practice on Four Continents*. Basingstoke: Palgrave Macmillan.

Joshee, R. and Johnson, L. (eds) (2007). *Multicultural Education Policies in Canada and the United States*. Vancouver: University of British Columbia Press.

Kalantzis, M. and Cope, B. (1999). Multicultural education: transforming the mainstream. In S. May (ed.), *Critical Multiculturalism: rethinking multicultural and antiracist education*, pp. 245–276. London: Routledge Falmer.

Kamboureli, S. (1998). The technology of ethnicity: Canadian multiculturalism and the language of the law. In D. Bennett (ed.), *Multicultural States: rethinking difference and identity*, pp. 208–222. London: Routledge.

Kane, J. (1997). From ethnic exclusion to ethnic diversity: the Australian path to multiculturalism. In I. Shapiro and W. Kymlicka (eds), *Ethnicity and Group Rights*, pp. 540–571. New York: New York University Press.

Kedourie, E. (1960). *Nationalism*. London: Hutchinson.

Kellough, J. (2006). *Understanding affirmative action: Politics, discrimination, and the search for justice*. Washington DC: Georgetown University Press.

Khubchandani, L. (2008). Language policy and education in the Indian subcontinent. In S. May and N. Hornberger (eds), *Encyclopedia of Language and Education, 2nd edn, Vol. 1: Language Policy and Political Issues in Education*, pp. 369–381. New York: Springer.

Kincheloe, J. and Steinberg, S. (1997). *Changing Multiculturalism*. Buckingham: Open University Press.

Kymlicka, W. (1989). *Liberalism, Community and Culture*. Oxford: Clarendon Press.

Kymlicka, W. (1995). *Multicultural citizenship: A liberal theory of minority rights*. Oxford: Clarendon Press.

Kymlicka, W. (1998). *Finding Our Way: rethinking ethnocultural relations in Canada*. Toronto: Oxford University Press.

Kymlicka, W. (2001). *Politics in the Vernacular: nationalism, multiculturalism, citizenship*. Oxford: Oxford University Press.

Kymlicka, W. (2007). *Multicultural Odysseys: navigating the new international politics of diversity*. Oxford: Oxford University Press.

Lo Bianco, J. (1987). *National Policy on Languages*. Canberra, Australia: Australian Government Publishing Service.

Lo Bianco, J. (2004). *A Site for Debate, Negotiation and Contest of National Identity: language policy in Australia*. Strasbourg, France: Council of Europe.

Lo Bianco, J. (2008). Language policy and education in Australia. In S. May and N. Hornberger (eds), *Encyclopedia of Language and Education, 2nd edn, Vol. 1: Language Policy and Political Issues in Education*, pp. 343–353. New York: Springer.

Mann, R. (2007). Negotiating the politics of language: language learning and civic identity in Wales. *Ethnicities* 7, 2, 208–224.

Maurais, J. (ed.). (1996). *Québec's Aboriginal Languages: history, planning, development*. Clevedon: Multilingual Matters.

May, S. (1994). *Making Multicultural Education Work*. Clevedon: Multilingual Matters.

May, S. (ed.) (1999). *Critical Multiculturalism: rethinking multicultural and antiracist education*. London and New York: Routledge Falmer.

May, S. (2002). Multiculturalism. In D. Goldberg and J. Solomos (eds), *A Companion to Racial and Ethnic Studies*, pp. 124–144. Oxford/Cambridge, MA: Blackwell.

May, S. (2008). Bilingual/immersion education: What the research tells us. In J. Cummins and N. Hornberger (eds), Bilingual education, *The Encyclopedia of Language and Education*, 2nd edn, Volume 5, pp. 19–34. New York: Springer.

May, S. (2010a). Curriculum and the education of cultural and linguistic minorities. In B. McGraw, E. Baker and P. Peterson (eds), *International Encyclopedia of Education*, 3rd edn, Vol. 1, pp. 293–298. Oxford: Elsevier.

May, S. (2010b). Aotearoa/New Zealand. In J. Fishman and O. Garcia (eds), *Handbook of Language and Ethnicity*, pp. 501–517. New York: Oxford University Press.

May, S. (2012). *Language and Minority Rights: ethnicity, nationalism and the politics of language* (2nd edn). New York: Routledge.

May, S. and Aikman, S. (eds) (2003). Special Issue. Indigenous education: addressing current issues and developments. *Comparative Education*, 39, 2.

May. S. and Sleeter, C. (eds) (2010). *Critical Multiculturalism: Theory and praxis*. New York: Routledge.

McCarty, T. (ed.) (2011). *Ethnography and Language Policy*. New York: Routledge.

McCrum, R. (2011). *Globish: how the English language became the world's language*. London: Penguin.

McGroarty, M. (2002). Evolving influences on education language policies. In J. Tollefson (ed.), *Language Policies in Education: Critical issues*, pp. 17–36. Mahwah, NJ: Lawrence Erlbaum Associates.

McGroarty, M. (2006). Neoliberal collusion or strategic simultaneity? On multiple rationales for language-in-education policies. *Language Policy* 5, 3–13.

McLaren, P. (1995). *Critical Pedagogy and Predatory Culture*. New York: Routledge.

McLaren, P. (1997). *Revolutionary Multiculturalism: pedagogies of dissent for the new millennium*. Boulder, CO: Westview Press.

Menken, K. and García, O. (eds). (2010). *Negotiating Language Policies in Schools: educators as policymakers*. New York: Routledge.

Modood, T. (2007). *Multiculturalism: A Civic Idea*. Cambridge: Polity Press.

Mohan, R. (1995). Multiculturalism in the nineties: pitfalls and possibilities. In C. Newfield and R. Strickland (eds), *After Political Correctness: the humanities and society in the 1990s*, pp. 372–388. Boulder, CO.: Westview Press.

Moodley, K. (1999). Antiracist education through political literacy: the case of Canada. In S. May (ed.), *Critical Multiculturalism: rethinking multicultural and antiracist education*, pp. 138–152. London and New York: Routledge Falmer.

Nelde, P., Strubell, M. and Williams, G. (1996). *Euromosaic: the production and reproduction of the minority language groups in the European Union*. Luxembourg: Office for Official Publications of the European Communities.

Nieto, S. and Bode, P. (2007). *Affirming Diversity: the sociopolitical context of multicultural education* (5th edn). New York: Allyn and Bacon.

Rawls, J. (1971). *A Theory of Justice*. Oxford: Oxford University Press.

Robbins, J. (2010). A nation within? Indigenous peoples, representation and sovereignty in Australia. *Ethnicities* 10, 2, 257–274.

Rodriguez, R. (1993). *Days of Obligation: an argument with my Mexican father*. London: Penguin.

Schermerhorn, R. (1970). *Comparative Ethnic Relations*. New York: Random House.

Schiffman, H. (1996). *Linguistic Culture and Language Policy*. London: Routledge.

Shields, C., Bishop, R. and Mazawi, A. (2005). *Pathologizing Practices: the impact of deficit thinking on education*. New York: Peter Lang.

Skutnabb-Kangas, T. (2000). *Linguistic Genocide in Education – or Worldwide Diversity and Human Rights?* Mahwah, NJ: Lawrence Erlbaum.

Skutnabb-Kangas, T. and Fernandes, D. (2008). Kurds in Turkey and in (Iraqi) Kurdistan: a comparison of Kurdish educational language policy in two situations of occupation. *Genocide Studies and Prevention* 3, 1, 4–73.

Skutnabb-Kangas, T., Phillipson, R., Mohanty, A. and Panda, M. (eds) (2009). *Social Justice through Multilingual Education*. Bristol: Multilingual Matters.

Stone, M. (1981). *The Education of the Black Child in Britain: the myth of multiracial education*. London: Collins Fontana.

Taylor, C. (1994). The Politics of Recognition. In A. Gutmann (ed.), *Multiculturalism: Examining the politics of recognition*, pp. 25–73. Princeton, NJ: Princeton University Press.

Tollefson, J. (1991). *Planning Language, Planning Inequality: language policy in the community*. London: Longman.

Vaish, V. (2008). *Biliteracy and Globalization: English language education in India*. Clevedon: Multilingual Matters.

Valencia, R. (ed.) (1997). *The Evolution of Deficit Thinking: educational thought and practice*. New York: Falmer Press.

Valencia, R. (2010). *Dismantling Contemporary Deficit Thinking: educational thought and practice*. New York: Routledge.

Verma, G. (ed.) (1989). *Education for All: a landmark in pluralism*. Lewes: Falmer Press.

Williams, Charlotte and De Lima, P. (2006). Devolution, multicultural citizenship and race equality: from laissez faire to nationally responsive policies. *Critical Social Policy* 26, 3, 498–522.

Williams, Colin (2008). *Linguistic Minorities in Democratic Context*. Basingstoke: Palgrave Macmillan.

OFELIA GARCÍA, NELSON FLORES AND
HEATHER HOMONOFF WOODLEY

3   Transgressing Monolingualism and
    Bilingual Dualities: Translanguaging Pedagogies[1]

Introduction

Throughout the world language minorities are most often educated in
schools that have been designed for language majorities. Usually they are
educated only through the medium of the dominant state language. But
even when they are given the opportunity to be educated bilingually, education programmes are most often built on models, frameworks and practices
that have been designed for schooling language majorities.

Building on what we have learned in a study of successful schools in
educating Latino youth who are developing English (García, Woodley,
Flores and Chu, 2011), this chapter explores the interactions of teachers and students in US public schools for Latino recent immigrants that
transgress the monolingual or traditional bilingual model of schooling.
We do so by exploring the classroom interaction of teachers and students
in these schools through their translanguaging practices; that is, discursive and pedagogical practices that break the hegemony of the dominant

1   We are grateful for the support given to Ofelia García and Nelson Flores by the
    Internationals Network for Public Schools for the study of PAIHS, and to the prin-
    cipals, Bridgit Bye Dyster and Marcella Barros, teachers and students for welcoming
    us into their schools. We are also grateful to Ramón Namnum, principal of High
    School of World Cultures, and for the teachers and students of the school, for the
    unrelenting support they have given Ofelia García and Heather Homonoff Woodley
    in our study of the school.

language in monolingual classrooms, and the isolation of languages in bilingual classrooms. Before we focus on these classrooms, however, we explore some of the theoretical frameworks that have to be transgressed in order to understand the power that translanguaging holds as a pedagogical practice by offering two theoretical alternatives – 1) transglossia, and 2) dynamic bilingualism. We also theorize about translanguaging itself, before we look at how it functions in the classroom.

From monolingualism and diglossia to transglossia

Language difference has been the purview of sociolinguistic studies since the mid-twentieth century, as studies explore how speakers make linguistic choices in social contexts. But the models that have been used often link one language choice to a speaker's identity on the basis of the domain in which language is used and the interlocutors (Fishman, 1967; Gumperz, 1982), or on account of social characteristics such as nationality, age, gender, or class (Labov, 1966). In many ways, sociolinguistic models of language choice have been diglossic, positing that one language variety (Ferguson, 1959) or one language (Fishman, 1967) or even one feature (Labov) is used for specific reasons, and that the choice of one feature, one variety, or even one language responds strictly to external characteristics or social contexts that function independently of others. Thus, a common sociolinguistic tenet is that language use is diglossic, meaning that one language variety (Ferguson, 1959) or one language (Fishman, 1964) is used in certain domains (or territories) with specific people and for unique purposes, and that the other language is used for different functions.

A diglossic arrangement has been the pillar of educational practices. In monolingual programmes, the dominant language of instruction, often a standard variety is most often kept separate and distinct from the ways in which students use language, and the students' home language practices are ignored. In bilingual programmes, the two languages being used as media of instruction are also most often kept completely separate. This monolingual or diglossic language use in the classroom was rampant in the twentieth century when 'speech communities' were understood as stable and homogeneous, reflecting the dominant language ideologies of the time embedded within the nation-state paradigm. Instruction was then usually teacher-centred, and students were given very little freedom to work collaboratively in groups or independently.

In the twenty-first century, the concept of diglossia has been called into question, as more situations of stable societal multilingualism without functional allocation have been described. Many have used the case of the complex and stable multilingualism of India and many African countries to question diglossic arrangements as the only way to achieve stable bilingualism (see, for example, Mohanty, 2006; Makoni and Pennycook, 2007; Pennycook, 2010). In the European Union the promotion of plurilingualism has posited that it is possible to acquire and use different language practices 'to varying degrees and for specific purposes' (Council of Europe, 2000). Plurilingualism also connotes that it is possible to use language practices without functional complementarity, and at the same time not threaten home language practices. The spread of English throughout a globalized world has also meant that more groups of people use English without giving up their language practices, and most often use English language practices and other language practices in interrelationship. Advanced technology has made the simultaneous use of multimodalities possible, thus different language practices can be displayed at the same time.

The greater movement of peoples and communication in the twenty-first century has also made us realize that the concept of a homogeneous speech community tied to a national territory is flawed. Instead of 'speech communities', what we have are 'communities of practices', groups of people who interact and communicate regularly. Acquiring different language practices then cannot be the result of transmission of knowledge and of language, but of collaborative social practices in which students try out ideas and actions (Lave and Wenger, 1991), and thus socially construct their learning (Vygotsky, 1978).

García (2009) has argued that a stable, and yet dynamic, communicative network in the twenty-first century, with the many language practices of different transnational groups in functional interrelationship, might be better called 'transglossia'. It is then important for schools to create transglossic spaces where students' multiple language practices in interrelationship can produce integrated knowledge, deep understandings, and coherent identifications and performances as bilinguals.

Transglossia has the potential to release ways of speaking of subaltern groups that have been previously fixed within static language identities and hierarchical language arrangements and that are constrained by the modern/colonial world system. Transglossia can develop what Mignolo (2000) calls 'an other tongue', 'the necessary condition for "an other thinking" and for the possibility of moving beyond the defense of national languages and national ideologies ...' (p. 249). Transglossia refers to the fluid, yet stable, language practices of groups of people. It questions traditional descriptions built on national ideologies and also interrogates the notion of two languages as autonomous systems (for a critique of the autonomous position of languages' position, see Makoni and Pennycook (2007)). In the next section we explore how transglossia allows us to construct dynamic understandings of bilingualism.

From subtractive or additive bilingualism to dynamic bilingualism

Bilingualism is often understood as linear. When the norm is monolingualism, groups are subjected to a subtractive form of bilingualism where the 'first' language is subtracted, as the 'second' language is added (Lambert, 1974). When the norm is a diglossic bilingualism, bilingualism is considered additive, with the 'second language' added to the first (Lambert, 1974). But in both traditional conceptions of bilingualism, bilingualism is not anything but a 'second language' added to or subtracted from a 'first language'.

This conceptualization of emergent bilinguals[2] as simply learners of a 'second language', and having a 'first language', a 'native language', a 'mother tongue', means that bilingualism in itself is not recognized. One could be a 'language learner', but one cannot be a 'bilingual' with a complex linguistic repertoire with features that transcend traditional descriptions of standard grammars. By reifying the concept of a 'second language', the language education field has negated bilingualism. On the other hand, by reifying the concept of a 'first' or 'native language', privilege or exclusion is assigned. For example, 'native' English speakers are often sought-after in Asian countries as English teachers, often meaning monolingual Americans, English, and Australians, preferably white, with other bilinguals excluded.

Speaking of 'mother tongue' Skutnabb-Kangas (1981) points out that depending on the criteria used, the term could mean different things. It could mean, as with 'first language', first learned. But even order of acquisition is problematic for bilinguals, since many bilinguals grow up with complex language practices that cannot be easily assigned to a 'first' or 'second language;' that is, there is bilingual first language acquisition (BFLA) (for more on this topic, see Genesee, 2003; see also De Houwer, 2009). According to Skutnabb-Kangas (1981), a mother tongue could also be, as with 'first language', the language one uses most, or the language one knows best, or the language with which one identifies, or the language with which others identify the speaker. But for bilinguals all of these different criteria could result in different answers or in no answer at all, since it is often impossible for bilinguals to categorize their language practices only as autonomous languages. Regardless of the complexity of criteria, the problem with all of these theoretical formulations is that they insist in shaping bilingualism according to monoglossic classifications of one or another autonomous language, when bilingual practices are a lot more complex and interrelated, especially in the globalized world of today.

2   We choose to speak about emergent bilinguals, rather than English language learn-ers, which is the term most often used in the United States. Following García (2009) and García and Kleifgen (2010), we emphasize the student's emergent bilingualism and the role that their home language practices play in their education.

The language practices of today's bilinguals do not respond to an additive or a subtractive model of bilingualism. In today's flows, language practices are multiple and ever adjusting to the multilingual multimodal terrain of the communicative act; that is, bilingualism is dynamic. A dynamic conceptualization of bilingualism (García, 2009) goes beyond the notion of two autonomous languages, of a first and a second language, and of additive or subtractive bilingualism. Instead, dynamic bilingualism suggests that the language practices of *all* bilinguals are complex and interrelated; they do not emerge in a linear way. As García (2009) has said, they do not result in either the balanced wheels of two bicycles (as in additive bilingualism) or in a monocycle (as in subtractive bilingualism), but instead bilingualism is like an all-terrain vehicle which adapts to both ridges and craters of communication in uneven terrains (see also García and Kleifgen, 2010). Dynamic bilingualism sees bilingualism not as two monolithic systems made up of discreet sets of features, but as a series of social linguistic practices that are embedded in a web of complex social relations (for a similar view on literacy practices, see Street, 1984; Pennycook 2010).

Within a dynamic conceptualization of bilingualism, bilinguals are valued for their differing multi-competence (Cook, 2002) because their lives, minds and actions are different from those of monolinguals. As Herdina and Jessner (2002) have pointed out, the interactions of bilinguals' interdependent language systems create new structures that are not found in monolingual systems. Learning is then not just the 'taking in' of linguistic forms by learners, but 'the constant adaptation of their linguistic resources in the service of meaning-making in response to the affordances that emerge in the communicative situation, which is, in turn, affected by learners' adaptability' (Larsen-Freeman and Cameron, 2008, p. 135).

A model of transglossia and of dynamic bilingualism needs a different pedagogy. In the next section, we develop what we consider the key to a different design for teaching emergent bilinguals – translanguaging as pedagogy.

Theorizing translanguaging

Jim Cummins' interdependence hypothesis posits that '[t]o the extent that instruction in Lx is effective in promoting proficiency in Lx, transfer of this proficiency to Ly will occur provided there is adequate exposure to Ly' (Cummins, 2000, p. 38). Resting on the interdependence of the languages of bilinguals, Cummins has moved away from discussing an L1/L2 dichotomy, characterizing the way in which languages had been conceptualized in Canadian immersion bilingual classrooms in the twentieth century as 'two solitudes' (Cummins, 2007), and calling for bilingual instructional strategies in the classroom as a way of promoting 'identities of competence among language learners from socially marginalized groups, thereby enabling them to engage more confidently with literacy and other academic work in both languages' (p. 238).

These bilingual instructional practices are related to the concept of translanguaging (García, 2009). The term translanguaging is the English translation given by Colin Baker (2001) to the Welsh concept of *trawsieithu*, a bilingual pedagogy designed by Cen Williams where the input is in one language and the output is in another. Since then, the term has been extended and used to talk about a flexible bilingual use in teaching and learning (Blackledge and Creese, 2010; Creese and Blackledge, 2010; García, 2009). Translanguaging for us refers to 'the complex discursive practices of all bilinguals, and the pedagogies that build on these discursive practices to release ways of speaking, being and knowing of bilingual subaltern communities' (García, 2011).

By emphasizing 'languaging', translanguaging focuses on language practices of people, and not on languages as defined by nation-states and its schools (for more on the concept of languaging, see Makoni and Pennycook, 2007; Shohamy, 2006). By focusing on its 'trans' aspects, translanguaging builds on the concept of 'transculturación' coined by Cuban ethnologist Fernando Ortiz in talking about Cuban culture: 'In all embraces of cultures there is something of what happens in the genetic copulation of individuals: the child always has something of both progenitors, but it is always different from each of them' (Ortiz, 1940, p. 96). Thus, to us, translanguaging is not simply a passive and rigid adaptation to one or more standard languages. Rather, new and complex language practices emerge. Translanguaging differs from code-switching in that it refers not simply to a shift between two languages, but to the use of original and complex discursive practices that cannot be easily assigned to one or another code. Bilingual students use these complex and fluid discursive practices to perform their learning – reading, writing, listening, discussing, taking notes, writing reports and essays, taking exams – by drawing on their entire linguistic repertoire. And teachers have the possibility of drawing on these translanguaging practices in their pedagogies.

Translanguaging as pedagogy refers then to building on bilingual students' language practices flexibly in order to develop new understandings and new language practices, including academic language practices. Translanguaging pedagogies are particularly important for language minority students who are emergent bilinguals because they build on students' strengths. They also reduce the risk of alienation at school by incorporating languaging and cultural references familiar to language minority students.

Translanguaging in a classroom is precisely a way of working in the gap between, on the one hand, the global designs of nation-states and their education systems, and on the other, the local histories of peoples who language differently. As we will see in the next section, translanguaging in US classrooms shows the tensions between the global design of the US in educating immigrants and language minorities, and the local histories of those students. In their design, classrooms most often exclude minority language practices, and when they do include them, they separate those discourses strictly from the dominant standard language of school. In reality, as we will see, teachers and students violate these compartmentalizations, acting on the new meanings of what it is to be an American bilingual. Before we describe translanguaging pedagogies in two educational spaces, we discuss the US national educational context in an effort to contextualize the reasons why teachers working with Latino recent immigrant youth transgress traditional practices of English as a second language or bilingual education programmes.

The national context and schools for immigrant adolescent newcomers

In the last decade, US schools have been faced with three competing demands – 1) an increase in the number of immigrant students, especially coming from Mexico and other Latin American countries, 2) the erasure of support for bilingual services and bilingual education, 3) a demand for higher achievement of all students. It is precisely the complexity of dealing with these three issues simultaneously that has spurred the increase in educational programmes that transgress traditional education models that are strictly monolingual or bilingual, as well as traditional pedagogies to develop a 'second language'. We explore each of these three issues below.

In the last decade the number of foreign-born Americans has soared, and in 2009 17 per cent of the population was born abroad (US Census, 2009). Latinos are the largest ethnic group and number 50.5 million, making up 16 per cent of the population in 2009 (US Census, 2010). Of Latinos who are over five years of age, approximately one quarter speak English-only at home, a sign of the varied language practices of US Latinos.

As the US linguistic landscape becomes evidently more bilingual, xenophobic ideologies have spurred campaigns supporting English-only, especially in education (for more on this history, see Crawford, 2008, and García and Kleifgen, 2010). English-only statutes that banned bilingual education were passed in two states with large Spanish-speaking populations – California in 1998, and Arizona in 2000. In 2002, Massachusetts also passed a proposition that replaced transitional bilingual education with 'structured English immersion programs'.

At the same time, the word 'bilingual' was struck out of every single name of federal education offices and projects, as well as legislation. For example, the Office of Bilingual and Minority Language Affairs came to be called the Office of English Language Acquisition. Likewise, the National Clearinghouse for Bilingual Education was renamed the National Clearinghouse for English Language Acquisition. Even more significant was that the Bilingual Education Act itself was substituted by Title III of the

No Child Behind Legislation of 2002, now named Language Instruction for Limited English proficient and Immigrant Students. The word 'bilingual' had become the 'B' word (Crawford, 2007, 2008), not mentioned because it is a 'bad word'.

At the same time that the number of emergent bilingual students was increasing and bilingual educational spaces were being closed, the country called for higher educational achievement for all, as well as for closing the achievement gap among racial, gender, linguistic and socioeconomic groups. Attention became focused on how those students that the federal government calls 'Limited English Proficient' were contributing to the gap in educational achievement. The education of emergent bilinguals became an important issue, as educators struggled with the shrinking of traditional bilingual education spaces. As a result, many educators started experimenting with bilingualism in education in the form of what we are here calling translanguaging (for more on this shift, see García, Flores and Chu, 2011).

The two educational spaces that we describe below are different, but they share some characteristics. They are public high schools that specialize in teaching recently-arrived immigrant adolescents who are emergent bilinguals, especially Latinos. Neither educational space is strictly an English-as-a-second language programme, nor a bilingual education programme. As such, teachers in both spaces are mostly content teachers, with some being Latinas/os, reflecting a city where 28 per cent of the population is Latino (US Census, 2009). All teachers speak English, and as good New Yorkers, many are not monolingual English-speakers, but fall within a Spanish–English bilingual continuum.

Below we describe the translanguaging practices used in these schools by teachers who fall at different points of the bilingual continuum. We look at how a translanguaging pedagogy scaffolds the instruction in English of Spanish-speaking adolescents who have recently immigrated to the United States. Specifically, in both educational spaces below we explore how translanguaging supports three functions – 1) the contextualization of key words and concepts, 2) the development of metalinguistic awareness, and 3) the creation of affective bonds with students.

High School of World Cultures

High School of World Cultures is a newcomer public high school in the Bronx. The purpose of this school is specifically to meet the needs of recently arrived immigrant youth. The student population of the school is about 90 per cent Spanish-speaking, and many classes are comprised of all Spanish-speakers. The school also focuses on affirming the diversity of its student population with school-wide displays of various flags, languages, multicultural festivals and celebrations. Students also take a class called Multicultural Studies where they explore issues of diversity, tolerance, learn about other cultures and countries represented in the school and community, and share as experts of their own home cultures.

The school's official instructional policy, according to the Language Allocation Policy that schools must have in New York City, is ESL, or English-only, but there are a select number of Spanish-speaking students who are on what the principal calls a 'dual language'[3] track which involves taking some of their courses in English, and some content courses in Spanish. Although the title of this programme insinuates a duality, the reality of the classroom is that languaging is fluid for teachers and students. One teacher in the 'dual language' bilingual programme, who we refer to as Ms R, is a global history teacher. Although the class is technically designated as a Spanish-instruction content area class, translanguaging abounds. In one particular lesson, Ms R wanted to explore issues of race and diversity in the United States with her students. As she found out during her planning of these lessons, there are few resources about such topics in Spanish that are appropriate for this age group. Therefore, she found an article in a teen publication written in English. She delivered her lesson in Spanish, which focused on historical contexts of interracial marriage and other race-based laws in the United States, accompanied by short read-aloud passages from

3   In the United States 'dual language' has been substituted discursively for 'bilingual' in an effort to silence the 'B word.' For more on this, see García, 2009; García and Kleifgen, 2010; García, forthcoming.

the article in English. This led to a class discussion, as the students shared their views, perspectives, and questions in Spanish. The class then moved on to a writing exercise. At this point, Ms R gave students the freedom to choose the language in which they wanted to write. She explained that this activity was 'about the content' and 'making connections', thus allowing students to express themselves and their understandings in different ways. Figures 1, 2 and 3 illustrate students' various language choices for writing in this class.

What is interesting about these samples of student writing is how they language fluidly. In Figure 1, the student writes the prompt in English, her response in Spanish, and in her heading uses the English title of 'Ms' for her teacher. In Figure 2, the student writes both the prompt and response in English, and then uses 'Sra' when designating his teacher's title. In Figure 3, the student writes the prompt in English, then uses Spanish for her written

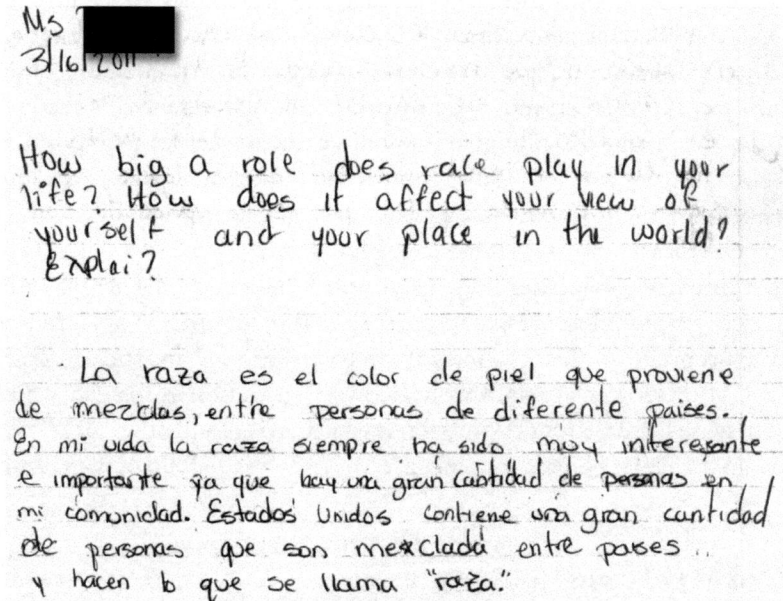

Ms
3/16/2011

How big a role does race play in your life? How does it affect your view of yourself and your place in the world? Explai?

La raza es el color de piel que proviene de mezclas, entre personas de diferente países. En mi vida la raza siempre ha sido muy interesante e importante ya que hay una gran cantidad de personas en mi comunidad. Estados Unidos contiene una gran cantidad de personas que son mezcladá entre países y hacen lo que se llama "raza."

Figure 1

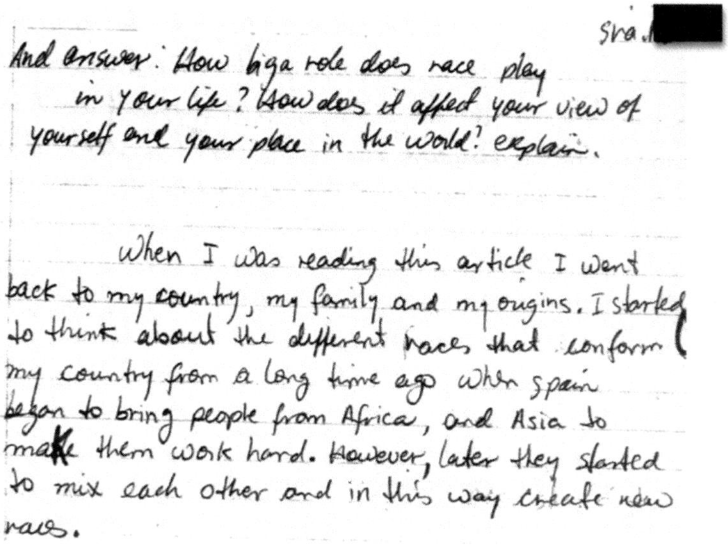

And answer: How biga role does race play
in your life? How does it affect your view of
yourself and your place in the world? explain.

When I was reading this article I went
back to my country, my family and my origins. I started
to think about the different races that conform
my country from a long time ago when Spain
began to bring people from Africa, and Asia to
make them work hard. However, later they started
to mix each other and in this way create new
races.

Figure 2

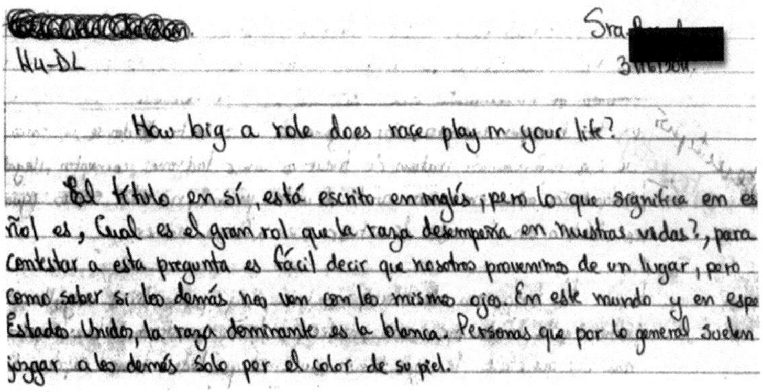

Hu-DL

How big a role does race play in your life?

El título en sí, está escrito en inglés, pero lo que significa en es
ñol es, Cual es el gran rol que la raza desempeña en nuestras vidas?, para
contestar a esta pregunta es fácil decir que nosotros provenimos de un lugar, pero
como saber si los demás nos ven con los mismos ojos. En este mundo y en espe
Estados Unidos, la raza dominante es la blanca. Personas que por lo general suelen
juzgar a los demás solo por el color de su piel.

Figure 3

response and 'Sra' for her teacher. These examples, as well as Ms R's lesson as a whole, illustrate the fluidity of language practices by students in this classroom. Spanish and English flow in this class through reading, writing, speaking, and listening, and the teacher provides this space of dynamic bilingualism in order to meet ultimate goals of student content learning, engagement, and expression.

For the majority of students in this school, however, class instruction is officially designated as English-only based on the school's instructional policy of 'bracketing English'; that is, of compartmentalizing languages so as to separate English strictly from Spanish (for a critique of this 'bracketing of English', see García and Kleifgen, 2010). However, 'English' classes build on translanguaging practices as students develop content understandings and English, as we will see below.

Each teacher in the lessons described below has a different ethnolinguistic background and falls at different points of the bilingual continuum. The classroom moments described below focus on singular lessons, but these translanguaging practices were common throughout days of observations within each of the teacher's classes. The cases here demonstrate how each teacher breaks from monolingual English only teaching, engaging the students and their own language practices. The three teachers integrate translanguaging in their classrooms at different moments and to different extent, but all serve three major functions – 1) the contextualization of key words and concepts, 2) the development of metalinguistic awareness, and 3) the creation of affective bonds with students.

Throughout the three classrooms, translanguaging was most often seen in the form of oral translation of key words and concepts in order to contextualize meaning. Ms D was born in the Dominican Republic, spoke Spanish at home and in school, began learning English in Dominican schools, and learned more upon moving to New York as a youth. In Ms D's 'English' class, the lesson focused on developing questions for an activity in which partners were to interview each other. As a whole group, the students brainstormed some possible questions to ask their partners, with students often contributing ideas in Spanish. Ms D wrote one of the student-generated ideas on the board: 'What do you do in the evening?' This led to the following conversation to ensure understanding of this question:

MS D:	Does everyone know what 'evening' means?
STUDENTS:	Noche.
MS D:	Expliquen 'evening' en español.
STUDENT:	Después de la tarde.
MS D:	Ahora, explíquenlo en inglés.
STUDENT:	After afternoon.

In asking students to translate this key word, Ms D created an interactive moment of translanguaging. Rather than just translating, the teacher asked for explanations of the word in Spanish and then in English, and engaged the students in the translation process to elicit their linguistic knowledge. Ms D finished reviewing the questions and, in Spanish, reminded the students that they could discuss the questions in Spanish first while planning what to ask, but to end with a question in English and write their answers in English. Here she made explicit the space for translanguaging in student-to-student conversations and in their learning process, as students are given the option to speak in ways they choose to make sense of their ideas prior to writing them in English.

After this discussion of planning questions, each pair of students began the process of creating their interview questions in English, negotiated in both Spanish and English. Students began to plan out their questions, frequently asking each other '¿Cómo se dice ...' followed by an answer by one of the partners; or if neither partner knew, the pair reached for a Spanish–English dictionary and searched for the word together. Several students asked Ms D in Spanish to confirm their understanding of a word, or the translation they found in their bilingual dictionary. At one point, a student looked up the word 'cuidar' in the bilingual dictionary. The translation she found was 'to care for', but she did not seem satisfied with this phrase. The student checked this with Ms D to see if this was correct, and Ms D told her 'dame toda la frase'. The student responded, 'A quién cuidas después de la escuela?' Ms D went on to explain in Spanish that in English, it is more common to say 'babysit' for what the student was insinuating here (caring for a younger sibling or neighbour). She then broke down the word 'babysit' to show that it refers to caring for someone who is younger, although not necessarily a baby. After these discussions, the pairs wrote their questions in English, followed by asking the questions and responding in English, peppered with Spanish clarifications. Then each member took turns asking one another the written questions in English, responded in English, and wrote down their partners' responses.

In these working pairs, Ms D utilized translanguaging to push the student to ask more meaningful questions; the students translanguaged for the purpose of assisting each other in completing the task. They also utilized bilingual print material to help make sense of their ideas. Ms D herself took the time to explain how a dictionary translation might not always be direct in the case of 'cuidar' and 'babysit', and elaborated this point in Spanish to ensure students' understanding of both an issue of vocabulary translation and metalinguistic awareness of a new English word.

Upon seeing that the pairs had finished, Ms D asked for volunteers to share what they learned about their partners from their interviews. One student shared, 'I learn that he has 15 years.' Ms D affirmed that this was a good piece of information to get in an interview, but went on to explain why in English, one would say, 'He is 15 years old.' Using Spanish, Ms D explained that when speaking in English, 'puede pensarse en él como que *es* de 15 años, pero en español, se dice *tiene* 15 años'. The students nodded their heads and several looked back at their writing and erased something on their papers, as if they too had made the same mistake. The next student to share information about her partner started with, 'She *is* 16 years old', putting emphasis on *is* that caused the class and Ms D to laugh, and Ms D to positively affirm the student's work, 'Good, just what we talked about.'

Ms D took this opportunity to use Spanish while explaining a linguistic difference between Spanish and English and to break down a confusing point for students based on mistranslation. Through translanguaging, the students were able to hear an explanation in their home language and to gain a sense of what a direct translation of the English phrase would literally be in Spanish, as Ms D tells them to think of how it should be in English as 'es de 15 años', although this is not how it is said in Spanish. The students understood this point and immediately applied it to their work, as seen in the second presenter who stressed her use of *is* when describing her partner's age. The responses of both classmates and the teacher show how a classroom context that embraces linguistic diversity and translanguaging in learning also helps to create supportive bonds between teachers and students.

Ms K grew up in the United States in a monolingual English-speaking home. She studied Spanish in school, but considers her time living and working in the Dominican Republic to be the place where she 'really learned' Spanish. In Ms K's class, students read books of their choice in English independently. As they read silently, Ms K rotates around the room and conferences one-on-one with students. She asks them various questions about vocabulary, comprehension, and their opinions about what they read. One day, a student asked Ms K, 'What does this mean, "driveway"?' She responded to the student in Spanish with a translation, 'entrada', and the student's eyes lit up with understanding, eagerly returning to his book. In another conference interaction, Ms K asked a student, 'Who is this character?' as she pointed to a page in the student's book. The student shrugged and Ms K repeated the question in Spanish, '¿Quién es esta persona?' The student responded with several sentences in Spanish, and Ms K then responded, 'Great description, now try in English.' The student gave a brief translation of her original response in English, and Ms K praised both her efforts and her improved English description.

In the one-on-one conference with the student above, Ms K's translation of the conferencing question into Spanish provided the student with an opportunity to express her reading comprehension in Spanish, which she was clearly more comfortable in, although she was reading in English. Having had the opportunity to express her thoughts first in Spanish gave this student a sense of validation that her ideas and answers were right, thus allowing her to take the next step of expressing her ideas in English with more confidence.

After about fifteen minutes of independent reading, students were told to write about inferences they could make about their reading, while also providing evidence from the text that supports their reasoning. Ms K began this class discussion by reviewing what it means to make an inference. She explained that an inference is 'something you can guess by the evidence you have'. She asked the students to make an inference about her.

STUDENT:	That you're nice.
MS K:	Interesting. What's your evidence?
STUDENT:	You speak nice, answer our questions, talk to us in Spanish.
MS K:	(with a laugh) Why is this nice?
STUDENT:	Other teacher, she yells at us, 'No Spanish', not very nice,
STUDENT:	In groups we speak Spanish and you let us, that's nice.
STUDENT:	Before I asked you what does 'driveway' mean and you told me. If you're not nice, you don't answer, or you don't let us speak Spanish in groups, or you yell at us.

The above conversation clearly demonstrates how students themselves have internalized the use of translanguaging as a sign of being 'nice' to students. The students juxtaposed Ms K with another teacher who yells 'No Spanish!' in her class. The use of translanguaging has created a positive environment in this class where students confirm that the presence and support of their home language practices contributes to positive rapport between the teacher and students.

Just down the hall Ms G is teaching writing. Ms G also grew up in a monolingual English-speaking home and studied French in school. She has begun speaking Spanish in the few years since coming to this school and learning from her students. Ms G's lesson focused on writing in the future tense. The students read a passage about a man and a woman who will be expecting a baby in the spring. There was some confusion about this phrase 'expecting a baby' and the students asked for clarification. Using both her hands to signify a large belly and the word she knew, Ms G said, 'You know, *embarazadas*.' The students all nod and said 'Yes, sí', but Ms G did not stop this lesson there. She continued what began as translanguaging for the purpose of translating one word, into a lesson on metalinguistic awareness. Ms G elaborated on the false cognates of *embarazadas* and embarrassed. 'But it's not like being embarrassed in English. What does that mean?' The students were silent, thus Ms G continued with examples to illustrate the meaning of embarrassed, 'If you do something and your face is red.' There was still silence, so she went on, 'If your mother comes to school and kisses you and all your friends see.' Ms G then acted this out and made an embarrassed face as the students giggled. One student raised his hand and shared, 'Miss, that's "avergonzado" in Spanish.' Unsure if this was the correct translation, Ms G directed this student to look up the word in the Spanish–English dictionary for confirmation. The student showed his teacher the dictionary entry confirming its meaning, and Ms G nodded and continued the lesson on metalinguistic awareness. She ended by noting, 'So even though we have a lot of words that sound the same in Spanish and English, they don't always mean the same thing, we have to be careful.'

Although Ms G is not fluent in Spanish, she does not let this stop the use of translanguaging. Relying on bilingual print resources such as Spanish–English dictionaries, Ms G uses student linguistic knowledge to contextualize meaning and build metalinguistic understandings. At several other times throughout the class, Ms G focused on the use of cognates for understanding new words in English, informing students that their knowledge of Spanish was helpful in understanding English.

After this lesson, Ms G moved on to independent work in the class where students worked in small groups to write a short paragraph. Before beginning the work, she reviewed the guidelines for group work. She wrote on the board, 'Take turns talking', and then asked for students to explain this in Spanish to the class. Several students volunteered; however, Ms G made a deliberate decision to call on two students who had not yet participated in class. These two students shared their explanations for the guideline, 'hablar de uno en uno' [talk one at a time], was one response, while another student elaborated with, 'no hablar cuando alguien está hablando' [not to talk when someone else is speaking]. Ms G then had the two students come to the board and write these Spanish phrases next to the English. She smiled as these students seemed eager to share with the class and write on the board. Ms G then shared with the class, 'See, you teach me things too.' A student responded to her with a smile, 'You're a good student', and the class laughed, but nodded in agreement as Ms G affirmed the positive interaction by adding, 'And you are good teachers.'

Because of her limited knowledge of Spanish, Ms G utilized the students as linguistic experts, which ultimately led to affective bonding between students and teacher. Ms G made it clear that she had something to learn from these students who are often seen as just lacking English. She deliberately used their home language practices to benefit not only other classmates, but her personally. Ms G used this as an opportunity to engage students who were not participating in the class, and utilized translanguaging to incorporate student knowledge and expertise into the class. In this interaction, Ms G bonded with the students as their teacher, and also as their student.

The classroom moments above illustrate the ways in which translanguaging occurs in three English classrooms with teachers across the continuum of bilingualism. They demonstrate how translanguaging can be utilized in ways that build English language development, metalinguistic awareness, as well as building affective bonds between students and teachers. Through translanguaging, students have the opportunity to expand their vocabulary, make sense of their own learning processes, and be linguistic experts. At the same time, students feel respected by their teachers as their home language expertise is affirmed. Each of these three teachers illustrates ways that teachers challenge the monolingual English-only instruction and the monoglossic ideology of diglossia in the education of emergent bilingual adolescents. These teachers push against linguistic boundaries as they strive to meet the needs of their students by embracing translanguaging in their classrooms.

The Pan American International Schools

The Pan American International Schools are two schools that are part of the Internationals Network for Public Schools, a network of schools that specialize in meeting the needs of immigrant students. All of the schools in this network pride themselves on the utilization of heterogeneous collaborative group work and a project-based approach to teaching and learning that culminates in a rigorous portfolio presentation process where students present their projects to a panel of teachers (see García and Sylvan, 2011 for more on these schools).

There is, however, one major difference between the Pan American International Schools and the other schools in the network. The majority of the schools in the network follow what the network refers to as the 'diverse language model' where students speak many different languages. In this model, English becomes the lingua franca for students, though whenever possible teachers work with students on the continued development of the home language. Because Latinos are the most numerous group of emergent bilinguals, and because they are concentrated in certain neighbourhoods, two Pan American International Schools were recently opened with a focus on serving Spanish-speaking Latino recent immigrants. In these two schools Spanish is the de facto language of communication for students and plays a more central role in the pedagogical repertoire of teachers.

Below are examples of how three 'English' teachers across the continuum of bilingualism translanguaged to help students in their development of English. The first teacher, who we call Ms C, was born in the US of Chilean parents and grew up speaking both English and Spanish. The second teacher, referred to here as Ms L, grew up speaking Italian and learned English as an additional language. The third teacher, referred to here as Ms S, is of South Asian background and is learning Spanish from her students. Each of these cases show how teachers break out of the borders suggested by the monolingualism of an English-only classroom or the duality of bilingual classrooms, while simultaneously showing that translanguaging is possible across the continuum of bilingualism and does not require an idealized bilingual teacher with balanced competence in two languages.

As we saw in the High School for World Cultures, one of the most common ways in which translanguaging is used by all of these teachers is in the contextualization of key words and concepts for students. This oftentimes emerges spontaneously through oral conversation in the classroom. For example, in one lesson, Ms C had students complete a 'Mind Mirror' based on the graphic novel *American Born Chinese*. This activity entails having students take a character from the text and delve into his or her personality through the identification of key quotes and the creation of symbols and original phrases to represent the character. This is all visually displayed on a representation of the character's face. As Ms C was trying to get students to create symbols to represent characters in the story that they were reading, some students were struggling with the concept of symbol. After explaining the concept in English and realizing that some students did not quite grasp it, she reinforced it for the students by explaining 'un symbol representa algo'. In this case, simply translating the meaning of the term helped ensure that students would be able to successfully complete the task and be able to eventually explain the reason they chose the symbol in English. In short, translanguaging is being used as a bridge toward a final product in academic English that would also demonstrate content mastery.

An equally common phenomenon during this lesson was for students to ask Ms C how to say certain key words in English. For example, when asking students to identify the relationship between background images and the character represented in the mind mirror, the following exchange occurred:

STUDENT: ¿Cómo se dice complemento?
MS C: Complement.
STUDENT: Because they complement the picture.

In this exchange, Ms C used her bilingualism to help a student successfully state her response in English. Again, Spanish, rather than being seen as an interference or crutch, is instead treated as a tool to facilitate English language development. Students are allowed to use their entire language repertoire to make meaning, while working to expand their discursive repertoires.

In addition, there were many times throughout the lesson where Ms C allowed students to use Spanish to negotiate meaning and ask questions, though she would respond to them in English, as demonstrated in the next example:

STUDENT: ¿Qué hay que poner aquí?
MS C: You have to put the setting.
STUDENT: ¿Hay que dibujarlo?
MS C: Yes.

In this exchange, a student is not quite sure what he is supposed to do and asks Ms C a procedural question. Ms C acknowledges that she understood what he said, but responds to him in English. In this way, the student is able to make sense of what he is supposed to do, while at the same time listening to English input.

Ms C also translanguages to develop the metalinguistic awareness of her students. For example, in response to a student's question about how to say 'conocer' in English, Ms C says 'knows', which then leads to a discussion about 'knows' versus 'nose' ['nariz']. Ms C explains that 'nariz' is written 'nose' in English. In another example, when explaining the meaning of the term 'background', Ms C explains it by saying '"back" means "espalda", so "background" is "behind".' Both of these examples gave students the opportunity to understand how their home language practices are used to facilitate the process of adding more English to their language repertoire – something that could not have happened in a strictly English-only classroom.

Yet, there was a substantive exchange during this lesson that went beyond the word level to larger ideas. This provided a moment of affective bonding between Ms C and a group of students in the class. This occurred when Ms C was brainstorming some ideas with one of the groups. One of the students asked her in Spanish if she could think of a symbol that they could use to represent China, which led to the following exchange:

MS C: Is she from China?
STUDENT: No. Japón. Pero es lo mismo. Hablan el mismo idioma y tienen los ojos así (moves her eyes to be narrower).
           [No, Japan. But its the same thing. They speak the same language and their eyes are like this.]
MS C: Hemos hablado de eso. Es como decir que todos los brasileños y peruanos son iguales ...
           We've talked about this. It is like saying that all Brazilians and Peruvians are the same.
(They then continue having an extended conversation in Spanish about stereotypes).

A student continued to express a stereotype that Ms C had been working with the students to unlearn throughout the entire unit. In order to ensure that this teachable moment was not wasted, Ms C used Spanish to ensure that there were no misunderstandings. She also provided examples from Latin America in Spanish to connect to students' own cultural backgrounds, so that they could see that this issue is also relevant to them.

The other two teachers are positioned at different points on the continuum of bilingualism than Ms C, and are, therefore, oftentimes not able to translanguage in the same spontaneous way. Ms L, however, is Italian, and is sometimes able to use her knowledge of Italian in helping students make meaning. One day they were preparing to watch the movie, *Twelve Angry Men*:

> MS L: Who decides if the defendant is guilty or not guilty?
> STUDENT: ¿Qué significa 'guilty'?
> MS L: Culpable.

At other points, Ms L relies on students to contextualize the meaning of key words and concepts through Spanish, as demonstrated in the following interaction during the same conversation:

> STUDENT: In the courthouse.
> MS L: Yes. In the courthouse. How do you say that in Spanish?
> STUDENT: ¡La corte!

Ms L utilizes the same principle of teaching as Ms C in that they both use translanguaging practices as a way of supporting students in their English language development.

Perhaps because of her inability to always respond spontaneously in providing home language support to students when they need it, Ms L also relies on written texts to help students make meaning of the concepts being explored in class. For example, in this same lesson on *Twelve Angry Men*, Ms L had students watch a short clip from the movie in English first, then again in English with Spanish subtitles. Students then engaged in a writing activity analysing what the judge said, with Ms L, providing students with the actual script of what he said, along with a Spanish translation. The resulting conversation was in English. In short, Ms L used written texts in Spanish to help students understand the content, and then utilized this understanding of the content to help them discuss it in English.

Like Ms C, Ms L also translanguaged for metalinguistic awareness. One way she did this was through pointing out cognates. Below is one example from this lesson where Ms L points out a cognate, while translanguaging to ensure that students are familiar with the concept in their home language:

MS L: This one ['verdict' is on the blackboard] is also close to Spanish.
STUDENT: Veredicto.
MS L: Can you tell us in Spanish in your own words what it means?
STUDENT: Una decisión, como la decisión final.

Once it is clear that students understand the concept in Spanish, they then can be supported in the process of discussing it in English.

Like with Ms C, there were also many examples of students using Spanish to negotiate meaning in their interactions with Ms L:

MS L: What is 'a reasonable doubt'?
STUDENT 1:   Cuando existe alguna duda.
MS L: About what?
STUDENT 2:   Cuando hay una duda en el caso.

In this exchange, Ms L is able to use her understanding of Italian to negotiate meaning with a student. In the next example, the translanguaging strategy helps a student eventually discuss the meaning of the key concept in English:

MS L: Who is the defendant?
STUDENT 1:   El defensor!
MS L: The defendant is not the lawyer.
STUDENT 2:   El defendido. The person that is accused.

Two things happen in this exchange that would not happen in a monolingual English-only approach or in a bilingual diglossic approach that strictly separates languages. First, Ms L is able to use her receptive skills in Spanish to clarify a student's misunderstanding of the meaning of the word 'defendant'. Secondly, after having negotiated meaning in Spanish, a student is then able to explain the meaning of the word in English. Once again, the student's Spanish is used to facilitate rather than hinder English language development.

Translanguaging also provided Ms L with the opportunity to affectively bond with her students. In particular, students appreciate her efforts using Spanish, and show interest in also learning about Italian. For example, one day she is working with a group of students who are struggling. As she reads with them, she contextualizes the lesson in Spanish. A student responds happily, 'Miss, you speak Spanish!' As she continues to work with them, she asks: 'How do you say "agree" in Spanish?' One student responds: 'De acuerdo.' But a second student says, 'In Italian it is d'accordo.' The translanguaging in this classroom allows Ms L to bond with students in a way that she otherwise might not be able to.

Ms S is of Indian descent and she is picking up Spanish from her students. As such, she relies on students to help her with the process of translanguaging more than the other two teachers. For example, in one exchange during a lesson focused on comparing and contrasting, Ms S has the students assist her in translating keywords to English:

MS S: How do you say 'find' in Spanish?
STUDENT: Buscar.

In another exchange, Ms S uses some Spanish but also relies on the students to assist her in getting her point across:

MS S: Can I please have Julio come on up ... (Julio comes up to the front of the room). Escribir una comparación with Julio and myself. Can someone say it in Spanish?
STUDENT 1: Que tienen que comparar a ellos.
STUDENT 2: Algo que ellos tienen en común.

In this exchange, Ms S uses students to communicate to others the concept she is trying to convey.

While there was a great deal of oral translanguaging that occurred in this classroom, with students playing an active role in this process, there were also written supports that Ms S provided to assist students in making meaning of key concepts. This written support came in the form of translating key words, as demonstrated in what was written on the board for students as they began class on one day:

AIM: Why do we compare ('comparar') and contrast ('diferenciar') things, ideas, or people?

DO NOW: To compare is to find similarities ('similares') in two things. To contrast is to find differences ('diferencias') in two things.

Here Ms S translated key terms that are essential for students to understand the major objective of the lesson. By introducing this at the beginning of class, Ms S activates students' prior knowledge and preps them for what they will be expected to do that day in class. In addition, because three of the words are cognates, Ms S also uses this as an opportunity to build their metalinguistic awareness and make them more conscious of the relationship between English and Spanish.

Despite her recent introduction to Spanish (or perhaps because of it), Ms S is able to translanguage to develop affective bonds with students. This is demonstrated in an interaction that occurred during a student portfolio presentation when at the end of the semester students orally present in English work they have done. One student completely shut down during her presentation and refused to speak. After the presentation, Ms S tried to encourage her to take risks. Originally, she was communicating through a translator, but ended up having a direct conversation with the student utilizing translanguaging strategies. Her message was completely understood as she expressed the importance of taking risks languaging. In so doing, she became a model of the very experimentation that she was encouraging in the student. This moment of bonding would not have been possible through a translator.

As in High School of World Cultures, the above analysis demonstrates the ways that translanguaging occurs in two similarly situated schools in classrooms for emergent bilingual students with teachers across the continuum of bilingualism. It demonstrates that translanguaging can be used in ways that both foster English language development and meta-linguistic awareness, while facilitating affective bonds and affirming the language practices with which students come. These educators demonstrate ways that teachers at PAIHS push against the English-Only paradigm of English language development. They challenge language borders in ways that are responsive to the needs of their students.

Conclusion

As language diversity becomes more complex as a result of globalization, technology and transnationalism, language education policies throughout the world have often become more intolerant of language differences. Thus, most students are increasingly taught in the dominant language of the state without harnessing the linguistic resources they bring. This is especially so in the United States where English-only instructional practices have silenced bilingual education practices that had been negotiated in an era of Civil Rights.

But a close look at ESL programmes reveals, however, that on the ground, Spanish–English bilingualism in the education of recent Latino immigrants to the United States has actually increased (see García, Woodley, Flores and Chu, 2011). Educators transgress English-only spaces in an effort to effectively educate Latino adolescents in an era of higher standards for all. This Spanish–English *bilingualism in education* is different from that of traditional *bilingual education* programmes where languages are kept separate. Instead, teachers and students use their discursive practices fluidly in order to educate effectively, building on translanguaging pedagogies.

For translanguaging pedagogies that we outline in this chapter to reach their full potential, we would need to let go of theoretical formulations of bilingualism that continue to dominate the field of language education. Our chapter questions diglossia and additive/subtractive conceptualizations of bilingualism, while offering the theoretical alternatives of transglossia and dynamic bilingualism. Within those alternative theoretical positions, translanguaging as pedagogy offers educators a way to harness the increased linguistic variation of students in the classrooms of today in order to educate meaningfully.

References

Baker, C. (2001). *Foundations of bilingual education and bilingualism*, 3rd edn. Clevedon: Multilingual Matters.

Blackledge, A. and Creese, A. (2010). *Multilingualism*. London: Continuum.

Cook, V. (2008). *Second Language Learning and Language Teaching*, 4th edn. London: Hodder Educational.

Council of Europe (2000). *Common European Framework of Reference for Languages: Learning, Teaching, Assessment*. Strasbourg: Language Policy Division.

Crawford, J. (2004). *Educating English learners: Language Diversity in Classrooms*. 5th edn. Washington, DC: Bilingual Education Services.

Crawford, J. (2007). The decline of bilingual education in the USA: How to reverse a troubling trend? *International Multilingual Research Journal*, *1*(1), 33–37.

Creese, A. and Blackledge, A. (2010). Translanguaging in the bilingual classroom: A pedagogy for learning and teaching? *Modern Language Journal* 94 (i), 103–115.

Cummins, J. (2000). *Language, power, and pedagogy: Bilingual children caught in the cross-fire*. Clevedon: Multilingual Matters.

Cummins, J. (2007). Rethinking monolingual instructional strategies in multilingual classrooms. *The Canadian Journal of Applied Linguistics*, *10*(2), 221–240.

De Houwer, A. (2009). *Bilingual First Language Acquisition*. Bristol: Multilingual Matters.

Ferguson, C. (1959). Diglossia. *Word* 15, 325–340.

Fishman, J.A. (1967). Bilingualism with and without diglossia: Diglossia with and without bilingualism. *Journal of Social Issues* 23(2): 29–38.

García, O. (2009). *Bilingual Education in the 21st Century: A global perspective*. Malden, MA: Wiley/Blackwell.

García, O. (2011). Transglossic classroom spaces, translanguaging classroom practices, and subaltern knowledge in the US. Keynote presentation at Mercator Conference. Leeuwarden, The Netherlands, 8 April 2011.

García, O. (forthcoming). Dual or dynamic bilingual education?: Empowering bilingual communities. In R. Rubdy and L. Alsagoff (eds), *The Global-Local Interface. Language choice and hybridity.* Bristol: Multilingual Matters.

García, O. and Kleifgen, J.A. (2010). *Educating Emergent Bilinguals: Policies, programs and practices for English Language Learners.* New York: Teachers College Press.

García, O., Flores, N. and Chu, H. (2011). Extending Bilingualism in U.S. Secondary Education: New variations. *International Multilingual Research Journal* 5(1): 1–18.

García, O., Woodley, H.H., Flores, N. and Chu, H. (2011). Latino Immigrant Newcomers in High Schools: Notions of Transcaring. Manuscript.

García, O. and Sylvan, C. with Witt, D. (2011). Pedagogies and practices in multilingual classrooms. Singularities in Pluralities. *Modern Language Journal* 95(iii): 385–400.

Genesee, F. (2003). Rethinking bilingual acquisition. In J.M. Dewaele (ed.). *Bilingualism: Challenges and Directions for Future Research.* Clevedon: Multilingual Matters.

Gumperz, J. (1982). *Discourse Strategies.* Cambridge: Cambridge University Press.

Herdina, P., and Jessner, U. (2002). *A Dynamic Model of Multilingualism.* Clevedon: Multilingual Matters.

Labov, W. (1966). *The Social Stratification of English in New York City.* Washington, D.C.: Center for Applied Linguistics.

Lambert, W.E. (1974). Culture and language as factors in learning and education. In F.E. Aboud and R.D. Meade (eds). *Cultural Factors in Learning and Education*, pp. 91–122. Bellingham, Washington: 5th Western Washington Symposium on Learning.

Larsen-Freeman, D. and Cameron, L. (2008). *Complex Systems and Applied Linguistics.* Cambridge: Cambridge University Press.

Lave, J. and Wenger, E. (1991). *Situated Learning: Legitimate peripheral participation.* Cambridge: Cambridge University Press.

Makoni, S. and Pennycook, A. (2007). *Disinventing and Reconstituting Languages.* Clevedon: Multilingual Matters.

Mignolo, W. (2000). *Local histories/Global designs. Coloniality, subaltern knowledges, and border thinking.* Princeton: Princeton University Press.

Mohanty, A.K. (2006). Multilingualism of the unequals and predicaments of education in India: Mother tongue or other tongue? In O. García, T. Skutnabb-Kangas and

M. Torres-Guzmán (eds), *Imagining multilingual schools: Languages in education and glocalization*, pp. 262–283. Clevedon: Multilingual Matters.

Ortiz, F. (1940/2002). *Contrapunteo cubano del tabaco y el azúcar [Tobacco and sugar: A Cuban counter point]*. Madrid: Cátedra.

Pennycook, A. (2010). *Language as a Local Practice*. London: Routledge.

Shohamy, E. (2006). *Language Policy: Hidden Agendas and new Approaches*. London: Routledge.

Skutnabb-Kangas, T. (1981). *Bilingualism or Not: The education of minorities*. Clevedon: Multilingual Matters.

Street, B. (1985). *Literacy in Theory and Practice*. Cambridge: Cambridge University Press.

US Census Bureau. (2009). *American Community Survey (ACS), 2008*. Washington, DC: US Government Printing Office.

US Census Bureau (2010). Decennial Census 2010. Washington, DC: US Government Printing Office.

Vygotsky, L.S. (1978). *Mind and Society*. Cambridge, MA: Harvard University Press.

SURESH CANAGARAJAH, MADHAV KAFLE AND
YUMI MATSUMOTO

4 World Englishes in Local Classrooms

Introduction

In the context of globalization and late-modernity, scholars have started asking how education can prepare students for transnational communication. English is touted as the global language par excellence, and claimed to guarantee communicative success in today's social and economic relationships. There is a stampede to acquire a good knowledge of English, and many countries are giving English teaching priority in their educational policies. However, it is often ignored that the global status of English comes with a price. English has also been appropriated by local communities for their own interests and purposes, and it has now become a heterogeneous language. 'Native-speaker' varieties, such as standard British or American English, have lost their status as the universal norm for proficiency. Multilingual people are negotiating their own varieties of English in their own terms to conduct business. Some linguists contend that English has diversified to such an extent that it is not one language, but 'a family of languages' (Crystal, 2004: 40). We use the term 'World Englishes' (WE, hereafter) broadly to capture this plurality of English language. As people are required to shuttle between communities and languages, proficiency in one's own variety of English is insufficient. One has to develop the competence to engage with diverse varieties of English worldwide. Such a perspective calls for a paradigm shift on thinking about the nature of English and ways of teaching it. In this article, we survey the attempts to address the plurality of English in classrooms worldwide through the burgeoning literature on WE.

It must be noted at the outset that studies on ways of teaching WE are fairly limited, as scholars are still preoccupied with modeling the changes English is going through and describing its varieties. Some are diffident to propose pedagogical practices because they feel that the changes of English have to be researched and described better before we proceed to teaching practice. In many excellent publications that track the global flow of English, such as Pennycook (2007) and Higgins (2009), the pedagogical implications are shoved to a final chapter. Such publications offer cursory reflections rather than robust findings from pedagogies that have been researched in a disciplined and systematic manner. Our survey of the literature on WE shows that the educational implications of the diversity of English need to be urgently addressed in our fields.

Theoretical foundations

Before we offer a perspective on teaching WE in diverse classrooms worldwide, we must review the ongoing debates on ways to theorize global English. Scholars are locked in heated polemics on how to model the changing nature of English language. Though we use WE in this article as an umbrella term to capture different ways of modeling English language, 'World Englishes' was coined to specifically label one of the earliest schools to theorize the diversity of English. Associated with the Indian linguist Braj Kachru (1984, 1985), this school is known for a tripartite model of the spread and diversity of English. Inner circle constituted the traditional owners of the language and they were called 'norm providing', as their norms were considered the reference point for others. Outer circle constituted the postcolonial communities such as India, Nigeria and Jamaica, where English was developing local norms, as it was actively used as a second language within those communities. They were called 'norm developing'. Expanding circle constituted communities which use English as a foreign language and, therefore, were presumed to adopt the norms of inner circle communities. Such communities as China, Brazil and Germany were called 'norm dependent'. Though the linguistic reality of these circles has now been questioned (see Canagarajah, 2006c), we will use this terminology to distinguish between different contexts of teaching English below.

Deviating from Kachru's model is the school of English as an International language (EIL). As Aya Matsuda clarifies, EIL is 'not a linguistic distinction, but it is rather a functional one' (2006: 160). Scholars who belong to this school perceive WE varieties as deriving from the same grammatical system. For them, English simply takes functional variations in different geographical contexts, the same ways registers and discourses of English are different in institutional, social and textual contexts. However, as Kachru's coining of the term 'Englishes' suggests, other scholars may consider the differences to go beyond mere functional variation.

Scholars of the ELF (English as a lingua franca) school believe that multilingual speakers have developed a grammar of English that differs from the norms of 'native' speakers (Jenkins, 2006a; Seidlhofer, 2004). These scholars are now attempting to describe the lingua franca core (LFC) that captures this emergent grammar of multilinguals who use English as a contact language for their transnational communication. ELF primarily relates to the usage of speakers in expanding circle communities. While Kachru's school perceives these communities as dependent on inner circle norms, it is significant that the ELF school perceives these communities as developing their own norms. ELF also takes the discussion of English beyond the fairly homogeneous national boundaries (and circles) of an English variety studied by Kachru's camp as it considers the use of English in transnational contact zones as more significant.

However, the search for a homogeneous and stable LFC is considered by some other scholars as misleading (see Pennycook, 2007; Canagarajah, 2007a; House, 2003a). Though they agree with the ELF camp that English usage beyond national borders varies from native speaker usage and that its variation needs to be given importance, they consider the norms in these interactions as fluid and hybrid. More importantly, they consider the norms as negotiated and evolving situationally in each specific interaction. Rather than looking for the core grammar of lingua franca English therefore, they attempt to study the strategies people adopt to negotiate the diverse norms multilinguals bring to the communication. Since these scholars look at lingua franca English as not a single variety, but a form of practice that negotiates diverse local varieties, they have labeled themselves the LFE (Lingua Franca English) school. Pennycook (2010) argues that the term English *as* a lingua franca gives the impression that this is a monolithic variety. LFE scholars also go beyond Kachru's camp in saying that English is more diverse than the listing and numbering of them as Indian English, Singaporean English and Nigerian English. For them, English is a form of local practice that is always creative and emergent, evolving in the context of the local values and interests of the people who use it worldwide for their purposes. The ability to communicate in this hybrid English does not depend on shared norms, but mutually recognized and reciprocated practices. The LFE school also goes beyond other models to argue that such negotiation is not limited to situations of English as a foreign language in the expanding circle. In the context of late-modern globalization, no community is self-enclosed. Apart from all communities having to negotiate language beyond their borders, the local is itself interpenetrated by the global. Therefore, those in the outer or inner circle cannot also rely upon their own national norms for communication in English. All of us have to adopt effective strategies to negotiate ever-present linguistic difference in global communication.

Pedagogical approaches

As we can imagine, the ways to teach WE would of course depend on the models scholars adhere to. Teaching is further complicated by the geographical setting (i.e., inner, outer, expanding circle, or the contact zones between all these communities), skill addressed (i.e., reading, writing, listening or speaking), and language competence aimed at (i.e., grammar, phonology, vocabulary, pragmatics, text features or discourse conventions). We discuss the pedagogical approaches in general below, while noting the distinguishing features related to specific geographical, skill and linguistic domains where relevant.

Promoting local English

At the most basic level, some teachers in local communities are focusing on developing a competence in the local varieties of English. Scholars in this school, mainly from the Kachruvian tradition, consider it important not to impose exonormative norms to develop and assess the English proficiency of their students. They recognize that their students learn English not necessarily to interact with native speakers in far away inner circle communities, but primarily to communicate in their own local contexts. This pedagogy works well for outer circle communities where there are recognizable local varieties (with a long history of usage) and institutionalized uses of English in local community. Teaching has focused on grammar, vocabulary, pronunciation and discourse conventions to make students competent in the local variety.

For example, Hino (2009) proposes teaching a de-Anglo-Americanized English as a means of expressing indigenous values in international communication. He adopts such teaching practices at one of the top national universities (Osaka University) in Japan. He encourages students to speak English with a Japanese mindset and exposes them to varieties of English and examples of nonnative speaker interactions in his course. His major teaching goal is to give confidence to Japanese learners by demonstrating that Japanese English is internationally functional. Thus he promotes this type of English as capable of expressing indigenous values while maintaining international intelligibility.

In the field of phonology, scholars like Levis (2005) are promoting the idea that pronunciation is connected to people's identities and relationships. Therefore, they are moving away from imposing a native speaker norm, and exploring ways of accommodating the accents and pronunciations diverse communities are comfortable with. A practical way to introduce local norms is discussed by Bruthiaux (2010). He argues that the teaching of English should remain based on one of the dominant models serving as a convenient starting point, with the localization of pronunciation supplied by teachers and the introduction of wider variation depending on students' proficiency. Given inadequate teaching materials featuring local norms and descriptions of local rules, many teachers would rather start with the dominant models and move on to localization at a later point. The danger is that this approach would treat WE as an add-on, marginalizing local norms and simplifying the profound issues of ownership that motivate the WE pedagogical paradigm shift.

The limitations in teaching materials and descriptions of local varieties of English are motivating others to combine research with teaching. Tsuzuki and Nakamura (2007) try to identify which phonological errors of Japanese student researchers in science majors might lead to miscommunication. Thereafter they fashion pedagogical implications that help learners notice which phonological features should be avoided in order to prevent communication failure. They have found out three types of mispronunciations which seriously impede intelligibility: 1) consonants such as plosives and l/r distinctions; 2) vowel length contrasts; 3) misplaced or lack of stress on words or phrases. These features are considered as phonological core features of Japanese influenced English, which may be the highest priority to teach in terms of pronunciation. They conclude that English curricula in Japanese school systems need to provide prioritized pronunciation education that is tailored to the needs of their local students.

The limitation of the above approach is that students cannot be satisfied with competence in local varieties in order to function as global citizens. Even communication in local communities involves interacting with international agencies and diverse ethnic groups who bring other varieties of English. An approach that addresses this limitation is intercultural sensitivity.

Intercultural awareness

Such pedagogical approaches sensitize students to the diversity of English worldwide. One might consider this approach a sensitivity training. The approach would help students develop positive attitudes towards their own varieties of English and develop tolerance towards other varieties. Such attitudes would increase their willingness and capacity to negotiate language diversity in their interactions. Morrison and White (2005) focus on nurturing their students as 'global listeners'. They describe a course offered in the World Englishes department at Chukyo University, Nagoya, Japan. The structure of the course is so designed that the students get real experience of interacting with English speakers around the world. To accomplish such goal students are taken to other countries to experience other WE varieties. Following a term-long class at Chukyo, groups of students travel to Singapore during school breaks in August, February or March. Part of the curriculum includes a three-week study tour at the Language Teaching Institute (LTI) at the Regional Language Center (RELC) in Singapore. The following academic year, all second year students are required to participate in a three-week course in one of the following destinations: Surrey, England; Boston, Massachusetts; or Sydney, Australia. Though this somewhat hands-on experience with WE is constructive, it requires considerable resources of time and money to make it succeed.

However, a limitation of sensitivity training is that knowing about WE is not the same thing as having competence in WE. It is important to consider ways of developing communicative competence through engagement with the language and through speech activities.

Intercultural competence

Such pedagogies address sociolinguistic sensitivity while also developing some competencies in negotiating diversity in intercultural communication. They situate English in specific cultures to consider how language use in these communities is shaped by local values and practices. Even in the case that there might be similarities in syntax structure or vocabulary, students can expect to experience differences in tone, thought patterns, idea development and conversational rules as they are shaped by the cultures concerned. Pedagogies informed by intercultural communication would develop the competence to negotiate these cultural differences in English communication. Alptekin (2002) argues for a pedagogy that introduces the local cultural situations in which students use English so that they develop the intercultural sensitivity to negotiate the different cultures informing the use of English in the context of globalization.

Teaching core grammars

Scholars informed by the ELF orientation would argue that one does not have to stop with an understanding of cultural values, but teach grammatical and phonological commonalities that characterize multilingual communication in English. Considering the intercultural approach as too open ended and process-oriented, they would advocate the teaching of LFC rules of grammar and phonology as more product-oriented and direct. Jenkins (2000, 2002, 2006a, 2006b) convincingly proposes a pedagogy based on LFC to fulfill a pluricentric approach to the teaching and use of English, and addresses the dual needs of international mutual intelligibility and local identity of ELF users. LFC provides empirically established phonological norms and classroom pronunciation models for teaching English as an international language rather than imposing Received Pronunciation or General American pronunciation on multilingual students. More specifically, Jenkins (2000) presents a five-phase accent addition programme. Note how her strategy differs from the traditional *accent reduction* programmes. She proposes:

1. Addition of core items to the learner's productive and receptive repertoire. This way, they can ensure intelligibility in diverse contexts.
2. Addition of a range of L2 (i.e., second language) English accents to the learner's receptive repertoire. In this manner, they can at least understand speakers who deviate from the LFC.
3. Addition of accommodation skills. This would enable speakers to fashion their speech in consideration of the norms their interlocutors bring with them.
4. Addition of non-core items to the learner's receptive repertoire. This too would help students to negotiate the speech of those who deviate from LFC.
5. Addition of a range of L1 (i.e., first language) English accents to the learner's receptive repertoire. This would enable them to communicate with native speakers who are often not adept at multilingual norms.

Jenkins thus proposes considering only core item deviation as error, and non-core item deviation as regional variation. In addition, she emphasizes the importance of developing learners' accommodation skills and language awareness so that they can engage with diverse groups of speakers.

Like Jenkins, many ELF scholars believe that the norms and practices of global English speakers have to be empirically studied in order to develop a suitable pedagogy. Seidlhofer (2001, 2004) introduces the corpus named VOICE (Vienna–Oxford International Corpus of English) and presents emerging ELF lexicogrammar characteristics which arise from this corpus to develop teaching practices. She focuses on ELF lexicogrammar among ELF users and analyses which items are used systematically and frequently without causing communication problems. She finds that typical grammatical errors are generally unproblematic among ELF interactions and pose no obstacle to communicative success. Therefore, deviations from native speaker norms do not necessarily cause communication problems among multilinguals.

Pragmatics

The limitation of the ELF approach is that students would rely too easily on commonalities and ignore the fact that English is changing and evolving in diverse local interactions. Furthermore, this approach may not allow multilinguals to negotiate with native speakers who would come armed with their traditional norms for communication. Students have to be prepared to negotiate any deviation from the norms they are trained to expect. To prepare students for such negotiation of difference, LFE scholars develop pedagogical approaches that focus on pragmatics. They feel that a focus on form fails to develop the competencies required to deal with the diversity of forms one would encounter in transnational encounters. Since it is impractical to expect that we can teach all the varieties of English under the sun, a more reasonable approach is to go beyond individual varieties to develop the competencies students need to deal with the difference in all possible encounters. To address this challenge, LFE scholars propose developing competencies such as the following:

Language awareness: this way, students do not focus only on learning single varieties but learn how all varieties are constituted. This awareness enables them to negotiate the different varieties their interlocutors bring to communication by decoding them and framing their own language to suit the interlocutor's expectations.

Interactional strategies: Rather than focusing on individual varieties, these strategies too would enable students to negotiate any variety speakers bring to an interaction. Scholarship such as accommodation theory (see Giles, 1984) has enlightened how interlocutors make adjustments to each other's difference in communication. Teaching accommodation strategies would help students tailor their speech to the norms of their interlocutors. Other strategies are emerging from ongoing research on lingua franca encounters, and are illustrated below.

House (2003b) shows how to develop pragmatic fluency in lingua franca English in the classroom based on intercultural research and her own multilingual subjects' interactional data. She provides the following detailed suggestions for developing pragmatic competence and fluency in WE: 1) Instruction should focus on training learners in using a variegated repertoire of interpretation and negotiation strategies; 2) The yardstick for measuring competence is the stable bilingual/multilingual speaker under comparable social, cultural, historical conditions of language use with comparable goals for interaction in different discourse domains and hybrid procedures in the teaching and learning of LFE; 3) Particular attention should be paid to LFE users' strategic competence and to training communication strategies such as code-switching and borrowing from other languages that the LFE users speak; 4) English language classrooms should empower learners to keep their own personalities and social persona, and linguistic and pragmatic knowledge for performance should be given primary importance in order to improve learners' pragmatic competence and pragmatic fluency; 5) It is important to stress the interactional usefulness of relevant routines in LFE; 6) Collaborative talk (discourse production) in LFE interactions should be capitalized in the teaching of pragmatic fluency; 7) For developing pragmatic fluency, it is essential to intensify the teaching of interactional phenomena in order to enable learners to manage smooth turn taking through sensitizing them to points of transitional relevance and to the lubricating and modificatory function of a rich repertoire of gambits and discourse strategies. In order to further increase metapragmatic awareness, House proposes that it is important to combine both research and teaching in pragmatics.

Others propose a teaching approach that recognizes the different pragmatic rules available in different communicative contexts. McKay (2005) proposes a pedagogy of pragmatics that recognizes the different conventions governing different WE circles. She argues that multilingual students should recognize the existence of native speaker norms in the inner circle, equally well established indigenous norms in the outer circle, and the co-construction of norms to negotiate a plurality of pragmatic norms in the expanding circle. She would be happy if students at least develop receptive competence in the conventions of other communities so that they can make themselves intelligible in intercultural communication. McKay outlines her pedagogy of pragmatics in the following manner:

1. Explicit attention should be given to introducing and practising repair strategies, such as asking for clarification, repetition and rephrasing, and allowing for wait time.
2. A variety of conversational gambits should be introduced and practised, including such items as managing turn-taking, back channeling and initiating topics of conversation.
3. Attention should be given to developing negotiation strategies that involve such features as suggesting alternatives arguing for a particular approach, and seeking consensus. (2009: 239)

Multilingual negotiation

Some in the LFE school go beyond English to advocate a negotiation with other languages for global communication. They are interested in constructing a multilingual pedagogy as they recognize that English co-exists with other languages in global communication. Higgins (2009), for example, advocates that we should teach students different kinds of code switching and hybrid communicative practices. She is critical of the current educational policy that stipulates that languages should be taught one at a time, separated from each other. In making this proposal, such scholars are motivated by everyday communicative practices in multilingual environments, where hybrid codes are common. Many scholars are in fact making the claim that pedagogy should be shaped around the creative multilingual practices of youth in popular culture, Internet and other new media environments. In this regard, the work of Pennycook (2007) on hip-hop communication is valuable. He criticizes the antipathy to popular culture in educational circles. Therefore, he proposes a pedagogy of 'teaching with the flow' – i.e., adopting the global flows of popular cultural forms. This form of pedagogy is not only multilingual, but also multimodal. Pennycook advocates teaching how to exploit the resources of media, music, the body and other semiotic resources to communicate in global English.

A pedagogy of appropriation

Though the teaching approaches above will help students be functional in contemporary contexts of global communication, some critical practitioners insist that we have to go beyond functional competence and develop the ability to appropriate English for students' own purposes according to their own values and interests. For this purpose, scholars are interested in developing a pedagogy of appropriation (Canagarajah, 2006a; Lin et al., 2005). It is arguable whether anyone can learn or use a language without appropriation. To speak is to people the language with one's own intentions, according to Bakhtin's well known theorization. Anything less than that is not to have voice in that language but to mimic it. Such appropriational pedagogical approaches have been developed in the teaching of writing much better rather than in speaking. Canagarajah (2006a, b) has argued that it is possible to teach students how to merge their own discourse patterns and codes with the dominant conventions of academic writing to construct hybrid texts. He has also shown how multilingual students lean towards such strategies of writing even without teacher intervention (Canagarajah, 1997, 2009). Though such writing strategy is rhetorically very demanding (i.e., students should know the dominant codes, their own codes, and appropriate ways to merge them), Canagarajah argues that multilingual students have developed such strategies through social practice in their own communicative environments. Appropriation is a well-practised communicative strategy in post-colonial contact zones (see Pratt, 1991). The task for teachers is to develop a reflective and critical attitude towards such practice so that students can develop their competence further.

A pedagogy of choices

Many scholars consider such an appropriation approach too idealistic and demanding. More importantly, they think that students will be penalized for deviating from dominant conventions. Short of teaching appropriation, they would teach students the range of options available to them and leave it to them to choose what is appropriate for their different communicative contexts. Matsuda and Matsuda (2010) propose a pedagogy for writing that involves the following options: i.e., teach the dominant language forms and functions; teach the nondominant language forms and functions; teach the boundary between what works and what does not; teach the principles and strategies for discourse negotiation; and teach the risks involved in using deviational features. Presumably, students will be able to adopt the strategies that are comfortable for them, with a full awareness of the risks and limitations of the different orientation towards established varieties of English.

It is clear that we have moved far from the traditional approach of developing universal expertise in the native speaker varieties of British or American standard, under the assumption that those norms are the ones that matter in international communication. The evolving pedagogical alternatives recognize that English has become deterritorialized and found new homes in diverse local contexts in the world. The global speakers of English are claiming ownership over the language and developing their own norms quite independently of native speakers. To be a global citizen in late-modernity involves the capacity to negotiate creatively and critically the plurality of norms characterizing English language.

Further research and educational development

Though scholars are expanding their work on constructing effective pedagogical approaches, students' attitudes towards local varieties of English
remain negative. Without positive or at least enlightened attitudes towards
the diversity of English, pedagogical intervention may not pay off. A few
scholars who have studied the attitudes of students in local communities
observe that students still give more value to native speaker varieties as the
desirable target for learning. Others find that students are also confused
about the differences between varieties of English. Though they feel that
native speaker norms are preferable, they cannot recognize the distinction
between varieties of English. Matsuda analyses the attitudes of the students
in Japan towards WE. She found that questions about varieties of English
confused students. They often replied, 'I don't know' and 'I'm not sure'
(2002a: 437) while answering questions about nonnative varieties. But the
students clearly expressed that American and Britain English were the only
standard varieties and they wanted to acquire these rather than outer circle
varieties such as Singapore English. The study suggests that there is a need
for pedagogical intervention to work hand in hand with language awareness, sociolinguistic sensitivity and ideological clarity. It is important for
teachers and researchers to consider if pedagogical intervention is resulting
in positive attitudes towards WE. If not, teachers have to pay equal attention to developing the type of attitudes that will help their students cope
with the diversity of English.

Along with working on positive attitudes among students, we have to
also empower nonnative teachers of English. It is well known that multilingual teachers have a high sense of linguistic anxiety and insecurity. Bolton
(2002) discusses the dominant discourses and attitudes of English language
teachers in Hong Kong. His findings from questionnaires show that there
is still a preference for native standard varieties in formal communication,
and English language teachers conceive Hong Kong English as inappropriate. Other scholars are working on creating a positive view of the skills and
knowledge brought by multilingual teachers for the teaching of English

(see Kirkpatrick, 2007). Though multilingual teachers do bring certain competencies that are useful for English teaching, they need guidance and clarity. McKay (2002) provides a useful manual for teachers on adopting the proper attitude towards WE, understanding the motivations for the paradigm shift, and devising creative strategies for teaching WE.

Furthermore, though it is now commonly accepted that inner circle communities also need the ability to negotiate WE, efforts to teach native speaker students WE are inadequate. As many scholars have noted, the inability to negotiate the diversity of English can result in inner circle students being disadvantaged in the new global job market (see Horner and Trimbur, 2002). A pilot project by Kubota is exemplary in this record. She aims at raising American high-school students' awareness of issues on WE and assisting them in exploring ways to better communicate with WE speakers (2001: 59). Her goals for her high school class in rural North Carolina were the following: (1) to help understand that there are many varieties of English used in the United States and in the world; (2) to provide a brief history of English; (3) to demonstrate the difficulty of acquiring native-like proficiency in a second language; (4) to explore ways to communicate effectively with WE speakers; and (5) to critically investigate implications of global spread of English (Kubota, 2001: 50–51). The project was conducted for eight sessions each of fifty-five minutes. Though Kubota states there are positive outcomes, she lists the following as the pedagogical and educational challenges of teaching WE in the inner circle that need to be addressed in the future: (1) the difficulty of critically examining the global spread of English; (2) the need for creating classroom interaction that is conducive to critical examination of the issue; (3) the need to use more experiential approaches when exploring cross-cultural communication strategies; (4) the need for earlier interventions for promoting cultural/linguistic diversities; and (5) the need for more emphasis on cross-cultural/linguistic awareness in foreign language learning (Kubota, 2001: 60).

In terms of skills developed, teaching of WE in reading instruction seems to be inadequate. This is intriguing as postcolonial literary writers have been using local varieties of English in their writing for a long time, and students and scholars of English literature have been exposed to many diverse varieties through the writings of Achebe, Soyinka, Walcott and Raja

Rao. It is possible that language teachers have failed to address reading as they have reserved this task to scholars in literature. It is also the case that reading specialists focus on expository and academic texts as coming under their purview, and treat these texts as still written in standard British or American English. From this perspective, they may consider their task as teaching the decoding of texts using traditional norms, and thus continue business as usual. In this regard, it is useful to merge the pedagogies of literature and multimodal communication with those of expository/academic texts to develop a richer literacy pedagogy.

Furthermore, while teaching strategies have developed well, researchers and scholars have not paid enough attention to teaching materials. This is a challenging area for intervention as textbook publishing is highly commercialized. Publishers would prefer to publish materials that can be marketed worldwide to diverse communities. Materials that are tailored to specific local communities require a lot of resources to research, write and produce. Materials in inner circle (traditional) norms are easier to produce. Adopting a pragmatic attitude, commercial publishers may also argue that it is the prestige varieties that are universally demanded by parents and students, and that they would sell more profitably. As a result, teachers are compelled to produce their own self-made materials for their classes.

However, even locally produced textbooks sometime fail to go far in accommodating local norms and culture. In her analysis of seventh-grade ministry-approved text books in Japan, Matsuda (2002b) found an inner circle emphasis in the textbooks' representation of users and uses of English. Of the 74 characters shown in the textbooks, most characters were from Japan (34), followed by inner circle country speakers (30). The remaining were from outer and expanding circle countries (10). However, there was a dissonance between the number of characters and their actual speech production. Despite being most in number, the Japanese speakers produced minimal utterances. In general, outer and expanding circle speakers produced nominal utterances. It is the inner circle speakers who dominate the conversation, denying the possibility of presenting the norms of other communities. The diversification of characters and situations, though welcome, fails to do much to provide a deeper vision of plural English. Perhaps based on this limited progress, Matsuda (2003, 2006) goes on to consider other ways of introducing diverse WE varieties in classrooms. She proposes using guest speakers from WE communities, student exchange programmes, Internet sites and multimedia resources to expose students to language diversity.

A final area for further research and development is testing. Though creative teaching practices are being devised in local classrooms, testing instruments are still traditional. They measure competence according to traditional native speaker norms. Such tests thus have the washback effect of shaping teaching and curriculum, setting back the advances made in teaching plural norms. The commercialization of the international testing industry creates constraints on the extent to which tests can be made open to plural Englishes. Tests like TOEFL and IELTS are held worldwide, and it is difficult for them to create different tests for different communities. Though there are a few examples of specialized tests for specific communities – such as the test for Indonesian teachers that focuses on local situations and language norms (Brown and Lumley, 1998) – we have to adopt more creative testing formats to assess if speakers can negotiate the diverse varieties they would encounter in transnational relations. For this, we have to move beyond the product-oriented and discrete-item tests to adopt more process-oriented and interactive instruments (see Canagarajah, 2006b). Proficiency today is not mastery of a single variety of English, but one's ability to negotiate the new and emerging norms one encounters in interactions.

Conclusion

As we have argued in this chapter, educational settings have to develop a plurilingual model that transcends the teaching of single varieties or monolithic grammars. The communicative context of late modernity compels us to develop language awareness among students and make them capable of negotiating the diverse varieties they will encounter in their everyday life in transnational settings. We have to therefore shift the pedagogical focus from individual varieties to repertoire building; product to process; mastery to negotiation; and grammar to pragmatics.

References

Alptekin, C. (2002). Towards intercultural communicative competence in ELT. *ELT Journal, 56*, 57–64.

Bolton, K. (2002). *Hong Kong English: Autonomy and creativity.* Hong Kong: Hong Kong University Press.

Brown, A. and Lumley, T. (1998). Linguistic and cultural norms in language testing: A case study. *Melbourne Papers in Language Testing, 7*(1), 80–96.

Bruthiaux, P. (2010). World Englishes and the classroom: an EFL perspective. *TESOL Quarterly. 44*, 365–369.

Canagarajah, A.S. (1997). Safe houses in the contact zone: Coping strategies of African-American students in the academy. *College Composition and Communication, 48*(2), 173–196.

Canagarajah, S. (2006a). The place of world Englishes in composition: Pluralization continued. *College Composition and Communication, 57*, 586–619.

Canagarajah, S. (2006b). Changing communicative needs, revised assessment objectives: Testing English as an International language. *Language Assessment Quarterly, 3*, 229–242.

Canagarajah, A. Suresh (2006c). TESOL at Forty: What are the Issues? *TESOL Quarterly, 40*/1: 9–34.

Canagarajah, S. (2007a). Lingua franca English, multilingual communities, and language acquisition. *Modern Language Journal, 91*, 923–939.

Canagarajah, S. (2007b). After disinvention: Possibilities for communication, community and competence. In S. Makoni and A. Pennycook (eds), *Disinventing and reconstituting languages*, 233–239. Clevedon: Multilingual Matters.

Canagarajah, S. (2009). Multilingual Strategies of Negotiating English: From Conversation to Writing. *Journal of Advanced Composition 29*, 17–48.

Crystal, D. (2004). *The language revolution.* Cambridge: Polity.

Giles, H. (ed). (1984). The dynamics of speech accommodation. *International Journal of the Sociology of Language 46*. (Special topic issue.)

Higgins, C. (2009). *English as a local language: Post-colonial identities and multilingual practices.* Bristol: Multilingual Matters.

Hino, N. (2009). The teaching of English as an international language in Japan: An answer to the dilemma of indigenous values and global needs in the expanding circle. *ALIA Review, 22,* 103–119.

Horner, B. and Trimbur. J. (2002). English Only and U.S. college composition. *College Composition and Communication,* 53, 594–630.

House, J. (2003a). English as a lingua franca: A threat to multilingualism? *Journal of Sociolinguistics,* 7 / 4, 556–578.

House, J. (2003b). Teaching and learning pragmatic fluency in a foreign language: The case of English as a lingua franca. In A. Martinez Flor, E. Usó Juan and A. Fernandez Guerra (eds), *Pragmatic competence and foreign language teaching,* 133–159. Castello de la Plana, Spain: Publications de la Universitat Jaume I.

Jenkins, J. (2000). *The phonology of English as an international language: New models, new goals.* Oxford: Oxford University Press.

Jenkins, J. (2002). A sociolinguistically based, empirically researched pronunciation syllabus for English as an international language. *Applied linguistics, 23,* 83–103.

Jenkins, J. (2006a). Current perspectives on teaching World Englishes and English as a lingua franca. *TESOL Quarterly, 40,* 157–181.

Jenkins, J. (2006b). Global intelligibility and local diversity: Possibility or Paradox? In R. Rudby and M. Saraceni (eds), *English in the world: Global rules, global roles,* 32–39. London: Continuum.

Kachru, B.B. (1984). World Englishes and the teaching of English to non-native speakers: contexts, attitudes, and concerns. *TESOL Newsletter,* 18(5), 25–26.

Kachru, B.B. (1985). The English language in a global context. In R. Quirk and H.G. Widdowson (eds), *English in the world,* 11–30. Cambridge: Cambridge University Press.

Kirkpatrick, A. (2007). *World Englishes: Implications for international communication and English language teaching.* Cambridge: Cambridge University Press.

Kubota, R. (2001). Teaching world Englishes to native speakers of English in the USA. *World Englishes, 20,* 47–64.

Levis, J. (2005). Changing contexts and shifting paradigms in pronunciation teaching. *TESOL Quarterly, 39,* 369–377.

Lin, A., et al. (2005). International TESOL professionals and teaching English for glocalized communication (TEGCOM). In Canagarajah, S. (ed.), *Reclaiming the local in language policy and practice,* 197–222. Mahwah: Erlbaum.

Matsuda, A. and Matsuda, P.K. (2010). World Englishes and the teaching of writing. *TESOL Quarterly.* 44, 369–374.

Matsuda, A. (2002a). 'International understanding' through teaching World Englishes. *World Englishes, 21(3)*, 436–440.

Matsuda, A. (2002b). Representation of users and uses of English in beginning Japanese EFL textbooks. *JALT Journal, 24(2)*, 182–200.

Matsuda, A. (2003). Incorporating World Englishes in teaching English as an international language. *TESOL Quarterly, 37(4)*, 719–729.

Matsuda, A. (2006). Negotiating ELT assumptions in EIL classrooms. In J. Edge (ed.) (Re)Locating TESOL in an age of empire, pp. 158–170. Hampshire: Palgrave Macmillan.

Mckay, L.S. (2002). *Teaching English as an international language: Rethinking goals and approaches*. Oxford: Oxford University Press.

Mckay, L.S. (2005). Teaching the pragmatics of English as an international language. *Guidelines, 27*, 3–9.

Mckay, L.S. (2009). Pragmatics and EIL pedagogy. In F. Sharifian. (Ed.), *English as an international language: perspectives and pedagogical issues*, 227–241. Clevedon: Multilingual Matters.

Morrison, R. and White, M. (2005). Nurturing global listeners: Increasing familiarity and appreciation for world Englishes. *World Englishes, 24*, 361–370.

Pennycook, A. (2007). *Global Englishes and transcultural flows*. London and New York: Routledge.

Pennycook, A. (2010). *Language as a local practice*. London and New York: Routledge.

Pratt, M.L. (1991). Arts of the contact zone. *Profession*, 33–40.

Seidlhofer, B. (2001). Closing a conceptual gap: the case for a description of English as a lingua franca. *International Journal of Applied Linguistics, 11*, 133–158.

Seidlhofer, B. (2004). Research perspectives on teaching English as a lingua franca. *Annual Review of Applied Linguistics, 24*, 209–239.

Tsuzuki, M. and Nakamura, S. (2007). Intelligibility assessment of Japanese accents: A phonological study of science major students' speech. In T. Hoffmann and L. Siebers (eds), *World Englishes – Problems, properties and prospects*, 239–261. Amsterdam: John Benjamins Publishing Company.

SANDRA LEE MCKAY

5 English as an International Language, Multilingualism and Language Planning

Introduction

The growing literature on English as an international language (EIL) (Crystal, 1997, 2003; McKay, 2002, 2008; Sharifian, 2009) attests to the widespread recognition that today English is a unique language with the greatest number of speakers in the world (if both L1 and L2 speakers are included) and the most widely distributed geographically. With the spread of English has come claims that the English language is undermining linguistic and cultural diversity (e.g., Nettle and Romaine, 2000; Phillipson, 1992, 2003; Skutnabb-Kangas, 2000). In this chapter I argue that the present loss of linguistic diversity involves a myriad of factors including individual perceptions, wants and needs, language-in-education policies, and most importantly the local linguistic landscape and the discourses surrounding English.

By way of illustrating how these various factors can affect the spread of English and linguistic diversity, the chapter describes two English language education policies. The first case describes Japanese policies regarding English education in which a belief that English is necessary for Japan to be an international player has led the Ministry of Education and local administrators to require the learning of English as a foreign language. The second case deals with the language education policies of South Africa where the government policy is highly supportive of multilingualism and multiculturalism. Both case studies will be examined to highlight the effects that language-in-education policies and the local linguistic landscape can have on the promotion of multilingualism. The final section of the chapter elaborates on a set of principles that should inform EIL pedagogy if it is to successfully enhance the learning of English and the maintenance of linguistic diversity.

Language loss

Nettle and Romaine (2000) note that there are several ways in which a language can die. The first is language loss through population loss, that is, when speakers of the language disappear through disease or wars, as was the case with some colonized indigenous populations. The second is through language shift, either a forced or voluntary shift. In forced language shift, populations are often required through colonization to acquire the language of the conqueror, a clear case of what Phillipson (1992) terms *linguistic imperialism*. There are many cases of forced language shift. Nettle and Romaine (2000), for example, document the loss of the Hawaiian languages and the decline of the Celtic languages. In voluntary shift, on the other hand, individuals perceive that it is to their benefit to acquire English. Both types of shift have contributed to the widespread growth of English; however, in many contexts aspects of both forced and voluntary shift are present, as was the case in the Philippines.

When the United States acquired the Philippines, it undertook an extensive documentation of the demographics of the country, noting some eighty-seven indigenous languages. Aware that the Spanish had had little impact in unifying the country linguistically, the Americans drafted a detailed plan to spread English within the country. At the base of the plan was a decision to use English as the sole means of instruction in the public schools. Whereas the official reports of the Bureau of Education contended that the plan would be successful so that within fifteen years, English would be the common unifying language of the country: 'in practice, the great majority of the population continued using local languages, despite the reported 97% of the Filipino children who passed through the colonial educational system by the late 1920s' (Brutt-Griffler, 2002: 36). Although the policy would seem to have been a failure from the American's perspective, the fact is that today English is widely used in Filipino society. The question is why.

Part of the answer lies in Nettle and Romaine's (2000) account of the influence of economic takeoff on languages. They distinguish the pull and push factor of economic development in the following manner:

> On the one hand, the developed economies have a strong pull factor, offering as they do the apparent possibility of wonderful new technologies, more profitable occupations, and a rising standard of living. On the other hand, economic takeoff gives the elite classes extraordinary power, by furnishing them with ever-better weapons, larger armies, and many other technologies for controlling and brainwashing people. Such elites have a strong interest in compelling people to join their sphere of economic interest – a larger sphere of interest means more profits – and they often do. This 'push' factor is just as significant as the intrinsic 'pull' of economic development in understanding subsequent history. (132)

Cases like the Philippines demonstrate that language shift or endangerment is often a far more complex process than some of the literature on linguistic imperialism would suggest. Drawing on examples of African colonization, Mufwene (2002), for example, contends that

> the vitality of a language often depends on factors other than merely power. They show that if power has any role to play, basic cost-and-benefit considerations having to do with what a speaker needs a particular language for, or to what extent a particular language facilitates survival in a changing socio-economic ecology, determine what particular languages are given up and doomed to attrition and eventual extinction. (164)

The case studies that follow illustrate the complexity of language loss and maintenance in an increasingly globalized world in which migration, language planning and prevalent discourses all have a significant influence on language loss and language acquisition.

Japan

Government policy

Like many countries in the world today, most young people in Japan take English as a foreign language. In fact in 2000, the Prime Minister's Commission on Japan's Goals in the Twenty-First Century recommended that all Japanese should acquire practical English skills and went so far as to suggest that in the future English may become the second official language of Japan (Kubota, 2010).

The most recent proposal regarding English education came from a Prime Minister advisory body termed the Educational Rebuilding Council, which issued three reports between 2007 and 2008. The reports recommended the introduction of English in the elementary school and a ten percent increase in the hours of English instruction. In addition, for the first time it made foreign language a required subject. Previously, foreign language was an elective, but virtually all schools offered English (Kubota, 2010).

Whereas most policy documents of the 1980s and 1990s mentioned teaching foreign languages other than English, policy discussions in the 2000s have tended to focus only on English language teaching. Perhaps because of this, only 14 per cent of the total number of senior high schools in Japan offers a language other than English. The fastest growing language is Chinese followed by Korean (Kubota, 2010). These languages, however, tend to be studied for their value in international contexts rather than to communicate with the existing Chinese and Korean population within Japan.

Although many believe that Japan is a monolingual country, in fact the number of registered foreigners in Japan has increased in the past thirty years so that as of 2007, foreigners accounted for 1.69 per cent of the total population. The country of origin of the largest group is China (28.2 per cent), followed by South/North Korea (27.6 per cent), Brazil (14.7 per cent), the Philippines (9.4 per cent), Peru (2.8 per cent), the US (2.4 per cent), and others (14.9 per cent) (Kubota, 2010). The growing number of Brazilians in Japan today is due to the 1990 enactment of the revised Immigration Control Law that allowed foreigners of Japanese descent down to the third generation to live and work legally in Japan.

Today Japan has a large number of students who need to acquire Japanese as a second language. Among this group of young people, the largest first language group is Portuguese speakers from Brazil, who account for 38.5 per cent of the number of students needing Japanese as a second language. It is this group that we turn to now in highlighting the complexity of English acquisition, multilingualism and language policy.

The case study is based on our investigation of one rural city in Japan that has been experiencing a rise of newcomers from non-English-speaking countries, creating an unprecedented kind of linguistic diversity. (See Kubota and McKay, 2009, for a complete description of the study.)

The local linguistic landscape

Hasu in Morino Prefecture (pseudonyms) is a mid-sized city with a population of approximately 160,000. Since the 1990s, Hasu has had an influx of foreign residents or so-called newcomers (as opposed to long-time residents of Korean descent), like some other cities in Japan. In 1990, the number of registered foreign residents in Hasu was approximately 700, whereas in 2006 it grew to over 6,000, constituting 3.7 per cent of the population. Of this population, approximately 50 per cent comes from Brazil, followed by China (17 per cent), Peru (8 per cent), Korea (6 per cent) and Thailand (4 per cent) (Kubota and McKay, 2009).

The rise of newcomers in the city of Hasu has pressed the longtime residents to reflect on local diversity. Our study of the community shows that while some residents welcome the newcomers, others view them as uninvited foreigners who do little to contribute to the internationalism of Japan. Some residents believe that the lingua franca of the local community should be English, though it is apparent in visiting the local schools that the Brazilian children had a much greater need for Japanese as a second language (JSL) than for English. For instance, on one visit to a junior high school, a tutor was working with a newly arrived seventh-grade boy. When asked about his birthday in Japanese, he struggled to understand. The assistant principal who was standing beside him tried to assist him by tossing out English words, such as 'birthday' and 'when?' Of course this was of little help because the student had studied English only for a couple of months at home.

The value that Portuguese has in the local community compared to the value of English is evident in one community leader's comment. When asked her opinion about having the local schools teach Portuguese as a foreign language, she responded:

> But you can't soar into the world with Portuguese. That's why international students from China can speak English. If you want to improve your research, you go to the US or Canada. ... Improving Japan with Portuguese won't let the country soar into the world. (Kubota and McKay, 2009: 604–605)

Perhaps this is why there is insufficient support for the newly arrived students in the area of mother tongue maintenance. Although mother tongue support is available in some schools with bilingual teachers or teachers' aides, the primary pedagogical approach is a transitional bilingual model (that is, initial mother tongue support in order to 'mainstream' students as soon as possible, rather than a developmental model for promoting bilingualism and bi-literacy). This points to the limited scope of the discourse of internationalization since it does not embrace or enhance the bilingualism that already exists in Japan.

It was clear from our investigation of the community that the spread of English in Japan in the form of increased emphasis on teaching and learning English does not in any way threaten the Japanese language. Instead, Japanese threatens the maintenance of the heritage languages of migrant workers in places like Hasu because of the monolingual and assimilationist orientation for newcomers. What is threatened or undermined by the spread of English seems to be mainstream people's willingness to learn other languages and embrace the linguistic and cultural heritage of minorities.

Prevalent discourses

In a good deal of the national and local discourse regarding language learning, many Japanese refer to their belief in the value of English for cross cultural communication. The prevalence of this idea is evident in the following government document called *Action plan to cultivate 'Japanese with English abilities'* (Ministry of Education, Culture, Sports, Science and Technology, 2003):

> English has played a central role as the common international language in linking people who have different mother tongues. ... it is essential for [children] to acquire communication abilities in English as a common international language. (Kubota and McKay, 2009: 595–596)

In this statement, English learning is encouraged because of its perceived value in communicating with people around the world. An obvious assumption here is that people in the world speak English. However, citing a projection of the demand for English in the education systems of the world, Graddol (2006) states that over 5 billion people globally do not speak English as either their first or second language. This means that over three quarters of the world population are non-English-speaking. Thus, contrary to the assumption held above, a majority of contexts for international communication do not allow English to serve as a lingua franca.

The assumption that English is a lingua franca among people with different mother tongues is a conspicuous aspect of the discourse of EIL. The prevalence of this assumption is perhaps related to the sole focus on the role of English in scholarly or non-scholarly discussions, with little attention paid to the possibility that English is not a lingua franca in many local contexts. In fact, more and more non-English-speaking people are crossing national boarders to seek employment in non-English-speaking countries. In such situations, the major lingua franca is usually the dominant language of the host country, not English.

The perceived international importance of English in Japan is also evident in the statements of many of the local leaders that the first author interviewed. One woman, for example, when asked about the value of studying languages other than English in the schools stated:

There aren't many foreigners and there is very little need for English, so speaking
Portuguese probably helps us get along with foreigners better. So the question is
why English? But English is becoming an international common language. ... My
neighbors are from Brazil and the Philippines. I sometimes speak in English with the
Filipino neighbors but they probably would feel more comfortable in Tagalog; and
English is useless with Brazilian people, so in terms of necessity, it's probably more
useful to learn Portuguese as a second language for co-living. But I think English
and computers are part of general education for all.

While recognizing the usefulness of Portuguese in the local context,
this community leader appears to believe that the usefulness of English in
an international context warrants it being a required foreign language for
all students. (Kubota and McKay, 2009: 608)

This same ambivalence regarding the relative value of Portuguese and
English was evident in another community leader's opinion, one who was
himself actually engaged in learning Portuguese. Referring to his future,
he stated:

I want to be involved in issues of education because I wanted to become a teacher. I
submitted my request to be transferred to the Department of Education ... Foreign
residents must have many concerns, like children's language learning, work, health,
and so on. I want to deal with their concerns. So to me, learning Portuguese has
become necessary. Of course English is important because it's a common language.
(Kubota and McKay, 2009: 610)

The discourse of both Japanese government documents and local community leaders affirms the international importance of learning English.
Government policies and local decisions regarding language learning and
the value of languages other than English are framed against a backdrop
of the perceived value of English internationally. In the end, government
policies and individual choices are being made by looking outward at Japan
in a global context rather than looking inward at local needs. The irony
of the situation is that while English is rarely used for cross-cultural communication in Japan, it exerts tremendous symbolic power when it comes
to preserving the diversity of languages that exist within Japan today. The
influence of prevalent discourses surrounding English will be an issue we
return to in discussing EIL pedagogical principles.

South Africa

Government policy

One of the major decisions that South Africa faced in the establishment of a post-apartheid government was the creation of an official language policy. Because the apartheid regime had promoted one ex-colonial language, Afrikaans, at the expense of the other, English, attitudes toward English amongst the majority of the African population in the apartheid era were, ironically, remarkably positive. Accordingly one policy option was to designate English as the sole official language as a way of promoting political unity and facilitating the country's ties with English-speaking nations. By doing so, however, the country would undermine the development of a sense of nationalism based on indigenous languages and culture and perhaps encourage interethnic conflict since those individuals not familiar with English would be at a distinct disadvantage in terms of social, economic and educational mobility. After much debate, South Africa decided to adopt the strategy of countries like India and the Philippines by designating several indigenous languages along with English as the official languages of the country. Hence, the new constitution states that English, Afrikaans and nine indigenous languages 'shall be the official South African languages at the national level, and conditions shall be created for their development and for the promotion of their equal use and enjoyment' (McKay and Chick, 2001: 395).

With the establishment of an official language policy, South Africa was then faced with a decision of how to implement this policy in the schools. In 1996 after a good deal of negotiation, a language planning task group submitted its final report in which it mapped out a national language plan for South Africa. Within the report, the task force specified the overall goals of a language-in-education policy for the new South Africa that contained the following goals. The report states that:

Language policy in the education sector should
(a) facilitate access to meaningful education for all South African students;
(b) promote multilingualism;
(c) promote the use of the students' primary languages as languages of learning and teaching in the context of an additive multilingual paradigm and with due regard to the wishes and attitudes of parents, teachers and students;
(d) encourage the acquisition by all South African students of at least two but preferably three South African languages, even if at different levels of proficiency, by means of a variety of additive bi-, or multilingual strategies; it is strongly recommended that where the student's L1 is either Afrikaans or English, an African language should be the additional language; .... (McKay and Chick, 2001: 395)

While providing for choice from a range of language-in-education policy models, the Act identifies additive bilingualism/multilingualism as the normative orientation of the language-in-education policy. It assumes that learners learn other languages (including the dominant language) most effectively when there is the continued educational use of the learners' first languages and, therefore, respect for the cultural assumptions and values implicit in them, that is, an additive approach.

The local linguistic landscape

Given South Africa's stated objective to promote multilingualism and multiculturalism in the schools, in 1999 we undertook a study of six schools in the Durban metropolitan area of the KwaZulu-Natal province of South Africa. (See McKay and Chick, 2001, for a full description of the study.) Our purpose was to investigate to what extent these schools are promoting the multilingualism and multiculturalism advocated in the official language-in-education policies.

To contextualize the study, under the apartheid system, there were basically five separate schools systems in KwaZulu-Natal – one for the white community (of a little over 500,000 people according to the 1996 census), one for the Indian community (of almost 800,000 people), one for the so-called coloured (or mixed-race) community (approximately 100,000 people), and two for the African community (approximately 7 million people). The available resources for the white schools far surpassed those of the black community in the townships and rural area. The Indian and coloured schools, while better funded than those of the black townships, still did not match those of the white community.

Because of this historical advantage, schools in the former white community have far better facilities than former Indian schools, Indian schools better than the coloured schools and the latter better than the African schools in the township and rural areas. As a consequence, following the establishment of a single educational authority, there has been a major flux of African students into the Indian (and coloured) schools located near African townships, and of many Indian students and some African students into former white schools. Since we assumed that the new multilingual/ multicultural policy would have greatest appeal and most chance of success in schools that have multilingual/multicultural populations, we focused on former white and Indian schools (two high schools and one primary school of each type) that have become dramatically more linguistically and culturally diverse following the desegregation of schools and other changes associated with the demise of apartheid.

Prevalent discourses

Given that the National Education Policy Act (Act 27) was released in 1996, in conducting our study, we assumed that progress towards multilingualism (or at least bilingualism) in desegregated schools in KwaZulu-Natal would be evident in increasing the teaching/learning of Zulu, the L1 of approximately 80 per cent of people in the province (McKay and Chick, 2001). We also assumed that in classrooms there would be considerable code switching between Zulu and English, which though the L1 of only about 16 per cent of people in the province, is the dominant language in education and many other prestigious domains. Yet this is not what we observed.

Rather it appeared that the use of Zulu was a site of struggle in which teachers, administrators and pupils attempted to negotiate their identity within the context of what can be termed an *English-only discourse*. This discourse supports the notion that learning English should start as early as possible, that the maintenance of first language is not necessary/desirable, and that the best way to acquire English is submersion.

What suggests that these ideological assumptions are widely taken-for-granted in the six KwaZulu-Natal schools we visited is the low levels of provision for the teaching of Zulu in these schools. The most generous provision is at one of the former Indian primary schools, where African learners make up 58 per cent of the learner population. There Zulu is taught as a subject in all grades. However it is taught by an English-speaking teacher whose own preparation for teaching Zulu was merely twelve one-hour lessons.

The ideological assumptions associated with English-only discourse are further evident in administrators' and teachers' explicit rejection of the use of Zulu in the classes, and the rationales they provided for their position. With the exception of the principal of the former Indian primary school, no principal was in favour of the use of Zulu in class. Most indicated that code switching from English to Zulu is not permitted except in such non-prestigious settings as the playground or where learners are viewed as 'deficient' in English. They offered a range of reasons for their position. The principal of the former white high school told us that since the school is an English medium school, learners are informed at a school assembly at the beginning of the year that they must use English in class. She argued that this policy is not discriminatory as it applies not just to Zulu but to all the first languages of learners at the school. She gave us a further reason for prohibiting the use of Zulu, that occasionally Zulu-speaking learners use Zulu to insult adults and other learners. The principal of a former white primary school indicated that learners at his school are actively discouraged from, as he put it, 'reverting' to the use of Zulu, and justified this by arguing that they need English for economic advancement in South Africa.

In general, our discussion with school principals on the place of Zulu and English in the schools suggested that the use of the language is related to issues of power. In the English-only discourse of most of these principals, English is represented as a unifying force; as a vehicle for economic advancement; and as the appropriate choice in prestigious domains such as the classroom. By contrast Zulu is represented as a potentially divisive force and as appropriate only for non-prestigious domains; that is, as more of a handicap than a resource. Learners who choose to use Zulu in class are represented as either rebellious or as deficient in English.

Most of the teachers in these schools expressed views that were closely aligned to those of the principals. For example, one of the teachers at the former Indian high school tells her students not to use Zulu in class, and will not let them explain things to one another in Zulu. She believes that if learners are to improve their English and be able to produce critical analyses in English, they must use English in class. Another teacher argued that if Zulu speakers have chosen an English medium school staffed by native English speakers, they must accept that Zulu will not be used in class. Some teachers also note that the use of Zulu can be used a symbol of rebellion by Zulu speakers and that its use in the classroom can be threatening to teachers and to other non-Zulu speakers.

In general our data suggest that the teachers and administrators at the schools we visited are promoting extensive and, at times, exclusive use of English under the banner that this is an English-medium school. By doing so, the schools promote the hegemony of English. Generally code switching is permitted only in non-prestigious domains such as the playground or when learners are viewed as lacking English proficiency. Thus in the schools we visited there is little indication that the additive policy of multilingualism promoted in the language-in-education policies of South Africa is being actively pursued. In this case, the South African language policy, which supports multilingualism, is being undermined by a local discourse that, unlike Japan, looks inward, advocating the use of English for economic advancement and inter-ethnic relations in South Africa, not outward for the international role of English.

Pedagogical implications

What does the above discussion on government policies, local linguistic landscapes and prevalent discourses regarding EIL in Japan and South Africa suggest for the teaching of EIL in these contexts? The intention of the following discussion is to highlight some of the major ramification of these cases on EIL pedagogy. Before doing so, however, it is important to emphasize the fact that the lack of support for multilingualism in both Japan and South Africa is due to a web of attitudes and beliefs regarding English. In the case of Japan, a widespread belief in the exclusive value of English in international contexts, coupled with a concern for the international role of Japan as a nation, have led government and local leaders to minimize the value of any foreign language learning, other than English, even when the local linguistic landscape warrants attention to other languages. In contrast, in South Africa, an informed language policy that supports multilingualism for all is being undermined by a local discourse that emphasizes the value of English for internal economic advancement and harmony.

A respect for and promotion of multilingualism

With colonialism and more recently with vast immigration to English-speaking countries, the ELT profession has frequently operated within an English-only framework in which any language other than English is discouraged in the English classroom. Phillipson (1992), in his widely circulated book, *Linguistic Imperialism*, documents past and present colonial policies enacted by Britain and the United States. He sets forth five tenets that he argues developed from colonial history and presently inform the English teaching profession.

> Tenet one: English is best taught monolingually.
> Tenet two: the ideal teacher of English is a native-speaker.
> Tenet three: the earlier English is taught, the better the results.

Tenet four: the more English is taught, the better the results.
Tenet five: if other languages are used much, standards of English will drop.

What are the disadvantages of supporting an English-only policy? First, such a policy fails to recognize the linguistic resources learners have and how these resources can be used to promote the acquisition of English. Second, by ignoring the learners' multilingual competencies, teachers lose an opportunity to promote learners' awareness of both the relationship between languages and the manner in which speakers make use of their mutilingualism.

Imagine how different the local schools in the Durban area would be if the English-only policy were replaced with one that recognized the multilingual competencies of the students. Zulu and the other local languages could be used judiciously to promote the learning of English in English classes. More importantly the uses of Zulu and English in the local community and school could form the basis for many student-initiated investigations in which students examine when, why and how the various languages they know are used in their daily life. Such tasks would promote in students an awareness of the complexity of language use, while affirming the skills they have as a multilingual individual.

A pedagogy that resonates with the local linguistic landscape

English today is being used by many kinds of speakers with many different purposes. In some cases, similar to Japan, English is being taught as a required subject in a context in which learners, seeing no apparent reasons for learning English, have little motivation to learn the language. In other contexts, similar to South Africa, learners are convinced that the acquisition of English will bring them significant rewards in terms of higher education opportunities, jobs, promotions and the acquisition of knowledge. Under such circumstances, it is clearly not possible to suggest a pedagogical approach that can serve all these needs.

Rather teachers need to consider factors such as the following in making pedagogical decisions.

- What languages are used in the local linguistic landscape and how are they used?
- What are prevalent attitudes toward these languages?
- What are the major purposes the learners have for learning another language?
- What is the proficiency level and age of the learner?

Imagine what a school in Hasu, Japan would be like if the language learning policies reflected the local linguistic landscape. Students could be encouraged to help one another learn each other's first languages. While Japanese-speaking students could help the Brazilian students learn Japanese, Brazilian students could be encouraged to help the Japanese students learn some Portuguese. This exchange could form the basis for a language awareness course in which students compare how things are expressed in the two languages.

The end result could be that the young people develop a greater understanding of and respect for their classmates and an appreciation for the kind of bilingualism that allows one to communicate cross-culturally in real situations. The learning of English then would take place against the backdrop of the students' growing awareness of the value of learning another language; in addition both the Japanese and Brazilian speakers would be on an equal playing field in which no students have more prestige because of their familiarity with the dominant language of the area.

A thorough examination of the discourse promoting the learning of English

One factor that has fueled the spread of English is a prevalent belief in the power of English. While in some instances, the learning of English can result in actual economic, educational and social advantages, in other cases, the discourse surrounding the use of English promises learners unrealistic accounts of what a knowledge of English can bring to their lives.

Such discourse is evident in public documents as, for example, when the Japanese Ministry of Education, Culture, Sports, Science and Technology strongly affirms the power of English in international contexts and in so doing undermines the value of other languages both on a local and international level:

> English has played a central role as the common international language in linking people who have different mother tongues. ... it is essential for [children] to acquire communication abilities in English as a common international language.

Such discourse is also evident in the rhetoric of local Japanese community leaders who contend that English has much greater power than other languages, and in that way more value than any other language:

> But you can't soar into the world with Portuguese. That's why international students from China can speak English. If you want to improve your research, you go to the US or Canada. ... Improving Japan with Portuguese won't let the country soar into the world.

Given such discourses, it is imperative that English educators present a realistic view of the benefits that the acquisition of English may bring. While in some instances English proficiency may be one factor that affects an individual's educational, economic and social standing, in most cases English proficiency is only one of a myriad of factors that affects the personal, social and professional status a person has.

If English is to spread in a manner which preserves the rich diversity of languages and cultures in the world today, EIL professionals and pedagogy must affirm the value of multiligualism by drawing on students' existing linguistic resources in the classroom, developing curricula that reflect the local linguistic landscape, and presenting a realistic account of the value of English learning.

References

Brutt-Griffler, J. (2002). *World Englishes: A study of its development.* Clevedon: Multilingual Matters.

Crystal, D. (1997, 2003). *English as a global language.* Cambridge: Cambridge University Press.

Graddol, D. (2006). *English next: Why global English may mean the end of 'English as a Foreign Language.'* London: British Council.

Kubota, R. and McKay, S.L. (2009). Globalization and language learning in rural Japan: The role of English in the local linguistic ecology. *TESOL Quarterly.* 43, 4: 593–619.

Kubota, R. (2010). The politics of school curriculum and assessment in Japan. In Y. Zhao, J. Lei, L. Guofang, M. He, K. Okano, D. Gamage, R. Hema and M. Nagwa (eds), *Handbook of Asian education.* New York: Routledge.

McKay, S.L. and K. Chick (2001). Positioning learners in post apartheid South African schools: A case study of selected multicultural Durban schools. *Linguistics and Education.* 12, 4: 393–408.

McKay, S.L. (2002). *Teaching English as an international language: Rethinking goals and approaches.* Oxford: Oxford University Press.

McKay, S.L. and W. Bokhorst-Heng (2008). *International English in its sociolinguistic contexts: Towards a socially sensitive pedagogy.* New York: Routledge.

MEXT. (2003). Action plan to cultivate 'Japanese with English abilities'. <http://www.mext.go.jp/english/topics/03072801.htm> (accessed 18 February 2008).

Mufwene, S. (2002). Colonisation, globalization, the future of language in the twenty-first century. *International journal on multicultural societies,* 4 (2), 162–193.

Nettle, D. and S. Romaine (2000). *Vanishing voices: The extinction of the world's languages.* Oxford: Oxford University Press.

Phillipson, R. (1992). *Linguistic imperialism.* Oxford: Oxford University Press.

Phillipson, R. (2003). *English only Europe? Challenging language policy.* London: Routledge.

Sharifian, F. (ed.) (2009). *English as an international language: Perspectives and pedagogical issues.* Bristol: Multilingual Matters.

Skutnabb-Kangas, T. (2000). *Linguistic genocide in education – Or worldwide diversity and human rights?* Mahwah, NJ: Lawrence Erlbaum Associates.

LINDA TSUNG

6 Rethinking Multilingual Education for Minority Students in China

Introduction

Enormous diversity characterizes the linguistic and cultural traditions of China's fifty-five legally recognized minority nationalities, which account for 106.43 million or 9.4 per cent of the population (NBSC, 2005). Each minority nationality has its own language, with the exception of the Hui and the Manchu who use the standard Chinese language – Putonghua. At least 128 languages are spoken among China's minorities (Sun et al., 2007). Some are bilingual, trilingual, or speak in a variety of different languages, some of which are completely different from one another (Tsung, 2009). The Constitution of China grants minority nationalities the freedom to use and preserve their native languages. An essential provision in China's policies toward minorities is that people of all ethnic groups are guaranteed equal rights to use their own languages in education, as specified in Act 4 of the People's Republic of China (PRC) Constitution. Administrative autonomy was adopted on 31 May 1984 in minority concentrated communities, and bilingual education (Chinese and a minority language) was implemented in the mid-1980s. Ethnic languages are now used in teaching, from kindergarten to high school, to preserve ethnic culture. Furthermore, diversity in multilingual education is prevalent in China, which reflects not only the diversity that exists among China's minority nationalities, but also an ambivalent attitude toward multilingual education: learning a minority language has been seen as a transitional measure aimed at facilitating mastery of the standard Chinese language (Lee, 2001; Stites, 1999; Tsung, 2009).

Ethnic minorities in China essentially face the choice of either preserving their language and culture, or acquiring requisite skills for upward
social mobility by gaining competency in the Chinese language (Zhou,
2004). The state allowing the use of minority languages in education can
be crucial to the formation of multilingual education. Currently, thirteen
national institutions in China permit minority students to take the college
entrance examination in their native language, a practice referred to as *min
kao min*. In addition, many comprehensive universities offer *minzu ban*
(ethnic group classes), which provide higher education courses to minority
students with their native language as the medium of instruction. However,
min kao min is only available in six minority languages, namely, Tibetan,
Uyghur, Mongolian, Korean, Kazakh and Kirghiz (Clothey, 2005).

This chapter discusses the current situation and explores the dilem-
mas in multilingual education, culture and identity that are encountered
by the ethnic minority students in Yunnan. In particular, we explore how
linguistic and cultural boundaries or differences have been constructed
as resources that serve as a bridge between the languages and cultures of
minority groups. To establish a framework for this exploration, the following section examines some of the complexities and tensions inherent to
Yunnan, as well as certain concepts regarding multilingual education.

Multilingual education in the context of Yunnan

Multilingual education (MLE) is typically referred to as 'first-language-
first' education, that is, schooling that begins with the use of one's mother
tongue. As learning progresses, language use transitions to other languages.
Typically, MLE programmes are employed in developing countries where
speakers of minority languages tend to be at a disadvantage in the mainstream education system. Scholars have categorized MLE programmes
into two types:

- 'Strong Foundation'. Research shows that children whose early education features the use of their first language tend to do better in later years of their education (Thomas and Collier, 1997).
- 'Strong Bridge'. This programme is characterized by guided transition from learning to use one's mother tongue to learning another language.

MLE emphasizes the child's mother tongue. This is the implicit validation of his/her cultural or ethnic identity by taking languages that were previously considered 'non-standard' and actively using these in class. In this sense, MLE underscores the importance of a child's worldview in shaping his/her learning.

MLE proponents stress that the second language acquisition component is a 'two-way' bridge, in which learners gain the ability to 'move back and forth' between their mother tongue and other languages, unlike a transitional literacy programme in which reading using one's mother tongue is abandoned at a certain stage in the educational process. The uniqueness of the former lies in the involvement of the community in creating their own curriculum and minimizing theoretical hegemony, thereby creating citizens who believe in the ethics of creating and sharing knowledge for society rather than limiting it to theoreticians.

MLE in China generally refers to schooling in which both the minority and majority languages, as well as foreign languages, are used in teaching or any other learning avenue. This description is a rather loose explanation compared with commonly cited definitions in literature, which state that MLE involves the promotion of literacy in the first language and the provision of further access to a language that enables wider communication and a broader linguistic community.

MLE policy making in China is usually viewed as consisting of four stages: the first pluralistic stage, in which education in minority languages is supported (1949–1957); the 'Chinese-monopolistic stage', which coincides with the Cultural Revolution (1958–1977); the second pluralistic stage (1978–1990); and the MLE declining stage, which promotes the teaching of standard Chinese – Putonghua (Tsung, 2009).

Known as China's southwestern gate, Yunnan Province shares its 4,060 km border with Vietnam, Laos and Burma. With twenty-five 'officially recognized' major ethnic minorities comprising 33.6 per cent of its population of 42.2 million, Yunnan is the most typical multi-ethnic province in China. Fifteen of the twenty-five recognized ethnic minorities are unique to Yunnan. In addition to the Hui, the Manchu and the Shui, who commonly use the Han language for daily communication, the remaining twenty-two groups speak more than twenty-six languages. Table 1 shows the language use pattern of fifteen major ethnic minority groups in Yunnan. Ninety-five per cent of Yunnan territory is surrounded by mountains, so that most ethnic minority communities live in harsh conditions in remote and poorly resourced areas. Among the disadvantages confronting them is the rate of illiteracy and semi-literacy, which is 1.7 times that of the national rate (Chen, 2006). These problems severely inhibit the socio-economic development of the region. The completion rate of nine-year compulsory education in Yunnan is about 14 per cent lower than the national rate, and twelve of the seventeen counties that are unable to provide compulsory education are ethnic autonomous localities.

The inability to communicate using standard Chinese (Putonghua or Mandarin) is another setback that prevents the minorities from seeking better educational and career prospects. For instance, 85.99 per cent of the Dulong people are unable to understand Putonghua (see Table 1), and among the entire ethnic minority population of Yunnan, only 12 per cent can communicate in Putonghua. In light of these statistics, MLE is one of the best vehicles for ethnic groups to obtain the basic early education they highly require because it 'contributes to enhanced mutual understanding and respect, as well as political and economic equality' (Teng and Wen, 2005: 268). With more than fifty years of development, and the past thirty characterized by rapid expansion, MLE is universally believed to be a critical method not only for facilitating the transmission, maintenance and development of native languages and cultures, but also for realizing equality among different nationalities. Thus, as the frequency and intensity of communication grow both within and between Yunnan and its foreign and provincial neighbors, and as local peoples witness for themselves the social, economic and political advantages of linguistic diversity, the importance of MLE for building a prosperous future becomes increasingly apparent.

Table 1. Ethnic minority groups and their language use in Yunnan (Tsang et al., 2005)

No.	Ethnic group	Mono-lingual population by 2005	%	Bilingual population by 2005	%	Speakers of a 3rd language (non-native nor Han) by 2005	%
1	Achang	10,060	49.23	7,516	36.78	2,857	13.98
2	Bai	414,891	36.64	615,333	54.35	102,000	9.01
3	Bulang	36,106	61.75	17,215	29.44	5,152	8.81
4	Dai	483,168	57.55	316,628	37.72	39,700	4.73
5	De'ang	7,132	58.00	4,591	37.33	574	4.67
6	Dulong	3,984	85.99	649	14.01	0	0
7	Hani	649,024	61.29	408,782	38.61	1,000	0.001
8	Jingpo	60,979	65.59	31,997	34.41	0	0
9	Jinuo	5,836	48.79	6,126	51.21	0	0
10	Lahu	202,277	66.48	89,981	29.57	11,998	3.94
11	Lisu	384,058	79.70	96,826	20.09	1,000	0.21
12	Naxi	110,465	43.91	131,127	52.12	10,000	3.07
13	Nu	6,971	30.45	4,525	19.76	11,400	49.79
14	Pumi	6,749	27.85	10,289	42.45	7,200	29.70
15	Va	198,466	66.46	83,489	27.96	16,656	5.58

In general, basic education in Yunnan lags behind that in the rest of China, and basic education in Yunnan's ethnic minority communities is nearly ten years behind that in its non-ethnic minority communities. The 5th National Population Census in 2000 (National Bureau of Statistics of China, 2002) revealed that the average year of schooling in China is 7.27 years, but 5.96 years in Yunnan, ranking it the twenty-ninth among China's thirty-one provinces and autonomous regions. Furthermore, the average number of years of schooling in Yunnan's ethnic minority communities is 2 per cent to 3 per cent lower than the provincial average. In their 2007 survey, Xu and Wu found that the average number of years of schooling among the Lahu, Va, Bulang, Dulong and Nu minority groups is three years or less. Illiteracy and semi-illiteracy among these minority groups constitute 15.9 per cent of the national level (fourth place in China) and 25.4 per cent of the Yunnan provincial level.

The recent economic boom in China appears to have widened the economic gap between minority and Han majority with differential effects on the educational outcomes in East and West China, where forty-four of the fifty-five minority groups are located (Yang, 2005). In 1998, the average GDP per capita was 4,159 RMB in western provinces compared with 11,533 RMB in the east (National Statistics Bureau Department of Synthesis, 2000, in Yang, 2005). Coastal regions in China attracted 93 per cent of foreign investments in the 1990s compared with the western regions, which attracted below 3 per cent (Fan, 2002). The decentralization of education administration in 1985 imposed increasing financial responsibility on local governments in terms of implementing basic education; this decentralization resulted in an 11 per cent decrease in the central government's contribution to total educational expenditure by the late 1990s (Hu, 2003; Ross, 2000; Wang, 2002). Much evidence indicates that the gap in financial resources for education has widened between the western and Han regions of China, and that minority education is still characterized by insufficient resourcing and teacher training (Postiglione, 2000; Tsung, 2009).

Recent economic and social developments have brought about a shift in government policy and community attitudes toward the MLE system. The national language, Putonghua, has come to be regarded in western regions as the language of power and access to economic wellbeing. This perception has led to greater demand by minorities for education in Putonghua and a consequent shift from minority schools to majority Putonghua-medium schools.

Ethnic minorities are disadvantaged in terms of participation in education and employment. One reason for this impediment is their lack of Chinese language skills (i.e., spoken Putonghua and written Chinese). The mastery of Chinese language is considerably related to successful participation in the mainstream economy. Thus, minority students have developed a positive attitude toward and motivation for learning the Chinese language as they perceive this to be their gateway to educational success, economic benefits and integration into mainstream society.

Meanwhile, government policy seems to have shifted away from supporting MLE, particularly in the 1990s. At this time, the proponents of MLE vigorously and effectively promoted this educational system during the first few years, but the campaign was suddenly confronted with a serious setback. Ironically, impediments to its development were caused by indiscriminate promotion of the nine-year compulsory education that aims to standardize instruction and curriculum all over the country. Considerable media attention has been paid to the lower outcomes in the education of minority students, with the blame falling on MLE (Tsung, 2009). This shift in attitudes has led to a renewed policy push for Putonghua and Chinese teaching and learning.

Two issues remain unaddressed: whether the popular belief that MLE plays a key role in the poor outcomes of minority education is in fact accurate, and whether the shift to monolingual teaching will in any way address these problems. Is the Putonghua teaching policy moving toward monolingual education or will MLE prevail?

The following section focuses on the situation of Yunnan. We draw from case study data on two schools, a Tibetan school and a Dai school in a rural area. We also examine the factors that affect the outcomes of minority education. The study works from an ecological framework approach to language education research, relying on data from interviews with teachers, parents and students, as well as observational and documentary evidence, use of available statistical data and policy/documentary analysis.

This approach places considerably more emphasis on contextual and environmental factors in investigating MLE and its policies rather than relying on predetermined structuralist models (Hornberger, 2002). The current research aims to advance knowledge on MLE, explore the gaps between policy and practice, and present the issues of power relationships for potential policy improvement.

Methodology

In this research, a mixed-method approach was adopted in collecting multiple sources of data from the two field studies. The current study was conducted from 2008 to 2010 in two primary schools located in Shangri-la and Luxi Counties in Yunnan. The two schools employ Tibetan and Dai programmes. Data were drawn from in-depth interviews with four principals and twenty-two teachers.

The interviewees, fifteen males and eleven females, were from four nationalities, namely, Han, Dai, Tibetan and Jingpo.

School 1 is located in the town centre of Shangri-la County in Diqing Tibetan Autonomous Prefecture. The school, established in 1980, is a boarding school with 273 students (during the study period), 73 per cent of whom are from Tibetan families. The school only takes in students from Grades 4 to 6. Ninety-five per cent of the students' parents are farmers.

One Tibetan language class was observed to provide additional information on the programme. To obtain views that are as wide-ranging as possible from various stakeholders, we also approached and interviewed an official at the Department of Ethnic Minority Education of the Yunnan Provincial Education Committee.

School 2, which uses the Dai programme, is in Luxi County, Dehong Dai and Jingpo Autonomous Prefecture. At the time of the study, the school had 413 enrolled students, 97 per cent of whom are of Dai nationality and hail from Dehong. Most of the students come from farming families.

The medium of instruction in the school is Putonghua, except for the Dai Language class (Figure 2). Dai language textbooks were produced locally by the Education Department of the Dehong Dai and Jingpo Autonomous Prefecture.

Findings

Two modes of MLE: foundation or bridge?

School 1 in Shangri-la has a strong Tibetan foundation programme. The principal, the vice principal, two Tibetan language teachers, and a fourth year student were interviewed to trace the latest developments in the MLE programmes of the school. The principal is responsible for the strategic development of the school, whereas the vice principal is in charge of teaching affairs.

The interviewee who offered the most important information was a female Tibetan teacher who has taught in School 1 for over ten years. After completing her Tibetan education in Aba Prefecture in Sichuan Province, she was recruited as a full-time Tibetan teacher more than ten years ago. In addition to teaching Tibetan literacy to around 200 students from Years 4 to 6, she also served as the head teacher of a Tibetan teaching group, a campus radio host and a Tibetan dance teacher.

The Tibetan programme in the school required the use of the Tibetan language as the medium of instruction for the Tibetan language and culture. Putonghua was the medium of instruction for all the other subjects. The Tibetan language was taught for fourteen sessions per week. Students who chose to study Tibetan had to take seven more periods compared with other students. A Tibetan teacher said that to satisfy the requirements set by the Tibetan language syllabus, he needed to take on extra classes (Figure 1).

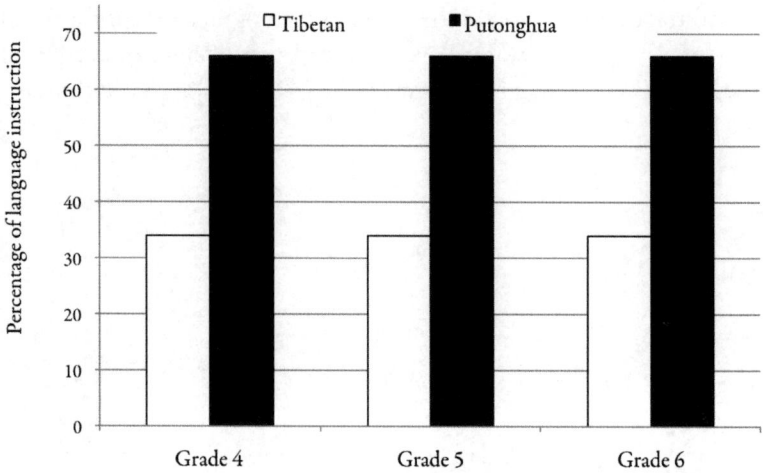

Figure 1. Minority and Han language instruction in School 1
(the Tibetan-Han programme)

School 2 differs in terms of objectives and teaching mode. It focuses
on second language learning. The school's objectives are to help Dai children learn Putonghua and develop the children's cognitive skills. Students
received thirty bonus marks for Dai language learning in their high school
entrance examination.

This programme provides 'a strong' or 'two-way' bridge for minority
students. This type of MLE programme is very common in Yunnan. For
example, bilingual and mono-literacy programmes use a minority language
such as Naxi, coupled with Putonghua, as the medium of instruction, and
develop Chinese literacy. These programmes serve as forms of transitional
bilingual education. Bilingual and bi-literacy programmes, also called
shuangyu shuangwen or *shuangyuwen*, are forms of maintenance bilingual
education that involve the development of oral competency and literacy
in two languages (one minority language and Chinese).

The findings of the present study indicate that linguistic diversity
is used as a resource in the MLE programmes, which are popular among
ethnic groups with long-standing native languages and writing systems,

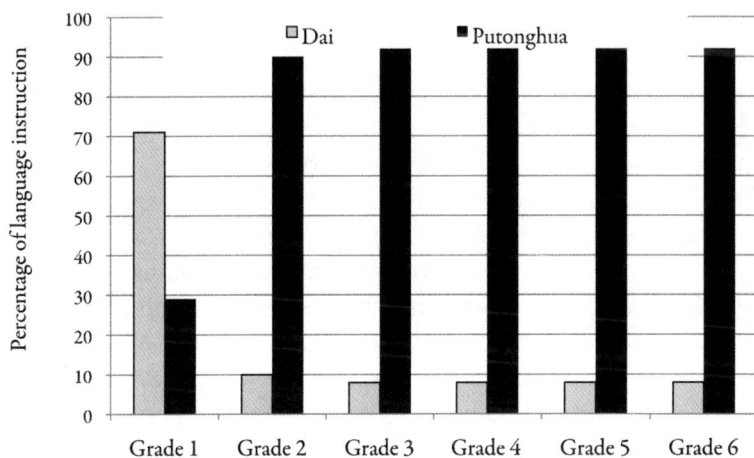

Figure 2. Minority and Han language instruction in School 2
(the Dai-Han bilingual programme)

such as those evident in Tibetan programmes. The diversity in linguistic and cultural features of its minority nationalities, such as diverse scripts, oral traditions and religions, among others, determines whether the programme establishes a strong foundation for the improvement of educational outcomes or builds a bridge for the acquisition of a second language, i.e., Chinese.

Development of multilingual textbooks

The development of multilingual textbooks has dramatically improved in the last ten years. By the end of 2007, 203 newly revised multilingual textbooks in eighteen minority languages were approved and distributed free of charge to students in multilingual programmes. To date, 276 bilingual textbooks and references have been written in or translated into 18 minority languages with 980,000 copies in circulation. Textbooks on mathematics and on individual minority languages are available in 18 minority languages to students in Years 1, 2 and 3, and in five minority languages to students in Year 4.

In addition to allocating multilingual course books to ethnic minority students in poor and backward areas free of charge, 4,282 bilingual teachers have been trained to teach students of various year levels to satisfy the requirements of local schools (China Education Daily, 27 September 2007). Apart from the support from the central government, local governments have also taken a number of concrete steps to promote bilingual education. In 2006, Dehong Prefecture issued the *Recommendations Strengthening the Bilingual Education in Rural Ethnic Minority Inhabiting Areas*, and every year the educational administration of Qujing municipal government provides awards to bilingual schools for outstanding performance in local examinations.

The data further reveal that the MLE system has experienced rapid development over the last few years in Zhongdian, where several years ago, only one Tibetan class was offered to about twenty students in School 1. It now has five Tibetan classes with 250 students. The main reason and motivation for the learners is that local civil servants (who hold coveted roles) must take a test in the Tibetan language to qualify for government positions.

The encouraging developments in MLE in Yunnan can be better viewed from the 2008 Yunnan Educational Committee (YEC) report (Table 2).

The report indicates that the government has exerted considerable effort in promoting MLE in Yunnan in the form of bilingual education. Not only has this programme provided minority students an avenue in which to learn their languages, it has also built a bridge for them to acquire competence in the national language. The latter is believed to be the ultimate goal of government policy.

Table 2. Achievements of bilingual education in Yunnan (YEC, 2008)

Number of bilingual schools	4,056 893 (bilingual and bi-literate) 3,163 (bilingual and mono-literate)
Number of students in bilingual schools	157,979 36,508 (bilingual and bi-literate) 121,471 (bilingual and mono-literate)
Number of bilingual teachers	9,361 2,129 (bilingual and bi-literate) 7,232 (bilingual and mono-literate)
Coverage of bilingual education	74 counties in 15 prefectures
Textbooks issued	276 203 new editions for the new curriculum 980,000 copies in circulation
Fees waived for tuition and textbooks	RMB 8.62 million
Teachers trained	4,282 (2001–2007)
Ethnic minorities involved	14
Ethnic minority languages involved	18

Gaps between policy and practice

Although MLE in Yunnan has made great progress in recent years, many problems concerning policies, perceptions, textbooks and teacher education still require addressing. The interview data reveal that many ethnic minority parents had a great deal of difficulty affording additional educational expenses because of their poor socio-economic conditions. In 2005, the average net income among ethnic minorities in Yunnan was RMB 2,041 (The State Ethnic Affairs Commission, 2006). If the net income of an average family is RMB 2,041, the maximum allocation for a typical four-member farming family would be around RMB 500 per member. Deducting the ever-increasing costs of production (fertilizers, pesticides and so on) and standards of living, the remaining income will be insufficient to cover the costs of education.

Interestingly, although most of the ethnic minority populations in Yunnan live on farming, the latest report of the National Information Center (2007) reveals the consumer price index (CPI) of farmers in Yunnan was 3.9 per cent from January to May in 2007, higher than the 3.4 per cent CPI of city dwellers. Meanwhile, the production costs of farming in 2007 were 2.9 per cent higher than those of the previous year. In light of these statistics, compulsory education (which covers primary and junior high school) that is not provided free of charge would increase, rather than alleviate, the financial burden of farmers. On the other hand, local schools cannot augment the huge deficits incurred from bilingual education without subsidies from local and/or central governments. On the basis of the interview data gathered from this research, the vice principal of School 1 explained that although the school can accommodate a quota of 300 boarding students because of subsidies from three government units (municipal, county and township), School 1 had to shoulder RMB 240,000 to cover the costs of an additional 120 boarding students. Nevertheless, School 1 is forced to turn away some school-aged Tibetan children because of limited accommodations and teaching resources.

Since 2001, the Chinese government has implemented an education-funding policy referred to as *liangmian yibu* (two exemptions and one subsidy) through which children of compulsory education age from poor families in rural areas are exempted from paying tuition and textbook fees; the living expenses of boarding students are also gradually subsidized. The central government is responsible for providing free textbooks, whereas the local government takes care of the tuition fees and subsidies for boarding students. In 2006, this policy was expanded to cover all rural children of compulsory education age; as many as 48.8 million students benefited from this policy by the end of the year. However, the data in the present study indicate that the government policy implemented in recent years has not been as successful.

Perceptions and attitudes toward MLE

The adoption of MLE programmes is considerably influenced by the attitudes and beliefs of local administrators and parents. The current study reveals the existence of two detrimental mentalities, i.e., the 'great Han mentality', as Lin put it (1997), and the 'pragmatic mentality'. The great Han mentality can be very harmful to the implementation of MLE. A local Tibetan middle school was reported to turn away one of the top students from School 1 not because his grade in the Tibetan language was poor – he actually earned the highest mark in the language in the secondary school enrollment exam – but because he failed in Chinese and Mathematics. The Tibetan middle school was concerned that the poor foundation of the student in Chinese and Mathematics may diminish the overall performance of the Tibetan students in the examination. This student was later admitted to a Chinese middle school. Meanwhile, as one Tibetan teacher observed, if graduates from schools such as School 1 are not sufficiently proficient in the Tibetan language to gain admittance to Tibetan middle schools, their learning of the language may have to end, because not enough focus is devoted to learning it.

The pragmatic mentality, which is also detrimental to the adoption of MLE in ethnic minority communities, is prevalent among some local administrators of MLE education programmes and many ethnic minority parents. This mentality reflects the belief that Putonghua is more important and beneficial to one's academic record and future employment opportunities.

An arbitrary removal of MLE programmes is also common; such indiscriminate exclusion not only violates government policies of promoting MLE, but also subverts the will of local ethnic minorities as it may lead to the extinction of native languages and loss of cultural identity. The Jinuo people in Yunnan are an example. This ethnic minority originally had its own language. During the early stage of China's modernization, local Jinuo leaders adopted a policy of assimilation and integration into Han mainstream culture. They made extensive efforts to develop educational programmes in Chinese and encouraged young people to learn Han culture, hoping that they would 'encounter fewer cultural and social obstacles and participate in social and economic spheres of activity without constraints' (Teng and Wen, 2005: 273). In the end, however, the Jinuo were completely assimilated to Han culture and their native language became extinct.

Religious education

Religious and cultural factors also have a tremendous effect on the attitudes and actions of ethnic minority parents and their children. Religious practices have been viewed as social capitals and resources by parents. Reports by interviewees in School 2 indicate that temples and public schools in some areas of Yunnan compete in attracting school-aged students. Interviewees stated that two years ago in Dehong Prefecture, some Burmese monks offered free instruction of Dai script, but the teaching abruptly ended as the monk transferred to another temple. The Dai classes were very popular and had a large number of local Dai students. One of the monks complained that the children who come to learn were very noisy and appeared to break the tranquility of the sacred temple.

In School 2, the data reveal that students have problems learning Chinese and other subjects. When public school students encounter difficulties in their studies, they often quit and attend temple schools instead. Therefore, their parents become more willing to provide financial support to temple or church schools rather than public schools. Our findings reveal that most Dai are Hinayana Buddhists and that Dai parents typically send their children to a temple to study the ethnic language. Sending teenagers to temples to study Dai script is in fact a custom, so that the students may later become monks. The Dai prefer to donate money to build temples for worship and services rather than establish schools.

In School 1, interviews also reveal the challenge that monastery education pose to public school education. A Tibetan teacher argues that

The Tibetan language is an important part of the cultural heritage of the Tibetan people. Parents wish their children to maintain both our written and oral traditions. This is the reason why parents send their children to monasteries. Parents place more value on Tibetan education than Han education. An educated Tibetan must be literate in Tibetan script. I teach children our Tibetan culture. They are very motivated to learn the Tibetan language.

Language teaching/learning and culture are inseparable given that language is the carrier of culture. Language instruction without cultural knowledge delivery confuses learners. As Hannum and Park (2002: 11) observed:

> Messages about the value of minority culture—negative and positive—transmitted through schools can have powerful effects on the academic engagement and achievement of minority students. Minority children in remote rural settings often find a vast distance between their experiences of daily life and the contents of school learning.

Some interviewees believe that MLE is best practised by helping minority students achieve better educational outcomes and effective pedagogy for learning a second language, i.e., Chinese. There is a close relationship between MLE and national stability.

An issue worth considering is that some foreign political and religious forces along Yunnan's national boundaries are seeking to steer school-aged children toward various ideologies that promote visions of transnational homogeneous languages and cultures. Some (anti-unitary Chinese) forces are seeking to recruit ethnic minority students, broadcasting propaganda in minority languages, organizing (clandestine) training classes and awarding native language books. In this sense, MLE has become an instrument for promoting intercultural understanding, safeguarding national unity and preserving frontier stability.

Textbook issues

A number of classes were observed during the second field study. One of the Tibetan language classes demonstrated highly interesting and effective learning among the Tibetan students. It was a forty-five-minute lesson on the Tibetan language, with the topic 'the spring is coming'. The female teacher, who was very organized in her teaching, successfully linked teaching content with the Tibetan community's views on spring and the students' actual experiences.

However, teachers consider problems on the quantity and quality of textbooks unsolved. The number of Tibetan textbooks, reference books and readers are far below demand. Tibetan textbooks are generally of very low quality. Only about sixty multilingual textbooks are devoted to eleven ethnic minority languages, and most of these have been compiled or translated for students in Years 1, 2 and 3. Because most of these multilingual textbooks focus on the development of the first language or mother tongue literacy, and do not cover other subjects such as Mathematics and Liberal Arts, native speakers of other languages cannot use them. Reference books written in ethnic minority languages are almost entirely unavailable.

In addition to literacy, the teachers we interviewed expect certain ethnic group knowledge such as fables, folklores and festivals to be introduced in the mother tongue. The school-based curriculum can at least include some of the aforementioned content.

Most of the existing minority language textbooks are outdated or inappropriate. In School 2, we observed that the latest year-one literacy textbook for Dai students that was published in 2005 by Yunnan Nationality Press contains the following poem and story about snow.

> It is snowing, snowing hard,
> Here comes a group of young painters afar.
> Chicks are drawing bamboo leaves.
> Puppies are drawing plum buds.
> ... ...
> Why is the frog absent?
> He is snoozing in his hole.
> (*Translation of an excerpt from Lesson 17 – Young Painters in the Snow Ground*)
>
> It snowed all day and all night. The houses, trees and grounds were coated white. Mom Rabbit had to go out seeking food. She built a snow child to play with her baby rabbit ... the snow child saved the baby rabbit from the big fire but he melted, as it was too hot.
> (*Translation of an excerpt from Lesson 19 – Snow Child*)

Given that Dai students live in a tropical environment and have never seen snow, imagining what snow looks like and relating it to their daily lives is rather difficult for them to accomplish. A Jingpo teacher commented:

> I believe the most important and interesting things for children to learn are those that they see around them – the vocabulary and phrases they use every day, the stories they hear from their parents and grandparents. We don't teach them these. The State textbook for nine-year basic education has very little content related to children's lives here. The most difficult subject is Ideology and Character Building. There are too many words with abstract concepts, which are difficult to explain to children.

With respect to these problems, more effort is needed in revising old textbooks and compiling new ones, with particular attention to both structure and content. For instance, multilingual textbooks should contain topics relevant to the lives and cultures of ethnic minorities. If possible, they can integrate practical knowledge concerning farming, local cuisine, holidays and festivals, and local handicrafts. Above all, local schools should be given greater autonomy in developing regional textbooks or selecting from national ones. Local teachers should be empowered and encouraged to compile minority language textbooks and reference books that have more relevance to the customs, emotions and social lives of their students.

Shortage of teachers and diminishing quality of teaching

The quantity and effectiveness of bilingual teachers (who can speak Chinese and one of the first languages of minority students) is another pressing problem. According to a survey by Tsang et al. (2005), 10,635 of Yunnan's 12,936 bilingual teachers are mono-literate and only 2,301 are bi-literate; only 5.6 per cent of Yunnan's 218,969 primary school teachers are bilingual.

Given the increasing number of multilingual programmes and growing student enrollment, bilingual teachers, especially bi-literate ones, are in great demand. In reality, however, students often complain that their teachers are either proficient in Putonghua but not in their native languages or are proficient in their native languages but not in Putonghua. Thus, a growing need for more and better-trained teachers is foreseen in the coming years. Shangri-la Primary School, for example, is experiencing a serious shortage of qualified teachers for its bilingual programme that it now has only two Tibetan language teachers teaching two courses to more than 250 students.

Unfortunately, few new teachers are willing to work in such bilingual schools because most are located in remote and poorly resourced mountainous areas with very harsh living conditions. Low salaries, slim chances for promotion, and limited training opportunities also hinder the recruitment of competent bilingual teachers. At the same time, many in-service bilingual teachers are not fully competent in both languages, and the number of bilingually competent teachers is gradually decreasing. Over the last three years, five newly recruited male teachers have left School 1 after a short period of teaching in the school, as indicated by one respondent in the study.

Curriculum deficiencies

Despite the increasing number of bilingual students, School 1 is confronted with the possibility of having to reduce the number of its weekly Tibetan language classes and the overwhelming task of teaching six textbooks in three years. Ten years ago, students had seven Tibetan classes a week, but now have only five classes per week. The respondents stated that students could not finish all the required textbooks within a given term. A similar situation was also observed in other bilingual schools. The minority students will most likely be able to complete only one or two textbooks in three years.

After graduating from elementary school and enrolling in a Tibetan middle school, students have to begin studying the Tibetan language. Although teachers tend to view this as a waste of time and resources, students interpret it as a second chance to catch up with others if they had not learned Tibetan well in elementary school. Moreover, yearly changes in textbooks and little or no communication between in-service native language teachers and test writers render bilingual education even more difficult.

Discussion and conclusion

Similar to authentic multiculturalism, MLE demands dual recognition, i.e., equality and difference (Banks, 1989). It emphasizes that all aspects of school, including policies, teachers' attitudes, instructional materials, assessment methods, counseling and teaching styles, have to evolve and be continually examined (Banks, 1981, 1989). The transformation of the school system becomes necessary provided the education it offers responds to the challenges of diversity, and creates equal conditions under which social members may effectively participate in the economic, social and cultural life of society while maintaining their distinctive cultural and linguistic heritage.

The present study also reveals that although MLE has made obvious progress in Yunnan, it continues to encounter many practical barriers and challenges. In the long run, more rational plans and strategies are needed to integrate national policies and local needs. As Sposky (1980) argues, 'the choice of language education policy is among the most critical and complicated issues facing the modern society' (13). For Yunnan in particular, government policies and school practices can broaden the spectrum of MLE in terms of linguistic resources, as well as cultural and social capitals for local communities; improve the quality and efficiency of fundamental education; and benefit the political, economic, cultural and religious interests of ethnic minority groups.

MLE is substantially more expensive than monolingual education because it requires additional funding for developing courses and textbooks, as well as teacher training. However, it is not only a method of instruction, but also a yardstick for measuring the government's policies on protecting the languages and identities of individual ethnic minorities, as well as its commitment to humanitarian concerns, linguistic human rights and social justice in general. Policy makers should always strive for fairness and justice, considering not only the welfare of the majority, but also that of the minority, and striking a balance between economic gains and social justice.

With the diverse challenges confronting the promotion of MLE in Yunnan, its continued development necessitates policy support, as well as substantial and sustained financial aid. Both central and local governments should allocate more funding to support MLE programmes and take measures to alleviate the financial burden that MLE imposes on ethnic minority families.

As an emerging global economic power, China should promote MLE policy and regularly review MLE practices to advance more rational and humanistic approaches that will develop the harmony and prosperity of both majority Han communities and ethnic minority communities for national stability.

References

Banks, J. (1981). *Education in the 80s: Multiethnic education.* Washington, DC: National Education Association.

Banks, J. (1989). Multicultural education: Characteristics and goals. In J. Banks and C. Banks (eds), *Multicultural education: Issues and perspectives.* Boston: Allyn and Bacon.

Chen, S.D. (2006). Qieshi ba minzu jiaoyu baizai youxian fazhan diwei [Making minority education a priority in development]. *People's Daily.* 29 June 2006.

Hannum, E. and Park, A. (2002). Educating China's rural children in the 21st century. *Havard China Review. 3*(2), 8–14.

Hornberger, N. (2002). Multilingual language policies and the continua of biliteracy: An ecological approach. *Language Policy* 1, 27–51.

Hu, Y.P. (2004). Shaoshu minzu nütong yu shuangyu jiaoyu [Minority nationality girls and bilingual education]. *Zhonghua Nüzi Xueyuan Xuebao (Journal of National Women's University of China),* 16(3), 19–24.

Lin, J. (1997). Policies and politics of bilingual education in China. *Journal of Multilingual Multicultural Development, 18* (3), 193–205.

NBSC (2002). National Bureau of Statistics of China. Beijing: China Statistics Press.

NBSC (2005). *China Statistical Yearbook.* Beijing: China Statistical Press.

National Information Center (2007). Yunnansheng 2007 nian 1–5 yue jumin xiaofei jiage shuiping jianxi (An analysis of CPI in Yunnan from January to May of 2007). <http://party.cei.gov.cn/index/dqbg/showdoc.asp?blockcode=DQBGYNFX andfilename=2007070324442> (accessed 22 November 2008).

Postiglione, G.A. (2000). National minority regions: Studying school discontinuation. In J. Liu, H.A. Ross, and D.P. Kelly (eds), *The Ethnographic Eye: Interpretive Studies of Education in China*, 51–72. New York: Falmer Press.

Postiglione, G.A., Jiao, B. and Manlaji (2007). Language in Tibetan education: The case of the Neidiban. In A. Feng (ed.), *Bilingual education in China: Practices, policies and concepts*, 49–71. New York: Multilingual Matters.

Skutnabb-Kangas, T. and Phillipson, R. (eds) (1995). *Linguistic Human Rights: Overcoming Linguistic Discrimination*. Berlin/New York: Mouton de Gruyter.

Sposky, B. (1980). Foreword. In E.G. Lewis (ed.), *Bilingualism and bilingual education: A comparative study*, xiii–xv. Albuquerque: University of New Mexico Press.

The State Council Leading Group Office of Poverty Alleviation and Development (2007). 2006 nian Yunnan nongcun pinkun renkou jianshaoliang ju quanguo di'er [The poverty alleviation in Yunnan ranked the second in 2006]. <http://www.cpad.gov.cn/data/2007/0627/article_334846.htm> (accessed 9 November 2008).

The State Ethnic Affairs Commission of the PRC (2006). 2005 nian shaoshu minzu diqu nongcun pinkun jiance jieguo [Poverty report on the ethnic minority inhabiting areas 2005]. <http://www.seac.gov.cn/gjmw/xwzx/2006-07-10/1170411119478198.htm> (accessed 23 December 2008).

Sun, H., Hu, Z. and Huang, X. (2007). *Zhongguo de yuyan [The languages of China]*. Beijing: The Commercial Press.

Teng, X. (2001). Objects, characteristics, content, and methods of research in ethnic minority bilingual education in China. *Chinese Education and Society*. 34(2), 54–75.

Teng, X. and Wen, Y.H. (2005). Bilingualism and bilingual education in China. In N.K. Shimahara et al. (eds), *Ethnicity race, and nationality in education: A global perspective*, 259–278. NJ: Lawrence Erlbaum.

Thomas, W.P. and Collier, V. (1997). *School Effectiveness for Language Minority Students*. Washington DC: National Clearinghouse for Bilingual Education.

Tsang, M.C. et al. (2005). Yunnan shaoshu minzu jiaoyu: fazhan, tiaozhan he zhengce [Minority education in Yunnan: Developments, challenges and policies]. <http://www.tc.edu/centers/coce/pdf_files/a11.pdf> (accessed 17 November 2008).

Tsung, L. (1999). Minorities in China: Language policy and education. Unpublished PhD thesis, University of Sydney.

Tsung, L. (2009). *Minority languages, education and communities in China.* New York: Palgrave Macmillan.

UNESCO (2003). Education in a multicultural world. <http://unesdoc.unesco.org/images/0012/001297/129728e.pdf> (accessed 8 April 2008).

Yang, J. (2005). English as a third language among China's ethnic minorities. *International Journal of Bilingual Education and Bilingualism,* 8 (6), 552–567.

Yang, Q. and Song, Y. (2006). Bai-han shuangyu beijingxia yingyu jiaoxue yanjiu pingshu [A survey of English teaching in the Bai-Han bilingual context]. *Dali Xueyuan Xuebao (Journal of Dali College).* 6 (9), 70–73.

Yang, X.L. (2004). Yi-Han shuangyuban zhengfu wangzhan kaitong gaishu [Brief introduction to government Yi-Chinese bilingual website]. *Xinan Minzu Daxue Xuebao (Journal of Southwest University for Nationalities).* 30 (2), 245–249.

Yi, L. (2005). Choosing between ethnic and Chinese citizenship. In V.L. Fong and R. Murphy (eds), *Chinese citizenship: Views from the margins,* 41–67. London and New York: Routledge.

Yunnan Educational Committee. (2008). Shaoshu minzu diqu shuangyu shuangwen jiaoyu jianjie [Brief introduction to the bilingual and bi-literacy education in the ethnic minority inhabiting areas]. *A News Briefing.*

Zhu, C.X. (2003). Shuangyu xianxiang yu zhongguo shaoshu minzu shuangyu jiaoyu tizhi he jiaoxue moshi [Bilingualism and the system and teaching mode of bilingual education of ethnic minorities in China]. *Minzu Jiaoyu Yanjiu (Journal of Research on Education for Ethnic Minorities),* 14(6), 73–77.

PETER GARRETT, JOSEP M. COTS, DAVID LASAGABASTER AND
ENRIC LLURDA

7 Internationalization and the Place of Minority Languages in Universities in Three European Bilingual Contexts: A Comparison of Student Perspectives in the Basque Country, Catalonia and Wales

Introduction

The globalization of higher education in part involves a massive displacement of students between countries to follow study programmes, typically for a period of half an academic year or for the entire period of study. It is a relatively recent phenomenon for many European institutions, in part stimulated by the establishment of the Erasmus Programme in 1987. The constantly increasing number of students sojourning in universities of a different European country reached the figure of 198,523 in 2008/2009. Spain and the UK are the countries with the highest number of incoming students (4,997 and 4,785 students, respectively) that year, followed by Germany (4,210) and France (3,659) (European Commission, 2009). In the UK, the non-EU student population (most of whom follow complete degree programmes) is almost five times greater than the EU students (UK Council for International student affairs, n.d.) and all together represent 15 per cent of the student population. No figure could be found for Spain, but the figure for the Autonomous University of Madrid, which has a relatively large student number, is 6.1 per cent.

European higher education institutions generally have a strong commitment to internationalization (Woodfield, 2010: 170), viewing it as a double opportunity to enter the global educational market as well as (i) to raise an important indicator of academic excellence such as the demand for the products/services they offer, and (ii) in the case of non-EU full-fee paying students, for financial benefits. However, institutions do not always regard internationalization as an opportunity to the same degree, since they need to accommodate a new population arriving with specific expectations. One expectation has to do with language use and the socio-linguistic profile of the students' new institutional environment. This is especially relevant for universities in some bilingual communities, where the minority language may have a long history of repression and struggle. The minority language is not always given due consideration and may be the source of tension and ambiguities both within the local community and institutions such as universities. In this chapter, we report a study which forms part of a project involving the University of the Basque Country (Basque Autonomous Community), Cardiff University (Wales) and the University of Lleida (Catalonia). Here, we compare the attitudes and the practices of students in relation to the minority language in these three contexts. We begin by briefly describing the three institutions, their socio-linguistic context and their respective language policies (these are more fully considered in Cots, Lasagabaster and Garrett, in press).

University of the Basque Country

The University of the Basque Country (UBC) is located in the Basque Autonomous Community (BAC) in the north of Spain. The population of the BAC is 2,200,000, half of whom live in the Bilbao conurbation. The BAC is an officially bilingual region, with Basque the minority language and Spanish the majority language. According to the last survey available (Basque Government, 2008), 30.1 per cent of those aged sixteen and above are fluent Basque speakers, 18.3 per cent passive speakers, and 51.5 per cent do not speak Basque. Mainly due to the compulsory presence of Basque in all the levels of the educational system and the increasing popularity of bilingual programmes with Basque as a means of instruction, there has been a steady increase in the percentage of bilingual speakers in the last two decades: 24.1 per cent in 1991, 27.7 per cent in 1996, 29.5 per cent in 2001 and 30.1 per cent in 2006. The highest percentage of Basque speakers is in the sixteen to twenty-four age range (57.5 per cent), decreasing to 25 per cent in those aged sixty-five and above. Conversely, Spanish is spoken by all the population as there are no remaining monolingual Basque speakers. Only 20 per cent of the population habitually speak Basque. Hence, despite the progress made, there is still far to go in the normalization process of the minority language.

As an officially bilingual university and a pioneer in the normalization of Basque, one of the UBC's main objectives is to provide Basque society with bilingual graduates in different specializations. In 2010, the UBC had more than 5,000 teaching staff and around 45,000 students, 1,200 of whom were international students completing part of their degrees through various mobility programmes such as the PAP-Erasmus programme. To promote the normalization of Basque, the Director Plan for Basque at the UBC 2007/08–2011/12 (University of the Basque Country, 2007) establishes objectives to be attained by the end of 2012: at least 43 per cent of the teaching staff should be bilingual, obligatory subjects should be offered in Basque, knowledge of Basque among the administrative person-nel should increase, the linguistic quality of courses delivered in Basque should be ensured, Basque language courses should be available to teaching and administrative staff, the use of Basque should be promoted at all levels (personal, academic, webpages, etc.), and there should be more teaching materials in Basque. In addition, the UBC is implementing the so-called Multilingualism Plan (MP) aimed at increasing the presence of foreign languages as means of instruction. There are currently 132 subjects included in the MP. Twelve are taught in French and the remainder in English.

University of Lleida

The University of Lleida (UdL) situated in the city of Lleida lies within the Catalan/Spanish bilingual territory of Catalonia, which has a popula-tion of 7.5 million. In 2010, the population of Lleida was 138,136 (Institut d'Estadística de Catalunya (Idescat), n.d.). The university student body in the academic year 2009–2010 comprised 9,504 students (Universitat de Lleida, 2009), which is 4 per cent of the university student population in Catalonia (Idescat, n.d.). The population of the western part of Catalonia, where UdL is located, accounts for 5.8 per cent of the population and 64 per cent of them consider Catalan as their usual language (Generalitat de Catalunya, 2009). These two figures contrast markedly with those of the metropolitan area of Barcelona, which has 73.5 per cent of the entire population and with only 27.8 per cent defining Catalan as their usual language (Generalitat de Catalunya, 2009). Catalan is also the dominant language at UdL; 67.3 per cent of the instructors used it in 2008–2009 as the language of instruction. Contrary to what one might expect from the bilingual situation in the local environment, this percentage is only slightly lower in two universities located in the Barcelona metropolitan area – Universitat Pompeu Fabra (2010) (61.6 per cent in 2009–2010) and Universitat de Barcelona (2010) (64.32 per cent in 2008–2009) – which shows the high degree of normalization of Catalan in the academic environment of Catalonia.

The language policy document of UdL (Universitat de Lleida, 2008) represents a vindication of multilingualism. The very first paragraph connects with internationalization by presenting it as an institutional strategy for the future of the university to face the 'universalization of culture and science, on the one hand, and the growing cultural and linguistic complexity of our society' (ibid: 8; authors' translation). Even though Catalan is defined as the university's institutional language (*llengua pròpia*), when it comes to regulating the use of languages, the document contemplates a trilingual situation, in which students are expected to be fully competent in Catalan and Spanish at a first stage and in English at a later stage. International student recruitment is one of the main elements of UdL's Internationalization Programme (Universitat de Lleida, 2006). In the academic year 2009–2010, there were 233 exchange students (most following undergraduate programmes), who accounted for 2.4 per cent of undergraduates (Universitat de Lleida, 2010), a lower figure compared to other universities in Catalonia (e.g. Universitat Autònoma de Barcelona, with 5 per cent of exchange students). In the goal of attracting more international students, the university's Internationalization Programme recommends making all information available in English, introducing instruction in 'other widespread languages' (apart from Spanish and Catalan), and increasing the multilingual competence of the members of the academic community. The minority language, Catalan, is mentioned only when it comes to promoting the integration of international students within the academic community through offering Catalan and Spanish courses, which seems to indicate concern about a possible decrease in its presence.

Cardiff University

Cardiff is the capital of Wales, with a population of about 325,000 in 2011, which is about 11 per cent of the population of Wales. The decline in number of Welsh language speakers through the first half of the twentieth century (54 per cent of people in Wales in 1891, 21 per cent in 1971, and 19 per cent in 1981 and 1991) has been followed by signs of a revitalization, with about 21 per cent of the population of Wales reporting using the Welsh language in the 2001 Census (see for example May, 2000). Cardiff is a relatively anglicized city, with about 11 per cent of its population speaking Welsh, and with the area around Cardiff University (CU), where many of the students reside, having a lower percentage than the city average (Aitchison and Carter, 2004).

As a Welsh public institution, CU has had to comply with the 1993 Welsh Language Act. This has involved developing and maintaining a Welsh Language Scheme, which sets out actions to promote the implementation and development of Welsh language provision in many domains of use: e.g. recruiting Welsh-speaking staff, communications with the public, translation services, the 'public face' of the University (e.g. web-site, official notices).

Cardiff is the largest of the Welsh higher educational institutions, with about 28,000 students in 2009–2010. As with many UK universities, Cardiff internationalization shows itself through the numbers of students from abroad, some on exchange schemes that allow them to spend a semester or year at Cardiff as part of their studies, but far more as international students taking CU degrees and so staying for three or more years. In 2009–2010, around 1.5 per cent of CU students were exchange students, and 10 per cent were international students.

Welsh is not at all prominent at CU. In CU's 2006–2011 Strategic Plan, for example, there is only one mention of the Welsh language, expressing support for using '... the Welsh language in the University in accordance with the Welsh Language Scheme' (section 9.7). In the more recent 2009–2014 Strategic Plan (Cardiff University 2009: 17), the Welsh language is mentioned once in relation to the provision of Welsh language teaching. Although there is a bilingual linguistic landscape in terms of signage across CU, information about the Welsh language on the university website is sparse (except, of course, in relation to the School of Welsh itself, and the language tuition provided in the Welsh for Adults Centre). On the CU website, four levels down from the home page, is a page called 'Welsh Language Information' (Cardiff University, 2011), where visitors are given reassurance that 'everybody in Wales speaks English, and all your lectures, seminars and coursework will be conducted through the medium of English. You will not be expected to have any knowledge of or learn Welsh (unless you want to).' The bilingual context in which CU is situated has substantial institutional support both at governmental and at some grassroots levels, but English is the dominant language in both Cardiff and Wales as a whole. Balfour (2007: 37) quotes a figure for 2003 of just 6 per cent of staff and students at CU using Welsh, and concludes that the hegemonic language (English) is the default language at CU.

We end this section by pointing to the significance of majority language speaker opposition to minority language policy in many bi- or multi-lingual contexts, which May (2003) and de Bres (2008) term 'tolerability'. De Bres notes that 'the psychological effects of past institutional and interpersonal repression of a minority language (or minority language group) can continue to inhibit minority language use even when overt repression has ceased and language regeneration efforts are under way' (465). Balfour (2007), in his study of university language policies, also maintains that language policies aimed at promoting minority language are either met with scepticism or seen as an obstacle for the expansion of the institution, including its internationalization. We compare the attitudes of the student populations in the three above described contexts in connection with the apparently conflicting forces involving the promotion of the minority language and the drive towards institutional internationalization.

Key variables and research questions

Literature on bilingual situations and bilingualism generally emphasizes that research findings differ considerably across contexts (e.g. Baker, 1988; Garrett, Griffiths, James and Scholfield, 1992; Hoffmann, 1991). This is of course a motivation for our own comparison of the three contexts. A recent set of studies in Lasagabaster and Huguet (2007) also demonstrated and examined such attitudinal differences. Attitudes towards three languages (the minority, the majority and the foreign language) were investigated in a range of European bilingual contexts that included Catalonia, the Basque Country and Wales. The studies used the same methodology and questionnaire across all contexts and gathered data from broadly comparable and relatively homogeneous samples of undergraduates studying education degrees in teacher training colleges (people who would later be in positions where they might be influencing the language attitudes of their pupils). In the study we report here, with its focus on students' attitudes and perceptions regarding the position of the minority language around them at the universities, our student sample extends across a greater range of disciplines, enabling us to investigate whether their responses vary with their academic discipline.

In the broader field of language attitudes research (see Garrett, 2010a), there are relatively few studies showing attitudinal differences between the sexes. But there have been some exceptions, and some of the survey work on schoolchildren and tertiary students in bilingual settings has shown some such differences on occasions. In Catalonia (Huguet, 2007) and the BAC (Lasagabaster, 2007), for example, attitudes did not differ on this variable. In contrast, in Wales (Laugharne, 2007), men were significantly more positive than women towards both English and the foreign language. And in the case of the Welsh language, there were indications of more positive attitudes amongst the women, which although not reaching statistical significance, echoes the findings of some of the earlier language attitude studies of schoolchildren in Wales (see, for example, Baker, 1992: 42 and 74). We take up this variable in the study we report in this chapter.

Language attitudes have been found to be influenced by the respondents' level of proficiency in the minority language. In a recent study in

Wales, 'knowledge of the minority language' was found to correlate positively with attitudes towards the Welsh language (Coupland, Bishop, Williams, Evans and Garrett, 2005). In the series of studies in Lasagabaster and Huguet (2007), some arguably related variables ('family language', 'linguistic model', 'predominant language in the context') were found to have a significant effect on language attitudes. Accordingly, we investigate whether knowledge of the minority language is a significant variable in these three contexts.

Hence, our research questions are:

1. In what ways do the perceptions and evaluations of the students with regard to the minority language situation differ across the three bilingual contexts?
2. Do male and female students have different perceptions and evaluations?
3. Do students pursuing different disciplines have different perceptions and evaluations?
4. Do students' perceptions and evaluations vary according to their level of knowledge of the respective minority language?

Method

Participants

Convenience samples totalling 1,622 students completed questionnaires at the three universities. The students were all 'home' (i.e. not international) students at each university.[1] Table 1 gives details of the whole sample, and

---

1   The original sample included an additional 339 international students. However, since some of their questionnaire items differed, and findings, perhaps due to relatively small numbers, were limited, we do not consider them in this report.

Tables 2 and 3 give a further breakdown. These details relate to the sex, level of knowledge of the minority language (Basque, Catalan, Welsh), and the subjects respondents were studying, grouped into a) languages or linguistics, b) humanities and social sciences, and c) sciences.

Table 1. Properties of the total respondent samples in the three contexts

	BAC	*UdL*	*CU*
Total respondents	*531*	*668*	*423*
Sex			
Males	44.1%	33.5%	30.5%
Females	54.8%	62.9%	67.8%
Ages			
18–25	87.8%	84.9%	96.7%
26–33	7.7%	10.8%	2.4%
Over 33	1.5%	3.3%	0.2%
Degrees			
Language	4.3%	12.3%	31.4%
Humanities/Soc. Sci.	71.4%	53.4%	10.6%
Science	22.0%	33.4%	57.0%
Knowledge of minority language			
No or little	28.6%	5.5%	86.5%
Good or very good	70.4%	94.5%	13.0%

Table 2. Percentages (and numbers) of respondents at each university taking each degree discipline type, broken down into males and females

Institution	Language		Humanities / Social Sciences		Sciences	
	Males	Females	Males	Females	Males	Females
UBC	1.6% (8)	2.7% (14)	29.0% (149)	44.0% (226)	14.2% (73)	8.6% (44)
UdL	1.7% (11)	10.8% (69)	18.0% (115)	36.0% (230)	15.0% (96)	18.5% (118)
CU	6.3% (26)	25.7% (106)	2.9% (12)	8.0% (33)	22.3% (92)	34.9% (144)

Table 3. Percentages (and numbers) of respondents in each context according to level of knowledge of minority language, broken down into males and females

Institution	None / a little		Good / very good	
	Males	Females	Males	Females
UBC	14.4% (75)	14.2% (74)	30.2% (157)	41.2% (214)
UdL	1.6% (10)	3.9% (25)	33.1% (213)	61.4% (395)
CU	25.1% (104)	61.6% (255)	5.8% (24)	7.5% (31)

Materials

We report the results for seven items from our questionnaire pertaining to the larger study. These items focus on the position of the respective minority languages in the three universities. They are listed below as they were used at CU in relation to Welsh. 'Welsh' was replaced by 'Basque' and 'Catalan' at UBC and UdL respectively. The abbreviations at the end of each item are those used when referring to them in the remainder of this chapter. The questionnaire also gathered the respondent details regarding the variables addressed by our research questions: context, sex, discipline / degree-type, and knowledge of the minority language.

1. The university should provide more opportunities to learn Welsh. (OPP)
2. There should be more teaching through Welsh. (TEACH)
3. If there were only three or four languages in the world, everything would be easier for everybody. (EASY)
4. The dominance of English at the university may be an obstacle for the recovery of Welsh. (DOM)
5. The language that I use most frequently in my academic work is Welsh. (UNI-USE)
6. The language that I use most frequently outside the academic environment is Welsh. (OUT-USE)
7. Most of the classes I have attended in this university are in Welsh. (CLASS)

We might regard items 1–3 as attitudinal, item 4 as a belief, and items 5–7 as being self-reported 'facts' about minority language use.

Procedure

Students were invited to participate in the study with questionnaires distributed and collected during lectures or workshops. Ethical issues were addressed by informing the students of the broad topic of the study, and giving them the opportunity to decline to be involved. They were told the questionnaires were anonymous, and not to write their names on them, and that completing and handing in the questionnaire would be taken as consent.

Results

MANOVAs were conducted to investigate the effects of context, sex, degree-type, and knowledge of minority language on the seven scales (OPP, TEACH, EASY, DOM, UNI-USE, OUT-USE, and CLASS).

Main effects were found for context (Wilks' 0.290 [14,2950] p<0.001 [eta²=461]), degree-type (Wilks' 0.923 [14,2900] p<0.001 [eta²=0.040]), minority language (Wilks' 0.734 [7,1466] p<0.001 [eta²=266]) and sex (Wilks' 0.967 [7,1437] p<0.001 [eta²=0.033]).

For context, ANOVAs showed context was significant on all seven scales (OPP F=43.129 [2,1481] p<0.001 [eta²=0.055]; TEACH F=85.447 [2,1481] p<0.001 [eta²=0.103]); EASY F=8.549 [2,1481] p<0.001 [eta²=0.011]); DOM F=77.569 [2,1481] p<0.001 [eta²=0.095]); UNI-USE F=588.807 [2,1481] p<0.001 [eta²=0.443]); OUT-USE F=614.175 [2,1481] p<0.001 [eta²=0.453]); CLASS F=688.511 [2,1481] p<0.001 [eta²=0.482]).

These significant effects are as follows. On all seven items except EASY, all three contexts were significantly different from each other. In the case of EASY, UBC (2.471, SD 1.43) differed from UdL and CU (which did not differ from each other, with respective means of 2.773, SD 1.48 and 2.844, SD 1.42). Hence, while students in all three contexts felt that life would not be easier if only three or four languages were spoken in the world, the UBC students felt this more strongly than the other groups. In all three contexts, students felt that the university should offer more opportunities to learn the minority language, with UBC showing the strongest support (mean = 4.060, SD 1.12), followed by UdL (3.609, SD 1.07) and CU (3.370, SD 1.18). As regards more teaching through the minority language, UBC showed the most support (3.712, SD 1.31), with UdL more neutral (3.036, SD 1.28), and CU not favourable overall (2.612, SD 1.10). The DOM item met with most agreement amongst CU students (3.409, SD 1.07), with UBC more neutral (3.007, SD 1.27), and UdL disagreeing (2.491, SD 1.14). In terms of language use, UdL students reported the most UNI-USE and OUT-USE (4.043, SD 1.34 and 4.014, SD 1.32), and also the most on the CLASS item (3.983, SD 1.00). In each of these three items, CU reported the least use (1.083, SD 0.45; 1.258, SD 0.79; 1.09, SD 0.42), with UBC students midway (3.032 SD 1.75; 2.518, SD 1.41; 2.963, SD 1.78).

For degree-type, significance was also found on all seven scales (OPP F=6.022 [2,1456] p=0.002 [eta²=0.008]; TEACH F=3.985 [2,1456] p=0.019 [eta²=0.005]; EASY F=22.437 [2,1456] p<0.001 [eta²=0.030]; DOM F=14.295 [2,1456] p<0.001 [eta²=0.019]; UNI-USE F=6.132 [2,1456] p=0.002 [eta²=0.008]; OUT-USE F=23.034 [2,1456] p<0.001 [eta²=0.031]; CLASS F=6.007 [2,1456] p=0.003 [eta²=0.008]).

Post-hoc analysis revealed that, while students following all three degree-types were in favour of OPP, the difference was between the humanities and social studies students (3.820, SD 1.11) and the other two groups. Language students (3.625, SD 1.15) and science students (3.534, SD 1.19) were not significantly differentiated. On TEACH, the humanities and social studies students were more in favour (3.312, SD 1.28) than the language (2.915, SD 1.35) and the science students (3.008, SD 1.33). All three degree-types differed from each other on the EASY question, with science degree students being comparatively neutral (2.957, SD 1.48), followed by humanities and social studies students being more negative (2.637, SD 1.44), followed by the language students (2.250, SD 1.32). Only the language students felt that the dominance of English might be an obstacle for the minority languages (3.228, SD 1.22), while there was no difference between the science (2.842, SD 1.22) and the humanities and social studies students (2.820, SD 1.21). The humanities and social studies students reported the most frequent UNI-USE (3.566, SD 1.68). The science students reported significantly less (2.530, SD 1.75) and the language students significantly less than the two others (2.165, SD 1.59). For OUT-USE, the humanities and social studies students reported more frequency (3.255, SD 1.59) than the language (2.487, SD 1.76) and the science (2.450, SD 1.63) students, who did not differ from each other quantitatively. Finally, the humanities and social studies students reported more CLASS (3.414, SD 1.57) than the science (2.575, SD 1.68) students, who reported more than the language students (2.165, SD 1.51).

For minority language competence, significance was also found on all scales (OPP F=105.043 [1,1472] p<0.001 [eta²=0.067]; TEACH F=217.217 [1,1472] p<0.001 [eta²=0.129]; EASY F=7.216 [1,1472] p=0.007 [eta²=0.005]; DOM F=36.346 [1,1472] p<0.001 [eta²=0.024]; UNI-

USE F=311.340 [1,1472] p<0.001 [eta^2=0.175]; OUT-USE F=431.434 [1,1472] p<0.001 [eta^2=0.227]; CLASS F=83.003 [1,1472] p<0.001 [eta^2=0.053]).

Post hoc analysis showed that those with a good or very good knowledge of the minority languages, compared to those with no or only a little knowledge, thought the universities should provide more opportunities for learning them (4.100, SD 1.03 compared to 3.189, SD 1.22) and more teaching through them (3.674. SD 1.27 compared to 2.260, SD 1.10). They felt more strongly that life would not be easier if there were only three or four languages in the world (2.616, SD 1.47 compared to 2.939, SD 1.41), and that the dominance of English was a greater obstacle to their minority languages (3.160, SD 1.24 compared to 2.581, SD 1.19). They also reported more frequent use of the minority languages in and outside their academic work and taking more classes taught through the minority languages than those with less knowledge (3.085, SD 1.48; 3.217, SD 1.41 and 2.943, SD 1.38 compared to 1.406, SD 0.54; 1.344, SD 0.52 and 2.130, SD 0.94).

Sex was significant for OPP, TEACH, and EASY only (OPP F=21.696 [1,1443] p<0.001 [eta^2=0.015]; TEACH F=4.767 [1,1443] p=0.029 [eta^2=0.003]; EASY F=27.305 [1,1443] p<0.001 [eta^2=0.019]). Post-hoc analysis showed females thought there should be more opportunities for learning the minority languages (3.779, SD 1.09) and more teaching through them (3.180, SD 1.27) than the males did (3.491, SD 1.22 and 3.028, SD 1.39), although males were not negatively disposed to either of these items. Females also felt more than males that life would not be easier with just three or four languages in the world (females 2.553, SD 1.39 and males 2.973, SD 1.55).

Significant interactions were found for context by degree-type (Wilks' 0.868 [28,5229.472] p<0.001 [eta^2=0.035]), context by knowledge of minority language (Wilks' 0.808 [14,2932] p<0.001 [eta^2=0.101], and context by sex (Wilks' 0.974 [14,2874] p<0.001 [eta^2=0.013]. Drop-down ANOVAs showed context by degree-type to be significant on OPP (F=3.368 [4,1456] p=0.009 [eta^2=0.009]), TEACH (F=4.648 [4,1456] p=0.001 [eta^2=0.013]), EASY (F=5.763 [4,1456] p<0.001 [eta^2=0.016]), and DOM (F=6.409 [4,1456] p<0.001 [eta^2=0.017]). Context by minority language was significant on OPP (F=4.067 [2,1472] p=0.017 [eta^2=0.005]), EASY (F=3.651 [2,1472] p=0.005 [eta^2=0.026], UNI-USE (F=55.715 [2,1472] p<0.001, OUT-USE (F=9.782 [2,1472] p<0.001 [eta²=0.013] and CLASS (F=89.091 [2,1472] p<0.001 [eta²=0.108]). Context by sex was found to be significant on OPP (F=4.555 [2,1443] p=0.011 [eta²=0.006] and EASY (F=5.455 [2,1443] p=0.004 [eta²=0.008]).

Context by degree-type

For interactions, cell means tests were conducted, as recommended by Toothaker, 1991. These showed that although language students in all three contexts agreed that their university should provide more opportunities to learn the minority language, this was a stronger sentiment among the language students in UBC (4.913, SD 0.42) than those in UdL (3.560, SD 1.13) and CU (3.43, SD 1.10), who did not differ from each other. The same relationship emerged for TEACH: the UBC language students were strongly favourable (4.783, SD 0.67), compared to the UdL (3.013, SD 1.45) and CU language degree students (2.516, SD 1.06), who did not differ significantly. There was also a difference among the humanities and social studies students, with the UBC students more in favour of TEACH (3.670, SD 1.31) than the UdL students (3.053, SD 1.18). In addition, the science students at UBC were also in favour of more such teaching (3.632, SD 1.38) than the CU science students (2.671, SD 1.32). On the EASY item, cell means tests revealed that the humanities and social studies students differed between UBC and UdL, with the UBC students disagreeing with this idea more strongly (2.448, SD 1.40) than those at UdL (2.883, SD 1.45). At CU, but not elsewhere, there was a significant difference between the language and the science students, with the former disagreeing with the statement (2.381, SD 1.30) and the latter agreeing with it (3.245, SD 1.37). And while science students at CU saw the dominance of English at the university as a possible obstacle to the recovery of the minority language (3.324, SD 1.16), those at UdL viewed it significantly less so (2.397, SD 1.17). At UBC, there was a division between language degree students and science degree students on this question, with the former seeing English as far more of a likely obstacle (4.261, SD 1.05) than the latter (2.755, SD 1.09). There was also a difference between the humanities and social studies students at UBC and UdL on this issue, with those at UdL seeing English as less of an obstacle (2.558, SD 1.10) than those at UBC (3.006, SD 1.30).

Context by knowledge of minority language

In all three contexts, students at both levels of knowledge of the minority languages were favourable to OPP. However, in the cases of UBC and CU, cell means tests showed a significant difference between those with high and low knowledge of the minority languages. In both contexts, those with high knowledge agreed more (UBC 4.360, SD 0.83 and CU 4.302, SD 0.85) with OPP than those with low knowledge (UBC 3.24, SD 1.37 and CU 3.213, SD 1.15). Also, those with high knowledge in UBC were significantly more favourable to this (4.360, SD 0.83) than those with high knowledge in UdL (3.638, SD 1.05).

Amongst those with high knowledge of their minority languages, the UBC students disagreed more with EASY (2.277, SD 1.38) than the UdL students (2.760, SD 1.47). The significant interaction for context by minority language on UNI-USE comprised differences in UBC and in UdL, where those with more knowledge reported more frequent use than those with least knowledge (UBC high = 3.711, SD 1.55 and low = 1.240, SD 0.64; UdL high = 4.165, SD 1.25 and low = 1.943, SD 1.056). In addition, there was differentiation of all three contexts. Those with good knowledge reported more use in UdL than in UBC and CU (CU high 1.377, SD 0.92), and those in UBC reported more use than those in CU. In terms of OUT-USE, in all three contexts, there was a difference between those with high and low knowledge of the minority languages, with the latter reporting less frequent use (UBC high 2.970, SD 1.34; low 1.320, SD 0.69; UdL high 4.152, SD 1.21; low 1.657, SD 0.80; CU high 2.528, SD 1.42; low 1.055, SD 0.37). Also, those with higher knowledge in UdL report much higher use (4.152, SD 1.21) than UBC (2.970, SD 1.34) and CU (2.528, SD 1.42), with no differentiation between UBC and CU. The interaction for CLASS showed a significant difference between the two levels of knowledge in UBC, where higher knowledge minority language users reported significantly more classes through the minority language

(3.586, SD 1.64) than the lower ones (1.304, SD 0.81). This difference was not found in the other two contexts. Alongside this, lower knowledge users in UdL reported more such classes (4.029, SD 1.04) than those in UBC (1.304, SD 0.81) and CU (1.058, SD 0.33), between which there was no significant difference. The higher knowledge users in the three contexts were all different from each other on this item. Those in UdL reported most classes through the minority language (3.980, SD 0.99), followed by UBC (3.586, SD 1.64) and then CU (1.264, SD 0.76).

Context by sex

Cell means analysis of the interactions between context and sex revealed that CU males were less favourable (2.983, SD 1.29) to OPP than any of the other groups (UBC males, 3.956, SD 1.14; UBC females, 4.140, SD 1.10; UdL males, 3.5349, SD 1.11; UdL females, 3.6499, SD 1.04; and CU females, 3.548, SD 1.06). A difference between the sexes on this item was found only at CU, and not at UBC or UdL. Also, females at UBC were more favourable to more opportunities (4.140, SD 1.10) than females at UdL (3.650, SD 1.04) and CU (3.548, SD 1.06). EASY received the strongest support from CU males (3.390, SD 1.44). The difference between their score and those of the other groups reached significance in the cases of the UBC males (2.631, SD 1.51), the UBC females (2.335, SD 1.34), and the CU females (2.583, SD 1.34). Again, it was only at CU that a difference was found between males and females on this item, not at UBC or UdL.

Discussion

Our first research question (RQ1) asked in what ways the perceptions and evaluations of our students differ in the three bilingual contexts. We found considerable differences.

The students in each of the contexts differ from each other on all of the items. On the UNI-USE, OUT-USE and CLASS items, a hierarchy emerged from the findings, with Catalan featuring more than Basque, which in turn featured more than Welsh. At this broad level, the sociolinguistic experience and activity of the students is in accord with the more general bilingual environment in each context that we described in our introduction. In this respect, university life does not appear, from this data at least, to be markedly different from that of the wider community. The same hierarchy emerges on the DOM item. There is more confidence at UdL that Catalan is not threatened by English, while UBC show uncertainty regarding Basque and CU see Welsh as more under threat. Although we can again see this as a reflection of the demography of minority language use in each context, there is for Wales a very long and continuous history over centuries of Welsh being threatened and attenuated by English. For Wales, the internationalization of universities, which motivates this question, is just a recent development in the relative positions of Welsh and English.

The contexts also differ from each other with regard to OPP and TEACH. Again, a hierarchy emerges, this time with UBC more strongly in support of these than UdL who in turn are more supportive than CU. Responses to the two items differ in degree, however. While all are positive towards more opportunities, only UBC is positive towards more teaching. UdL is relatively neutral, and CU is negative. This may be explained by a different baseline to their responses; there is already a comparatively high level of teaching through Catalan at UdL, and students might see this as already optimal. This aligns with De Rosselló and Boix' (2006) findings from students at the University of Barcelona: 'Catalan speakers do not perceive that the current background of linguistic uses of the University of Barcelona constitutes a threat for the continuity of the Catalan language. (...) they already feel that language is consolidated enough (...) so they think that they do not have to move a finger to promote if further' (167). In contrast, CU students might be mindful of other kinds of factors, including relatively low numbers and distribution of Welsh speakers, the fact that all Welsh speakers in Wales are (at least) bilingual in Welsh and English, and perhaps the fact that students from other countries are rarely Welsh-speakers and that many come to CU in part to study through English. These are powerful forces working against Welsh.

There are other factors to consider at this point, which will also be of value in relation to other results below. Catalan and Spanish are close in terms of linguistic typology, such that Spanish-speakers can be expected to attend classes delivered through Catalan. But there is considerable typological distance between Basque and Spanish, and also between Welsh and English. Hence Basque classes can only be attended by Basque-speakers and Welsh classes by Welsh-speakers. The differences we find between UBC and CU can in part also be attributed to the fact that a higher proportion of (non-international) undergraduates at UBC come from within the BAC (as also happens with UdL and Catalonia), whereas a considerable proportion of CU undergraduates come from England, and even those from Wales are usually non-Welsh speakers. At CU, the argument for providing more classes through Welsh is somewhat different in nature than at UBC or UdL.

It is congruent that the UBC students again stand out from the others on the EASY item. While students overall at each university disagree with this idea, UBC students disagree more than the others, and such a view doubtless underpins their comparatively strong drive for more learning opportunities and classes in Basque. These results coincide with Ros, Cano and Huici's (1994) comparison of Basque, Catalonian, Galician and Valencian university students. They concluded that Basque students showed a more ardent attitude towards the revitalization of their minority language. It is worth noting that, unlike the other questions, EASY does not refer to a specific or named language, and respondents can show their overall attitude towards linguistic diversity. From this, of the three groups, UBC students appear to be attributing the most importance to the preservation of minority languages, including their own.

Some of these context differences discussed above were found to be related to the sex of the students (RQ2), the type of discipline they were studying (RQ3), and their knowledge of the respective minority language (RQ4). Although all of our research questions are answered in the affirmative, some qualification is nevertheless needed.

Sex

Overall, females were more supportive than males on two of the attitudinal items: OPP and TEACH. They also disagreed more with the idea that life would be easier with only three or four languages in the world than the males did (who were relatively neutral to this overall). There were no sex differences on any of the other items (e.g. UNI-USE and OUT-USE). On the attitudinal items, then, we might see these findings as reflecting the occasional, if relatively consistent (when found) pattern of female favourability found in the studies reviewed earlier.

That aside, the interactions reveal a more complex pattern for OPP and EASY. To begin with, taking each university in isolation, there were differences between the sexes in only one of the universities: CU. Compared to the CU females, CU males were the less supportive of more opportunities for learning the minority language, and agreed the most with the view that life would be easier if there were only three or four languages in the world. And indeed, the CU males are the group seeming to account for most of these interactions, as they were more negative than all of the other groups (male and female) on the OPP item, and also more in agreement on the EASY item than the Basque males and females. There is no obvious single explanation as to why CU males should stand out to such a degree from other groups.

Illumination of these more specific differences between the sexes is to some extent impeded by the limited findings in the language attitudes literature (see Garrett, 2010a). Outside the multilingualism field, in the recent BBC Voices study in the UK, Bishop, Coupland and Garrett (2005) found that female respondents in the UK gave more positive evaluations than males of regional and foreign accented English in terms of status and social attractiveness, as if they were more favourably disposed to other ways of speaking than their own, and so to linguistic diversity. We might speculate that this trend could be evident in the differences between the judgements of the CU males and females, and that it is an attitudinal trend in the UK more than other cultural contexts. But the CU males are different from so many of the other groups on these two items. We choose therefore to avoid excessive speculation, and to leave further pursuance of this issue to further research.

Degree-type

On the 'use' items (in and outside academic life, and as a medium of instruction in classes), there are only main effects for degree-type, showing that across the three universities, it is the humanities and social science students who report the most use, more frequent use than the science students, who in turn find more minority language use in academic contexts than the language students. Degree-types do not work differently among the universities in this regard.

With the attitudinal questions, we see the humanities and social studies students most in favour of more opportunities and teaching, but the story begins to vary more across the universities. While it is arguably re-assuring to find the language-oriented students are all positive on the OPP item, the UBC language students stand out from those at UdL and CU as particularly positive on this question, as if feeling that their university might be short-changing the students in such provision. This again may reflect an overall perspective at UdL that, though more might be to some extent desirable, they are closer to an optimum already. And such optimum levels are doubtless seen very differently by the UdL students compared to CU.

The teaching question produces a similar pattern amongst these language groups, but this time UdL and CU scores are lower, showing a general neutrality amongst the UdL students, again suggesting perhaps that there is already adequate teaching provision there, and a negative stance amongst the CU students, perhaps implying that this would not be of benefit to them and might also in other ways not be a good direction for CU to take. There are also university differences, with the UBC language students far more likely to be studying Basque than the CU students are to be studying Welsh.

A further division occurs between the humanities and social studies students at UBC and UdL, and these differences again appear to reflect a greater sense of security amongst the UdL students as far as their minority language is concerned. Again, the desire for more university teaching through Catalan does not match the desire for more in Basque. UdL students see English as less of a potential hindrance to Catalan than the UBC students do with Basque. And, though negative, they are closer to lukewarm than the UBC students when it comes to the question of whether it might be better just to have three or four languages in the world.

Amongst the science students, the position of the CU science students is noteworthy. They see English dominance at the university as being a potential obstacle for the recovery of Welsh, contrasting with the UdL science students' scepticism about its threat to Catalan. Yet this does not lead them to the level of promotion of Welsh that one sees much more in relation to Basque; they are against more teaching through Welsh, contrasting significantly with the positivity of the UBC science students, and they are prepared to agree that life would be easier with only three or four languages (in contrast with the CU language students). It is notable that 16.7 per cent of the science degree respondents said they were good or very good at the Welsh language, a higher proportion than in the other CU degrees.

Minority language knowledge

Across all the items, and taking the respondents from all the contexts together, the level of knowledge of the minority language is significant, and there is a pattern of those with a higher knowledge reporting more frequency for UNI-USE, OUT-USE and CLASS. There is also a pattern of those with more knowledge being more favourable on the OPP, TEACH and DOM items, and also against the idea that things would be easier with only three or four languages. In this regard, our findings echo the link found in Coupland et al. (2005) between positive attitudes and high language competence levels. However, many of our findings interact with context to reveal a more complex picture. Hence, on OPP, those with greater knowledge are more enthusiastic than those with less knowledge in the case of Basque and Welsh, but there is no such distinction in the case of Catalan, again doubtless arising in part from vitality factors such as the broader demographic base and the already-existing opportunities.

In the academic environments (UNI-USE and CLASS), high and low level speakers only at UBC and UdL report differences. For the CU respondents, UNI-USE is not affected here by how much Welsh they know, but more constrained by the opportunities, conventions, expectations and competencies in the language environment itself. This contextual difference also shows itself in the way that high level speakers at UdL use Catalan in their academic environment significantly more than those at UBC use Basque and those at CU use Welsh (in this last case, a low frequency rating of 1.38).

For CLASS, the distinction between high and low level speakers only applies to the UBC students, with the high level speakers having more classes through Basque than the low level ones. As we saw in Table 1, 28.6 per cent of UBC students have little or no Basque, and given the typological distance from Spanish (compared to the closeness between Catalan and Spanish), they will not elect to take the classes conducted through Basque that are available on their courses. There is no such division between the high and low levels at UdL and CU, but for different reasons. At UdL, all students are expected to attend the Catalan classes, and there is a stronger demographic base to the competence in the language. At CU, on the other hand, it is relatively rare to find classes in Welsh for anyone to attend. It is outside the university where those with a greater knowledge of Welsh use it more than those with less. Indeed, in all three contexts, those who are better at their minority language use it outside the university more than those who know little. This is particularly the case with Catalan, as we might expect. With Basque and Welsh, it is worth noting that even those with a good knowledge of Basque report only moderate (around the scalar mid-point) OUT-USE, and those with a good knowledge of Welsh lower still (2.53).

Conclusion

Employing a single methodology, we have aimed to shed light on the diverse character of these bilingual contexts, and on how linguistic diversity and minority language maintenance are perceived within them. We have done this by examining responses regarding what we have termed 'self-reported facts' about language use within and outside the academic contexts, about attitudes to a greater presence in the university and also to language diversity, and about beliefs about the threat from English. Self-reported facts logically seemed to reflect the existing reality in each university's sociolinguistic context. Attitudinal findings supported some of those from previous studies. UBC students remain eager for more of their minority language at their university, whereas UdL students, despite their high linguistic identity, show a medium-low perceived need for more Catalan. Thus we can conclude that these trends found by Ros et al. (1994) findings have endured over the last two decades. In comparison, CU students seem to show a low Welsh linguistic identity and less motivation for more Welsh (similar to the Galician students in Ros et al.'s study).

All in all, there appears to be a complex interplay between attitudes, sociolinguistic reality and vitality. Use of the minority language is higher at UdL, followed by UBC, with far less at CU. The students' attitudinal responses show a more 'militant' approach in UBC, followed by UdL and in contrast to CU. In the case of UBC, lower use of Basque is accompanied by a desire for a greater use of the language, whereas in the case of CU, lower use of Welsh does not. Perceptions of the risk of English further damaging the minority language are highest among CU students, but this does not generate attitudinal responses.

Finally, it might seem reasonable to expect language students to show higher regard for linguistic diversity and for minority languages than students in other disciplines. Yet there is arguably no reason simply to assume that those who choose to pursue their degrees in other areas are less concerned about language.[2] And indeed, our data tell a story of the humanities and social studies students being more in favour than the language students of more opportunities to learn, and for more teaching through, the minority languages. Given the larger numbers of people working in these areas other than language, we believe such findings give cause for optimism.

Acknowledgement

This research is a part of the project *Internationalisation and multilingualism in universities in bilingual contexts: Catalonia, the Basque Country and Wales*. The project is funded by the Spanish Ministry of Science and Innovation (FFI2008–00585/FILO). For statistical advice and support, we are grateful to Angie Williams at the Centre for Language and Communication Research, Cardiff University.

References

Aitchison, J. and Carter, H. (2004). *Spreading the Word: the Welsh language 2001*. Talybont: Y Lolfa.
Baker, C. (1988). *Key Issues in Bilingualism and Bilingual Education*. Clevedon: Multilingual Matters.
Baker, C. (1992). *Attitudes and Language*. Clevedon: Multilingual Matters.
Balfour, R. (2007). University language policies, internationalism, multilingualism, and language development in the UK and South Africa. *Cambridge Journal of Education* 37, 35–49.

---

2   In a study of Chinese perceptions of 'globalization', for example, science students did not differ from arts students (who included language students) in what they had to say about impacts on language (Garrett, 2010b: 471).

Basque Government (2008). *Fourth Sociolinguistic Survey 2006.* Vitoria-Gasteiz: Basque Government.

Bishop, H., Coupland, N. and Garrett, P. (2005). Conceptual accent evaluation: thirty years of accent prejudice in the UK. *Acta Linguistica Hafniensia*, 37, 131–154.

Cardiff University (2009). *Strategy 2009/2010–2013/2014.* <http://www.cardiff. ac.uk/plann/resources/Cardiff%20Strategy%20-%20Final%20(english).pdf> (accessed 19 July 2011).

Cardiff University (2011). <http://www.cardiff.ac.uk/for/prospective/inter/study/ lifeatcardiff/welshlanguageinfo/index.html> (accessed 10 February 2011).

Cots, J., Lasagabaster, D. and Garrett, P. (in press). Multilingual policies and practices in bilingual regions in Europe. *International Journal of the Sociology of Language.*

Coupland, N., Bishop, H., Williams, A., Evans, B. and Garrett, P. (2005). Affiliation, engagement, language use and vitality: secondary school students' subjective orientations to Welsh and Welshness. *International Journal of Bilingual Education and Bilingualism*, 8, 1–24.

de Bres, J. (2008). Planning for tolerability in New Zealand, Wales and Catalonia. *Current Issues in Language Planning*, 9, 464–482.

De Rosselló, C. and Boix, E. (2006). An unbalanced trilingualism: linguistic ideologies at the University of Barcelona. *Catalan Review* 20, 1: 153–171.

European Commission (2009). *Lifelong learning programme. The Erasmus programme 2008/09. A statistical overview.* <http://ec.europa.eu/education/erasmus/doc/ stat/report0809.pdf> (accessed 12 February 2011).

Garrett, P. (2010a). *Attitudes to Language.* Cambridge: Cambridge University Press.

Garrett, P. (2010b). Meanings of 'globalisation': east and west. In N. Coupland (ed.), *The Handbook of Language and Globalization*, 447–474. Oxford: Wiley-Blackwell.

Garrett, P., Griffiths, Y., James, C. and Scholfield, P. (1992). Differences and similarities between and within bilingual settings: some British data. *Language, Culture and Curriculum*, 5, 99–115.

Generalitat de Catalunya (2009). *Enquesta d'usos linguistics de la población 2008.* <http://www20.gencat.cat/docs/Llengcat/Documents/Dades_territori_poblacio/Altres/Arxius/EULP2008.pdf> (accessed 15 February 2011).

Hoffmann, C. (1991). *An Introduction to Bilingualism.* London: Longman.

Huguet, Á. (2007). Language use and language attitudes in Catalonia. In D. Lasagabaster and Á. Huguet (eds), *Multilingualism in European Bilingual Contexts. Language Use and Attitudes*, 17–39. Clevedon: Multilingual Matters.

Institut d'Estadística de Catalunya (Idescat) (n.d). *El municipi en xifres.* <http://www. idescat.cat/dequavi/?TC=444&V0=4&V1=2> (accessed 15 February 2011).

Lasagabaster, D. (2003). *Trilingüismo en la enseñanza. Actitudes hacia la lengua minoritaria, la mayoritaria y la extranjera.* Lleida: Milenio Educación.

Lasagabaster, D. (2007). Language use and language attitudes in the Basque Country. In D. Lasagabaster and Á. Huguet (eds), *Multilingualism in European Bilingual Contexts. Language Use and Attitudes*, 65–89. Clevedon: Multilingual Matters.

Lasagabaster, D. and Huguet, Á. (eds) (2007). *Multilingualism in European Bilingual Contexts. Language Use and Attitudes.* Clevedon: Multilingual Matters.

Laugharne, J. (2007). Language use and language attitudes in Wales. In D. Lasagabaster and Á. Huguet (eds), *Multilingualism in European Bilingual Contexts. Language Use and Attitudes*, 208–233. Clevedon: Multilingual Matters.

May, S. (2000). Accommodating and resisting minority language policy: the case of Wales. *International Journal of Bilingual Education and Bilingualism*, 3, 101–128.

May, S. (2003). Re-articulating the case for minority language rights. *Current Issues in Language Planning*, 4, 95–125.

Ros, M., Cano, J.I. and Huici, C. (1994). Ethnolinguistic vitality and social identity: their impact on ingroup bias and social attribution. *International Journal of the Sociology of Language* 108, 145–166.

Toothaker, L. (1991). *Multiple Comparisons for Researchers.* Thousand Oaks, CA: Sage.

UK Council for International student affairs (n.d.). *Higher education statistics.* <http://www.ukcisa.org.uk/about/statistics_he.php#table7->

Universitat de Barcelona (2010). *Els usos lingüístics a la Universitat de Barcelona.* <http://www.ub.edu/sl/ca/socio/infcat.htm> (accessed 12 February 2011).

University of the Basque Country (2007). Plan director del euskara en la UPV/EHU (2007/08–2011/12)-UPV/EHUko euskararen plan gidaria (2007/08–2011/12) (Director Plan for Basque at the UBC (2007/8–2011/12)). Zarautz, Gipuzkoa: University of the Basque Country.

Universitat de Lleida (2006). *Programa d'internacionalització.* <http://www.udl.cat/serveis/ori/Fitxers_descxrrega/Pla_internacionalitzacio2.pdf> (accessed 7 August 2009).

Universitat de Lleida (2008). *Política lingüística de la UdL.* <http://web.udl.es/rectorat/sg/bou/bou101/acord153.htm> (accessed 15 February 2011).

Universitat de Lleida (2009). Memòria acadèmica de la Universitat de Lleida 2008/2009. <http://www.udl.cat/export/sites/UdL/organs/secretaria/Memoria-Academica/MemoriaGeneralUdL08–09breu.pdf> (accessed 12 February 2011).

Universitat de Lleida (2010). Memòria acadèmica de la Universitat de Lleida 2009/2010. <http://www.udl.cat/export/sites/UdL/organs/secretaria/ Memoria-Academica/MemoriaGeneralUdL09–10breu.pdf> (accessed 12 February 2011).

Universitat Pompeu Fabra (2010). *Dades lingüístiques de docència.* <http://www.upf. edu/llengues/infosocio/dades/> (accessed 12 February 2011).

Woodfield, S. (2010). Europe. In E. Egron-Polak and R. Hudson (eds), *Internationalization of Higher Education: Global Trends, Regional Perspectives,* 170–178. International Association of Universities 3rd Global Survey Report.

NKONKO M. KAMWANGAMALU

8 The Medium-of-Instruction Conundrum and 'Minority' Language Development in Africa

Introduction

This chapter discusses the perennial issue of choosing the medium of instruction in public schools in Africa. More specifically, language-policy makers in Africa have been grappling with the question whether the indigenous African languages should replace former colonial languages such as English, French, Portuguese and Spanish as the medium of instruction in public schools and, if so, at what cost?

The literature on language policy and planning in Africa has, over the years, attempted to shed light onto this issue of the medium of instruction in African education (Bamgbose, 1983; Kamanda, 2002; Heine, 1990; Prah, 1995). What this literature seems to have overlooked, however, is that language policy and planning is an interest-driven game, one in which the stakeholders all plan to win and value the outcomes differently. The term 'game' is borrowed from the 'game theory' (Harsanyi, 1977; Laitin, 1993). It is understood to refer to any situation in which there are at least two players, each with a number of possible options or strategies to choose from in order to achieve desirable, payoffs-driven, outcomes. The game theory itself is concerned with explaining how participants or players in a game, be they individuals, groups or organizations should act rather than with the question of how they will actually act in order to promote their interests (Harsanyi, 1977). The goal of the game theory is to predict and explain real-life human behaviour in various social situations. With respect to language planning, Harsanyi (1977) points out that the game theory has predictive power to determine whether a language policy will fail or succeed. In Africa, language policies designed to promote use of the indigenous languages in education, commonly known as mother-tongue-education policies, have failed (Adegbia, 1997; Laitin, 1992; Akinnaso, 1993). Laitin (1992: 43) explains that the policies have failed due, in part, to what he refers to as the private subversion of language planning, that is, the practice of agreeing with language policy publicly but subverting it privately. The policy-makers subvert mother-tongue-education policies by theoretically giving major indigenous languages official status that is equal to that of ex-colonial languages, but not allowing them and their speakers access to important domains (e.g., the educational system, socio-economic and political participation or access to employment) that an ex-colonial language and a minority of its speakers – the elite – have.

Eggington (in press, after Harding, 1998 and Diamond, 2005) describes this behavioural paradox, that is, committing to something but actually doing the opposite of that which one has committed to, as the 'tragedy of the commons'. This is the idea that a shared resource is eventually destroyed when many individuals act independently in their own short term self-interest although it is obvious to everyone that the destruction of the shared resource is harmful to everyone's long term interests. In Africa, the 'commons' refers to the indigenous languages that the stakeholders (policy-makers, parents, schools) share but ones that they all are ready to sacrifice, hence 'the tragedy', in favour of ex-colonial languages as the medium of instruction, for they view the latter as a commodity in which they have a good reason to invest. Even the illiterate labourer who sends his children to school knows that their prospects in life will improve immensely if they study through the medium of an ex-colonial language such as English (Mustafa, 2005). In other words, the stakeholders, irrespective of their social class, have strong incentives to aspire to or have an education through the medium of ex-colonial languages because of their economic payoffs, but they have none for the indigenous languages. In Africa, the tragedy of the commons is reinforced by the myth in language policy formulation that ex-colonial languages are politically and ethnically neutral and external languages; that is, they do not privilege any specific ethnic group but rather (dis)advantage everyone equally, both socio-economically and politically.

In an attempt to resolve the medium of instruction conundrum, I will draw on recent theoretical developments in language economics, a field of study whose focus is on the theoretical and empirical analysis of the ways in which linguistic and economic variables influence one another (Vaillancourt and Grin, 2000; Grin, 2001). Some of the issues raised in 'language economics' that are relevant to this chapter include the following: (i) the relevance of language as a defining element of economic processes such as production, distribution and consumption; (ii) the relevance of language as a commodity in the acquisition of which individual actors may have a good reason to invest; (iii) language teaching as a social investment, yielding net benefits (market-related or not); and (iv) the economic implications (costs and benefits) of language policies, whether these costs and benefits are market-related or not (Grin, 2001: 66). In addition, Grin (1994: 25) lists the following among the issues studied in language economics: the effect of language on income, language learning by immigrants, patterns of language maintenance and spread in multilingual societies, the selection and design of language policies, minority language protection and promotion, language use in the workplace and market equilibrium for language-specific goods and services.

In language economics and related frameworks, particularly critical linguistics, linguistic products such as language, language varieties, utterances and accents are seen not only as goods or commodities to which the market assigns a value, but as signs of wealth or capital, which receive their value only in relation to a market, characterized by a particular law of price formation (Bourdieu, 1991: 66–67). The term 'market' refers to the social context in which linguistic products are used. In a given linguistic market, some products are valued more highly than others. This means, as Bourdieu puts it, that the market fixes the price for a linguistic product or capital, the nature, and therefore the objective value of which the practical anticipation of this price helped to determine (1991: 77). The market value of a linguistic capital such as language or language variety is determined by a number of factors, all of which contribute to make language not only a medium but also an element of economic success (Coulmas, 1992: 77–89). Besides language economics, game theory and the tragedy of the commons, this chapter also draws on insights from language ecology

(Hornberger, 2003). Language ecology perspective is concerned with the maintenance of threatened languages and linguistic diversity and supports linguistic human rights. It adopts a resource-and-enrichment orientation towards indigenous languages and their speakers (King, 2004). Put differently, in this framework linguistic diversity or multilingualism is seen as resource rather than a problem. I will argue, however, that multilingualism in Africa or elsewhere is a resource in so far as all the languages – especially those targeted as potential media of instruction – are associated with an economic value in the linguistic market place.

Before I address this issue of the medium of instruction, it is imperative that I clarify a few concepts, among them minority and minoritized languages, majority and majoritized languages, mother tongue and mother tongue education, to name but a few, as they apply to language issues in education in the African context. As Adegbija (1997: 7) explains, there seems to be a fundamental difference in the Western and African situation of minorities. He notes that while in the West minorities result most of all, though not necessarily, from migration or political shifts of positions, in Africa, those referred to as minorities are predominantly native to the countries in which they, from the numerical, political and power-wielding standpoint, hold a minority status. But as Cenoz and Gorter (2001: 244) remark, the concept of minority languages does not necessarily have to be associated with the number of speakers of a language. They give the example of Catalan in Europe and Quechua in Latin America, noting that the two languages have millions of speakers but they are minority languages in their socio-demographic context.

In Africa, ex-colonial languages such as English, French, Portuguese and Spanish are demographically minority languages but, because of their comparatively higher economic status vis-à-vis the indigenous African languages, they are perceived as mainstream or majority languages, or what Skutnabb-Kangas (2006) calls 'majoritized languages' as opposed to 'minoritized languages' – the indigenous languages. Any discussion of the medium of instruction in public schools in Africa in particular must consider the distinction between economically majority languages and minority languages or 'majoritized languages' and 'minoritized languages', respectively. This distinction is necessary because the term majority-minority language entails a hierarchy which is neither a natural nor a linguistic process; rather, it is the result of power relations between languages in a given polity (May, 2001).

Other concepts commonly used in the discussion of the medium of instruction in Africa and elsewhere include 'mother tongue' and 'mother tongue education'. UNESCO ([1953] 1995), defines 'mother tongue' as 'the language which a person has acquired in early years and which normally has become his natural instrument of thought and communication'. It seems, however, that 'the concept of mother tongue has been so taken for granted that between the debates on language acquisition and language learning scholars have not found time to examine it carefully' (Pattanayak, 1998: 124). Pattanayak defines 'mother tongue' as 'that language with which one is emotionally identified. It is the language through which the child recognizes and organizes his [her] experience and environment around him [her]. It is the language used to express one's basic needs, ideas, thoughts, joys, sorrows and other feelings. [It is the language that,] if one gives it up, one may remain intellectually alive but would grow emotionally sterile' (Pattanayak, 1998: 129). Some scholars have been very critical of the concept of 'mother tongue', arguing that it is essentialist and therefore should be dropped from the linguist's set of professional myths about language (Ferguson, 1992). It is explained that 'much of the world's verbal communication takes place by means of languages that are not the users' "mother tongue," but their second, third, or nth language, acquired one way or another and used when appropriate' (Ferguson, 1992: xiii). This is precisely the point that UNESCO (1995) is making, when the organization points out that mother tongue 'need not be the language which a child's parents use; nor need it be the language he first learns to speak, since special circumstances may cause him to abandon this language more or less completely at an early age'. Even if UNESCO (1995) defines mother tongue education as 'education which uses as its medium of instruction a person's mother tongue', this does not, due to financial constraints especially in post-colonial settings in Africa in particular, entail that every child must or will necessarily have access to an education through the medium of his or her mother tongue. In this chapter, I use the concept of 'mother tongue education' to refer to an education that is imparted through the medium of an indigenous language, which may or may not be the mother tongue of all the student population in a polity. In the section that follows I discuss the rationale for mother tongue education to provide the background against which the issue of the medium of instruction in African education can be understood better. The next section discusses some of the ideologies that inform the debate around the medium of instruction in the African continent, with a focus on the ideology of decolonization and the ideology of development. The last section explores ways in which mother tongue education can be implemented successfully in Africa, drawing on the theoretical frameworks highlighted earlier, including language economics, the tragedy of the commons, the game theory and the ecology of language.

The medium of instruction conundrum and mother tongue education

The issue of the medium of instruction tends to take centre stage, in theory at least, in language policy decisions in most African countries, much as it does in postcolonial settings elsewhere in the world (Tollefson and Tsui, 2004; Lin and Martin, 2005; Evans, 2002). This is because, as Tollefson (1991: 2) points out, language has a fundamental importance in the organization of human societies; it affects people's lives in more ways than the people themselves realize; it has impact on family, friends, occupation, home and income. Along these same lines, Fishman (1971: 1) observes that 'language is a referent for loyalties and animosities, an indicator of social statuses and personal relationships, a marker of situations and topics as well as of the societal goals and the large-scale value-laden arenas of interaction that typify every speech community.'

In Africa, the debate around the medium of instruction is being rekindled by the widening gaps between the elite, who overtly profess but privately subvert the promotion of indigenous languages as the medium of instruction in favour of ex-colonial languages, as explained earlier; and the masses, who are marginalized because they have no access to the latter languages. This debate has its roots in the unrealized expectations in post-colonial Africa that in retaining former colonial languages as official languages, they would bring about national unity, develop into viable media of national communication, and spread as lingua franca and perhaps eventually as first language by replacing local languages, as was the case in large parts of Latin America (Heine, 1990: 176).

At the heart of the debate around the medium of instruction is the concept of 'mother tongue' and, with it, 'mother tongue education'. As Kamwangamalu (2005) observes, the renewed interest in mother tongue education appears to be informed by UNESCO's (1995) model of mother tongue literacy and by the findings, documented in several studies around the world, that children perform better at school when they are taught through the medium of their mother tongue or a related indigenous language rather than through the medium of a foreign language (Akinnaso, 1993; Auerbach, 1996; Lai and Bryan, 2003). With these findings in mind, it is not a coincidence, then, that in the West and in some Asian and Arab countries mother tongue education is the norm rather than the exception. We know, for instance, that the French, the Britons, the Germans, the Russians, the Polish, etc. are schooled through the medium of their respective mother tongues, viz. French, English, Polish, German, Russian; just like the Japanese, the Koreans, the Chinese and some Arabs are through theirs, namely Japanese, Korean, Chinese and Arabic, respectively. Put differently, in the West in particular no country utilizes a language for education and other national purposes which is of external origin and the mother tongue of none, or at most few, of its people (Spencer, 1985: 390). While in the West and elsewhere the majority of children are educated through the medium of their indigenous language, in Africa, however, linguistically minoritized children learn through the medium of an ex-colonial language such as French, English, Spanish or Portuguese. It follows that although colonialism ended in Africa decades ago, its legacy remains formidable and continues to impact post-colonial language policies, especially in education. It is this state of affairs that African countries have attempted to change, albeit unsuccessfully, by arguing for the decolonization of the educational system. The next section offers a brief introduction to language ideologies followed by a discussion of the ideology of decolonization and its competition, the ideology of development.

The medium of instruction conundrum and language ideologies

Linguistic practices, irrespective of domains including education, are shaped by language ideologies, as summarized in Kamwangamalu (in press). Language ideologies, or what Woolard and Schieffelin (1994: 55) refer to as 'cultural conceptions of the nature, structure and use of language', are ingrained, unquestionable beliefs that people have about language (Wolfram and Schilling-Estes, 2006: 35) and which influence their linguistic choices in various domains. As these beliefs continue to hold sway, they assume ever-greater force, regardless of their accuracy or correspondence to present realities (McGroarty, 2010). In this regard, Blommaert (1999: 10–11) remarks that the more a linguistic ideology is taken up in any setting, the more likely it is to undergo normalization, a hegemonic pattern in which the ideological claims are perceived as normal ways of thinking and acting. At their core, language ideologies represent the perception of language and discourse that is constructed in the interest of a specific social or cultural group; that is, they are rooted in the socio-economic power and vested interests of dominant groups and serve to sustain relations of domination and inequality (Thompson, 1984). Essentially, as Dyers and Abongdia (2010) note pointedly, language ideologies are reflected in actual language practice – how people talk, what they say about language and their actual language choices, and their sociopolitical positioning with regards to different languages. For instance, studies into the issue of the medium of instruction in public schools in Africa reveal that community members, parents and even the schools themselves oppose the use of indigenous languages as the medium of instruction (Mfum-Mensah, 2005; Kamanda, 2002). Most participants in Mfum-Mensah's study on language attitudes in Ghana, for instance, view the use of indigenous languages in education as a subtle strategy to perpetuate the communities' marginalization from the mainstream society, which is understood to use English as its dominant language and as a powerful tool for attaining dominance, power and prestige. One participant in the study comments as follows concerning the social status of English in the polity: 'Whenever you go to the bank or any other office in the regional capital, and you meet people, the first language that they use to communicate to you is English. They expect everybody who comes to such a place to know and speak English' (Mfum-Mensah, 2005: 310). Other participants, including parents in particular, question the usefulness of the mother tongue in education: 'The people feel that in order to get a job you must have a European language and that if you study African languages you have no employment opportunities'; 'What will my child do with that [African] language?' (2005: 310). The stakeholders' negative attitude towards the indigenous languages stems from their deep-seated perceptions about the diglossic relationship in which the indigenous languages and English co-exist in Ghanaian society and elsewhere in the African continent, with English being more hegemonic than the indigenous languages. Thus, language ideologies to be discussed in the next two sections – the ideology of decolonization of education and the ideology of development – form an essential frame of reference in terms of which individuals and groups in Africa evaluate their linguistic choices in domains such as education in particular.

The medium of instruction conundrum and the ideology of decolonization

Scholars and policy-makers who subscribe to the ideology of decolonization, which requires that minoritized African languages be used as the media of instruction in public schools, not only point to the cognitive advantages associated with the mother tongue of the learners, but they also argue that colonial schools deprived the African child of its cultural heritage (Alexander, 1997; Prah, 2005). Their argument draws support not only from current research findings on the use of the indigenous languages as the medium of instruction, but also from competing views by Western scholars on colonial language-in-education policies in Africa, with some opposing and others supporting the policies. In the colonial era, those who opposed the policies argued that it was imperative that Africans be educated through the medium of their indigenous languages. For instance, in a draft memorandum entitled 'The Place of the Vernacular in Native Education' in Africa, a Swiss born British linguist, Hanns Vischer, explains that 'a man's native speech is almost like his shadow, inseparable from his personality. Hence in all education, the primary place should be given to training in the exact and free use of the mother tongue' (Whitehead, 1995: 4). Significantly, Vischer and associates argue eloquently that 'by taking away a people's language we cripple or destroy its soul and kill its mental individuality ... If the African is to keep and to develop his own soul and is to become a separate personality, his education must not begin by inoculating him with a foreign civilization ... the vernacular ... is the vessel in which the whole national life is contained and through which it finds expression' (Whitehead, 1995: 4).

In the postcolonial era, we have witnessed similar statements by institutions such as the Organization of African Unity and its successor, the African Union. In particular, the organizations state that:

(1) All African children have the unalienable right to attend school and learn their mother tongues at all levels of education;
(2) The effective and rapid development of science and technology in Africa depends on the use of African languages;
(3) African languages are vital for the development of democracy based on equality and social justice;
(4) African languages are essential for the decolonization of African minds and for the African Renaissance.
(Asmara Declaration, 2000, <http//www.queensu.ca/snid/asmara. htm>)

The most recent efforts to promote the indigenous languages in the higher domains have resulted in the creation of the African Academy of Languages (ACALAN). This is a Pan-African organization founded in 2001 by Mali's then-president Alpha Oumar Konaré, under the auspices of the Organization of African Unity, now the African Union, to promote the usage and perpetuation of African languages among African people and to serve as a specialized scientific institution of the AU (see <en.wikipedia.org/wiki/African_Academy_of_Languages>). Bamgbose (2006) highlights the goals of ACALAN as follows:

(1) To foster the development of all African languages and empower some of the more dominant vehicular languages in Africa to the extent that they can serve as working languages in the African Union and its institutions.

(2) To increase the use of African languages in a variety of domains so that the languages become empowered and revalorized.

(3) To promote the adoption of African languages as languages of learning and teaching in the formal and non-formal school system.

(4) To promote the use of African languages for information dissemination and for political participation to ensure grassroots involvement in the political process and demystification of the elite.

Unlike previous language policies, the African Union's policies do not call for African languages to replace ex-colonial languages in education or other domains. Rather, it is expected that ex-colonial languages will assume a new role as partners to African languages, but not in an unequal relationship as is currently the case. In Article 88 of its constitution, the African Union reiterates its goal in education as follows:

The Systems of Education is [sic] crucial for the best possible training and development of future generations and to ensure the highest skills and abilities for all citizens of the Union. It shall remain a primary object of the Union to ensure that all children have access to a well rounded and sound education both in the fundamental knowledge systems of humanity, language and literature but also in the history and pride of their own culture.

These policy declarations, like their predecessors in the 1990s, are not matched with practical steps to use the indigenous languages in education. Instead, these languages remain confined to the cultural domains, much as they were in the colonial era. Unlike their Western counterparts, African policy-makers perpetuate the myth that the use of African languages in education and other higher domains is incompatible with socio-economic development. As a result, the ideology of development, to be discussed in the section that follows, has been put on a pedestal at the expense of the ideology of decolonization of education in the African continent.

The medium of instruction conundrum and the ideology of development

In the colonial era, one of the strategies that the discourse of development used in the unequal distribution of power and resources is what Brock-Utne (2001) refers to as the invalidation of non-material resources of the African people, including their languages and cultures. The colonial authorities invalidated the indigenous languages by stigmatizing them as unsuitable for higher learning and as a barrier to upward social mobility for the African people. This is evident from the following statement by a certain Sir Rivers-Smith, Director of Education in the then Tanganika (now Tanzania) who, unlike Haans Vischer (see earlier), argues that 'to insist on the use of the mother tongue in education would set back the clock of progress for many tribes' (Whitehead, 1995: 8). For Rivers-Smith: 'The vast majority of African dialects ... must be looked upon as educational cul de sacs [sic]... From a purely educational standpoint the decent interment of the vast majority of African dialects is to be desired, as they can never give the tribal unit access to any but a very limited literature ...' (1995: 8). Rivers-Smith also stresses the important link between language policy and economic growth, and argues that use of the vernacular could isolate a tribe from commercial intercourse: 'To limit a native to a knowledge of his tribal dialects is to burden him with an economic handicap under which he will always be at a disadvantage when compared with others who, on account of geographical distribution or by means of education, are able to hold intercourse with European or Asiatics' (1995: 8). Although the languages of the colonized people are typically described as subordinate and backward, lacking higher literary forms, and inadequate for socio-economic development (Newton, 1972), Tollefson (1991) warns that these assessments of value must be understood as reflections of relationships of power and domination rather than objective linguistic or historical facts.

Scholars and policy-makers who subscribe to the ideology of development view instruction in the language of the former colonial power as an approach that will lead to greater proficiency in that language, representing a further step towards economic development and participation in the international global economy (Mfum-Mensah, 2005). These expectations, however, have not materialized. Although European languages have been used in Africa for almost 400 years, their social distribution remains very limited and restricted to a minority elite group. In this regard, Alexander (1997: 88) remarks that efforts to make Western languages accessible to the masses have been resounding failures: the majority remains on the fringe; language-based division has increased; economic development has not reached the majority; and the illiteracy rate among the populace remains high. Likewise, Tollefson (1991) points out that though vast resources are directed toward language teaching and bilingualism involving European languages and indigenous languages, more people than ever are unable to acquire the language skills they need in order to enter and succeed in school, obtain satisfactory employment, and participate politically and socially in the life of their communities.

Research reports from around the African continent bear testimony to the failure of Western education in Africa. The statistics show that in 1990, for instance, there were 138.8 million illiterate persons in sub-Saharan Africa (UNESCO, 1995). Although no recent statistics on literacy are available, one can but assume that illiteracy figures must have gone up, especially in a continent where regression, not progress, is the norm rather than the exception. It is reported that in Anglophone Africa, for instance, only a thin percentage of between 5 per cent and 20 per cent can communicate in

English (Samuels, 1995: 31). Along these lines, in a relatively recent study on literacy in South Africa, Balfour (1999) refers to a manuscript by Barbara Ludman entitled 'A rainbow nation of illiterates', which reveals that 80 per cent of Black South Africans and about 40 per cent of Whites are illiterate and innumerate at Standard Five level (i.e. Grade 7). Previous studies into literacy in Africa anticipated these new developments about literacy decline in the continent. For instance, Siachitema's (1992: 19) and Tripathi's (1990: 38) investigations of literacy in Zambia reveal that since independence the number of Zambians competent in the use of English has shrunk. The situation in Lusophone and Francophone Africa is not any different. Heines (1992: 27) notes that less than 10 per cent of people are able to function through Portuguese, and so does Kamwangamalu (1997a, after Rubango, 1986) with regard to literacy in Francophone Africa. Therefore, since competence in ex-colonial languages is a prerequisite for participation in the national political and economic system, the majority of the people, most of whom live in rural areas, have been left out in the cold, on the fringe of the privileged, political action.

In Anglophone, Francophone and Lusophone Africa, the prominence given to English, French and Portuguese respectively has virtually rendered the local languages instrumentally valueless. Phillipson (1988: 350) attributes the failure of Western education in the developing world to its inappropriateness. He argues convincingly that ELT (English Language Teaching), for instance, has failed because linguicism operates covertly to ensure that the third world educational systems, by following Western models, tend to advantage a small elite and disadvantage the majority and that where English in these contexts dominates, the vast majority of children get little benefit from schooling, either in terms of acquiring the necessary language proficiency or in terms of the content. Linguicism is defined as 'ideologies and structures which are used to legitimate, effectuate and reproduce an unequal division of power and resources between groups which are defined on the basis of language (on the basis of their mother tongues)' (Skutnabb-Kangas, 1988: 13). It is noted that linguicism is always linked to pressure towards monolingualism and a denial of the reality that multilingualism is a global norm. In this regard, Western aid packages to Africa are accompanied by linguicism in the sense that they place a high status on the former colonial language, and a low status on local languages. These packages tend to support subtractive rather than additive bilingualism. Heugh (1995: 333) explains that local languages, having a low status vis-à-vis the ex-colonial languages, are given little validity in the educational system and, consequently, knowledge which children have in these languages, or what the French linguist Revel (1988) aptly calls *la connaissance inutile* (useless knowledge), is ignored in the school system. And since ex-colonial languages are not equally accessible to all, they do not equalize opportunities but rather reproduce inequality.

The question that needs to be raised at this juncture is this: how do we resolve the medium of instruction conundrum in Africa? Is replacing ex-colonial languages with the indigenous languages as the medium of instruction the answer? The next and last section of this chapter will revisit this issue of the medium of instruction against the background of the theoretical frameworks highlighted earlier, namely, the game theory, the tragedy of the commons, the ecology of language and language economics.

Building on these frameworks, I argue strongly against an 'either/or' perspective to the medium of instruction conundrum in African education, and question the dichotomy between tradition and modernism, on which the ideologies of decolonization and development appear to be subtly based. Instead, I call for new language-in-education policies that recognize the relationship between language and the economy and ensure that African languages become, for their speakers and potential users, the languages of upward social mobility, much as the ex-colonial languages are for those who have access to them in Africa and other post-colonial settings.

The medium of instruction conundrum: which way forward?

Irrespective of the ideology one embraces, whether the ideology of decolonization or the ideology of development, the whole debate around the medium of instruction appears to be based on a wanting dichotomy: socioeconomic development is possible only through the medium of European languages versus indigenous African languages are good only for preserving African cultures and traditions. Blaut (1993: 10) critically describes the former view of development from the perspective of what he calls the colonizer's model of the world, also known as Eurocentric Diffusionism. This is a western-based paradigm once used to justify colonialism and the repression of indigenous peoples and one according to which 'all good things, including dominant languages, develop first in the West, and are then "diffused" to the periphery, based on Western models' (Blaut, 2000: 11). Viewed from this perspective, mother tongue education ideologies are tied to political economies or resource allocations and control over goods (Friedrich, 1989: 298). Recall from the work of Bourdieu (1991) and others that linguistic products, and these include mother tongues, are goods or capital to which the market or language users assign a value; and that 'on a given linguistic market some products are valued more highly than others' (Bourdieu, 1991: 18). Recall also from language economics that the value of a linguistic product such as the mother tongue is determined in relation to other languages in the planetary economy. In postcolonial Africa, however, ex-colonial languages have more economic value than the indigenous African languages. It is this imbalance that must be corrected if indigenous languages are to have or achieve any value in the linguistic market place and thus be accepted as medium of instruction by the stakeholders.

In response to this imbalance, Kamwangamalu (1997b: 247; 2003: 78) has suggested, for South Africa, what he calls 'mother tongue education cleansing', a process whereby indigenous African languages are vested with some of the advantages and prerequisites that are currently associated only with English and/or Afrikaans. The idea of 'mother tongue education cleansing' can be implemented in any post-colonial setting. A requirement, for instance, that a certified (i.e. school-acquired) knowledge of the indigenous languages become one of the criteria for upward social mobility, for political participation, and for access to employment in the civil service will, in my view, contribute significantly to mother-tongue-education cleansing. After all, people do not learn languages for language learning' sake; they do so in the hope that the knowledge of a particular language will pay off in the linguistic market place. As Laitin (1994: 625) points out with respect to the medium of instruction in Ghana, the payoffs for educating one's child in English when all official business is conducted in English are far higher than the payoffs for educating the child through the medium of an indigenous language. The literature provides useful case studies of indigenous language promotion in education and other higher domains that show that when a language is associated with an economic value, language consumers will strive to acquire or be schooled through it irrespective of whether or not it is their mother tongue.

A case in point is the Macedonian language, as discussed in Tollefson (2002). Tollefson points out that when the Republic of Macedonia was created within Yugoslavia, the Macedonian language served as the medium of government operations and education. The use of Macedonian in these higher domains guaranteed access to jobs in the administration and schools, and the communication industries enjoyed more clients for their books, newspapers and music. In a related study, Kamwangamalu (2010: 13–15) cites several case studies of indigenous language promotion in education that show that parents in particular support education in indigenous languages if it is associated with economic outcomes. One such case is reported in Reagan and Schreffler's (2005) study of an institutional policy adopted by the Istanbul Technical University (ITU) in Turkey. The report is made against the background of the dilemma often facing tertiary institutions in developing countries, whether to use a language of wider communication as the principal medium of instruction and, in so doing, succumb to linguistic imperialism; or to use a local language and, in this process, cut off students from the international scholarly community. It is noted that, traditionally, ITU has used Turkish as the medium of instruction. However and given the influence and power of English globally, the institution has adopted a language policy that requires students to complete one-third of their university courses in English. The policy is intended to ensure that students acquire competence in English to be able to compete in what has become an English-dominant world, while at the same time maintaining a scholarly and academic context in which the Turkish language remains viable. It follows that any language policy that seeks to promote the indigenous languages in education must demonstrate economic advantages if it is to be successful. In Africa, unless the indigenous languages are associated with tangible economic outcomes, any attempts to promote their use in education or to resolve the medium of instruction conundrum will remain symbolic at best.

References

Adegbija, E. (1997). The identity, survival, and promotion of minority languages in Nigeria. *International Journal of the Sociology of Language* 125: 5–27.

Akinnaso, F. Niyi (1993). Policy and experiment in mother tongue literacy in Nigeria. *International Review of Education* 39,4: 255–285.

Alexander, N. (1997). Language policy and planning in the new South Africa. *African Sociological Review* 1(1): 82–98.

Auerbach, E.R. (1996). Re-examining English-only in the ESL classroom. *TESOL Quarterly* 27(1): 9–32.

Balfour, R.J. (1999). Naming the father: re-examining the role of English as a medium of instruction in South African education. *Changing English* 6, 1: 103–113.

Bamgbose, A. (1983). Education in indigenous languages: The West African Model of language education. *Journal of Negro Education*, 52, 1: 57–64.

Bamgbose, A. (2006). Multilingualism and exclusion: policy, practice and prospects. Keynote address at the Symposium on Multilingualism and Exclusion. University of the Free State. Bloemfontein, South Africa, 24–26 April 2006.

Blaut, J.M. (1993). *The colonizer's model of the world: Geographical diffusionism and Eurocentric history*. New York, NY: The Guilford Press.

Blommaert, J. (1994). The metaphors of development and modernization in Tanzanian language policy and research. In R. Fardon and G. Furniss (eds), *African languages, development and the state*, 213–26. London: Routledge.

Blommaert, J. (1999). The debate is open. In J. Blommaert (ed.), *Language Ideological Debates*, 1–38. Berlin: Mouton de Gruyter.

Bourdieu, P. (1991). *Language and Symbolic Power*. Cambridge: Polity Press.

Brock-Utne, B. (2000). *Whose education for all? The recolonization of the African mind*. New York: Falmer Press.

Cenoz, J. and Gorter, D. (2010). Diversity of multilingualism in education. *International Journal of the Sociology of Language* 205: 37–53.

Coulmas, F. (1992). *Language and the Economy*. Oxford: Blackwell.

Diamond, J. (2005). *Collapse: How Societies Choose to Fail or Succeed.* London: Penguin.

Dyers, C. and Abongdia, J-F. (2010). An exploration of the relationship between language attitudes and ideologies in a study of Francophone students of English in Cameroon. *Journal of Multilingual and Multicultural Development* 31, 2: 119–134.

Eggington, W. (in press). Towards Accommodating the 'Tragedy of the Commons' Effect in Language Policy Development. In R. Baldauf, R. Kaplan and N.M. Kamwangamalu (eds), *Language planning and its problems, a special issue of Current Issues in Language Planning.* New York: Routledge.

Evans, S. (2002). The medium of instruction in Hong Kong: policy and practice in the new English and Chinese streams. *Research Papers in Education* 17, 1: 97–120.

Ferguson, C.A. (1992). Foreword to the First Edition. In B.B. Kachru (ed.), *The Other Tongue: English Across Cultures (2nd edn)*, xiii–xvii. Delhi: Oxford University Press.

Fishman, J.A. (1971). *Sociolinguistics: A brief introduction.* Rowley: Newbury House Publishers.

Friedrick, P. (1989). Language, ideology and political economy. *American Anthropologist* 91: 295–312.

Grin, F. (1994). The economics of language: Match or mismatch? *International Political Science Review* 15, 1: 25–42.

Grin, F. (2001). English as economic value. *World Englishes* 20, 1: 65–78.

Grin, F. (2006). Economic considerations in language policy. In T. Ricento (ed.), *An Introduction to Language Policy: Theory and Method*, 77–94. Malden, MA: Blackwell.

Hardin, G. (1998). Essays on science and society: Extensions of 'The Tragedy of the Commons'. *Science* 280: 682–683.

Harsanyi, J.C. (1977). *Rational Behavior and Bargaining Equilibrium in Games and Social Situations.* New York: Cambridge University Press.

Heine, B. (1990). Language policy in Africa. In B. Weinstein (ed.), *Language Policy and Political Development*, 167–184. Norwood, NJ: Ablex Publishing Corporation.

Heugh, K. (1995). Disabling and enabling: implications of language policy trends in South Africa. In R. Mesthrie (ed.), *Language and social history: studies in South African sociolinguistics*, 329–350. Cape Town: David Philip.

Hornberger, N.H. (ed.) (2003). *Continua of biliteracy: An ecological framework for educational policy, research, and practice.* Clevedon: Multilingual Matters.

Kamanda, M.C. (2002). Mother tongue education and transitional literacy in Sierra Leone: Prospects and challenges in the 21st Century. *Language and Education* 16, 3: 195–211.

Kamwangamalu, N.M. (1997a). The colonial legacy and language planning in sub-Saharan Africa. *Applied Linguistics* 18, 1: 69–85.

Kamwangamalu, N.M. (1997b). Multilingualism and education policy in post-apartheid South Africa. *Language Problems and Language Planning*, 21, 3: 234–253.

Kamwangamalu, N.M. (2003). Globalization of English, and language maintenance and shift in South Africa. *International Journal of the Sociology of Language*164: 65–81.

Kamwangamalu, N.M. (2005). Mother tongues and Language planning in Africa. *TESOL Quarterly* 39, 4: 734–738.

Kamwangamalu, N.M. (2010). Vernacularization, globalization, and language economics in non-English-speaking countries in Africa. *Language Problems and Language Planning* 34, 1: 1–23.

Kamwangamalu, N.M. (in press, a). Language planning: Approaches and Methods. In E. Hinkel (ed.), *The Handbook of Research in Second Language Teaching and Learning, Volume II*, 888–904. New York, NY: Routledge.

Kamwangamalu, N.M. (in press, b). Language policy and ideologies in Africa. In R. Bayley, R. Cameron and C. Lucas (eds), *The Oxford Handbook of Scoiolinguistics*. Oxford: Oxford University Press.

King, K. (2004). Language policy and local planning in South America: New directions for enrichment bilingual education in the Andes. *Bilingual Education and Bilingualism* 7, 5: 334–347.

Lai, P-S. and Bryan, M. (2003). The politics of bilingualism: a reproduction analysis of the policy of mother tongue education in Hong Kong after 1997. *Compare* 33, 2: 315–334.

Laitin, D.D. (1993). The game theory of language regime. *International Political Science Review* 14, 3: 227–239.

Laitin, D. (1992). *Language Repertoires and State Construction in Africa*. Cambridge, MA: Cambridge University Press.

Lin, A.M.Y. and Martin, P. (2005, eds). *Decolonization, Globalization: Language-in-Education Policy and Practice*. Clevedon: Multilingual Matters.

May, S. (2001). *Language and Minority Rights: Ethnicity, Nationalism and the Politics of Language*. Longman: London.

McGroarty, M. (2010). Language and ideology. In N. Hornberger and S. McKay (eds), *Sociolinguistics and Language Education*, 3–39. Bristol: Multilingual Matters.

Mfum-Mensah, O. (2005). The impact of colonial and postcolonial Ghanaian language policies on vernacular use in schools in two northern Ghanaian communities. *Comparative Education* 41, 1: 71–85.

Mustafa, Z. (2005). Debate on medium of instruction (in Pakistan). *The Dawn*, 16 November 2005, <http://www.apnaorg.com/articles/dawn-11/>.

Newton, E.S. (1972). Linguistic pluralism: Third World impediment to Universal literacy. *The Journal of Negro Education* 41, 3: 248–254.

Phillipson, R. (1988). Linguicism: structures and ideologies in linguistic imperialism. In T. Skutnabb-Kangas and J. Cummins (eds), *Minority Education: From Shame to Struggle*. Clevedon: Multingual Matters.

Prah, K. (1995). *African languages for the mass education of Africans*. Bonn: German Foundation for International Development, Education, Science and Documentation Center.

Reagan, T. and Scheffler, S. (2005). Higher education language policy and the challenge of linguistic imperialism: A Turkish case study. In A.M.Y. Lin and P. Martin (2005, eds), *Decolonization, Globalization: Language-in-Education Policy and Practice*, 115–130. Clevedon: Multilingual Matters.

Revel, J-F. (1988). *La Connaissance inutile*. Paris: Grasset.

Rubango, N. (1986). Le Francais au Zaire: Langue 'superieure' et chances de 'survie' dans un pays Africain. *Language Problems and Language Planning* 10, 3: 253–271.

Samuels, J. (1995). Multilingualism in the Emerging Educational Dispensation. *Proceedings of SAALA* 15: 75–84. Stellenbosch University, South Africa.

Siatchitema, A.K. (1992). When nationalism conflicts with nationalist goals: Zambia. In N.T. Crawhall (ed.), *Democratically Speaking*. Cape Town: National Language Project.

Skutnabb-Kangas, T. (2006). Language policy and linguistic human rights. In T. Ricento (ed.), *An Introduction to Language Policy: Theory and Method*, 273–291. Malden, MA: Blackwell.

Skutnabb-Kangas, T. (1988). Multilingualism and the education of minority children. In T. Skutnabb-Kangas and J. Cummins (eds), *Minority Education: From Shame to Struggle*. Clevedon: Multilingual Matters.

Spencer, J. (1985). Language and Development in Africa: The unequal equation. In N. Wolfson and J. Manes (eds), *Language of Inequality*, 387–397. New York: Mouton.

Tollefson, J.W. and Tsui, A.B. (eds) (2004). *Medium of Instruction Policies: Which Agenda? Whose Agenda?* Mahwah, NJ: Erlbaum.

Tollefson, J.W. (2002). Language rights and the destruction of Yugoslavia. In J.W. Tollefson (ed.), *Language Policies in Education: Critical Issues*, 179–199. Mahwah, NJ: Lawrence Erlbaum Associates.

Tollefson, J. (1991). *Planning Language, Planning Inequality*. London: Longman.

Thompson, J. (1984). *Studies in the theory of ideology*. Berkeley: University of California Press.

Tripathi, P.D. (1990). English in Zambia: The nature and prospects of one of Africa's 'new Englishes'. *English Today* 6, 3: 34–38.

UNESCO ([1953]1995). *The use of vernacular languages in education*. Paris: UNESCO.

Vaillancourt, F. and Grin, F. (2000). *The Choice of a Language of Instruction: The Economic Aspects. Distance learning course on language instruction in basic education*. Washington, DC: World Bank Institute.

Weinstein, B. (ed.) (1990). *Language Policy and Political Development*. Norwood, NJ: Ablex Publishing Corporation.

Whitehead, C. (1995). The medium of instruction in British colonial education: a case of cultural imperialism or enlightened paternalism. *History of Education* 24, 1: 1–15.

Wolfram, W. and Schilling-Estes, N. (2006). *American English: Dialect and variation (2nd edn)*. Malden, MA: Blackwell.

Woolard, K.A. and Schieffelin, B.B. (1994). Language ideology. *Annual Review of Anthropology* 23: 55–82.

JESSICA BALL AND BARBARA MAY HANFORD BERNHARDT

9 Standard English as a Second Dialect: A Canadian Perspective

During the years I spent kayaking along the coast of British Columbia and Southeast Alaska, I observed that the local raven populations spoke in distinct dialects. Ravens from Kwakiutl, Tsimshian, Haida, and Tlingit territory sounded different from one another, especially in their characteristic 'tok' and 'tlik'. (Dyson, 2006: 136)

Introduction

Over 40 per cent of Aboriginal[1] children in Canada do not receive a secondary school diploma (Gilmore, 2010; Mendelson, 2006), and dialectal variation may play a key role. Combined with significant gaps in quality of life for First Nation[2] children in Canada, dialect differences between some First Nation children and mainstream educators likely contribute to inequitable outcomes for First Nation youngsters on many dimensions, including education, health and social inclusion (Ball, 2008; Salée, 2006). High rates of identification of First Nation children as 'at risk' for difficulties in school and teacher referrals of these children for assessment and treatment

---

1   In Canada, the term *Aboriginal* refers to three groups of original inhabitants: First Nation, Métis and Inuit peoples. Many original inhabitants now prefer to be called Indigenous when not referred to by their specific cultural community.
2   First Nation is an ethnic identifier that can apply both to individuals and to communities on or off of reserve lands and in urban or rural/remote settings. In contrast, a First Nation is a culturally distinct, federally registered entity comprised, at least in part, of registered status Indians living on lands reserved for them by the Canadian federal government.

of perceived speech and language delays and disorders (Sterzuk, 2008) may reflect, in part, a pervasive lack of understanding that these children's first language is a nonstandard dialect of the language used in school.

Despite the importance of these issues, little research has investigated the nature, acquisition or implications of nonstandard English dialects among Indigenous people in Canada.[3] At the prompting of several First Nation leaders in the Canadian province of British Columbia, Ball, Bernhardt and Deby (2007; Ball and Bernhardt, 2008; Bernhardt, Ball and Deby, 2007) explored this topic. Their project gleaned anecdotal evidence through two forums involving Indigenous educators, school-based clinicians and investigators who have explored dialect variation and its implications through their applied practice in schools and speech-language service settings in Canada. Insights were also gained from a survey of speech-language pathologists (Ball and Lewis, 2005) and an interview study of First Nation parents and Elders (Ball and Lewis, 2005).

Because of the lack of systematic research on this topic, this chapter is intended to raise awareness, stimulate dialogue and promote considerations of the implications for children who enter school speaking a nonstandard variety of the school language. Ideas are explored for providing these children with a welcoming, culturally safe transition and supporting them in learning the standard dialect while respecting and recognizing the value of their home dialect.

The Canadian context of language loss

Three groups of original inhabitants of the land now called Canada are recognized by the federal government as Aboriginal: First Nation, Métis and Inuit. In the 2006 census, 1,172,790 people self-identified as Aboriginal,

---

3   There is scattered interest in these phenomena among Native Americans in the US and a growing body of work of an ethnographic and anecdotal nature on Aboriginal English in Australia.

representing 3.8 per cent of the total population. Of these, 700,000 self-identified as First Nation (Statistics Canada, 2006). Although a minority of First Nation people live in French-speaking areas of Canada, this chapter focuses specifically on what is known about First Nation English dialects because this is the population where at least some research effort has been directed. About one-third of First Nation children live in rural, remote or on-reserve settings, and 5 per cent live in rural off-reserve communities (Statistics Canada, 2006). It is generally believed that non-standard English dialects are most likely to be the first language these youngsters learn.

First Nation English dialects in Canada are situated within an overall context of language loss and revitalization. About fifty different First Nation languages from eleven major language families are spoken today.[4] Sociohistorical and linguistic conditions have resulted in steadily declining intergenerational transmission of Indigenous languages. Today, only about 16 per cent of Aboriginal children in Canada learn their Indigenous language first (Bougie, 2010; Norris, 2007), and this number is decreasing (Norris, 2007).

Language loss is a global crisis; over half of the world's 6,000 languages have been lost (Crystal, 2000; Dixon, 1997; Moseley, 2010). The losses occur for many reasons, including the pressures exerted by a dominant language. In Canada, the loss of First Nation languages is the result of several interacting factors, beginning with colonial government polices over the past two centuries that aggressively interrupted the intergenerational transmission of language. The most disruptive interventions were the forced removal of Indigenous communities from their traditional territories to designated (reserve) lands, which often congregated culturally and linguistically different populations together, and the forced removal of Indigenous children from their families to be raised by the staff of Indian

4   Algonquin, Athapaskan and Inuktitut are the largest language families, or linguistic isolates, accounting for 93 per cent of the Indigenous languages learned as first languages (Norris and Jantzen, 2002). According to the 2006 Census, Cree, Inuktitut and Ojibway are the largest of the fifty Indigenous languages currently spoken, with approximately 70,000, 29,000 and 21,000 speakers respectively.

residential schools. Children in the schools were compelled to learn English or French and were punished for speaking their own language (Lawrence, 2004; Miller, 1996; Royal Commission on Aboriginal Peoples, 1996). An ongoing practice of removing First Nation children from their homes and placing them in foster or adoptive care with English- and French-speaking families also contributes to First Nation language loss (First Nations Child and Family Caring Society of Canada, 2005).

Some Indigenous scholars and communities have declared a major collective push to end oppressive policies and practices that keep Indigenous cultural knowledges and languages in the shadows (e.g., Fettes and Norton, 2000). They see a linguistic renaissance[5] as an integral part of the evolution toward Indigenous self-government and the restoration of spiritual and physical health to First Nation communities (Assembly of First Nations, 1990, 1992; Canadian Heritage, 2005; Crawford, 1996; Fishman, 2001). This renaissance includes more choices for Indigenous parents in regard to their children's education either in mainstream schools or in Indigenous-controlled school settings.

The persistence of First Nation English dialects might seem to conflict with Indigenous language revitalization; the existence of these dialects and their use within First Nation communities is powerful evidence of the cultural hegemony of English and of the settler society's disruption of the intergenerational transmission of First Nation languages. Paradoxically, however, because a dialect may be the only remaining trace of an Indigenous language, dialects may play an important role in language revitalization (Ball and Bernhardt, 2008). By preserving not only grammatical aspects, but unique discourse and narrative features, First Nation English dialects may contribute to transmission of Indigenous cultures and identities. Fluency in the dialect might provide speakers who want to learn – or relearn – an

5   In British Columbia, for example, the First Peoples' Cultural Foundation raises awareness and funding for Indigenous language revitalization (First Peoples' Cultural Foundation, 2007). A major initiative of the foundation is First Voices, <http://www.fpcf.ca/language-index.html>, an on-line language archive.

ancestral language an easier entry point. And, over time, dialects may evolve in independent directions, reinforcing cultural distinctiveness.

First Nation English dialects reside uneasily in the space between language loss and revitalization, and between Indigenous calls for more Indigenous control of education for their children and a nationwide concern with improving Indigenous children's success in mainstream education and the economy. On one hand, First Nation English dialects reflect a history in which English was – and remains – the primary colonizing language. On the other hand, they may be seen as important linguistic markers of Indigenous identity and belonging.

Pidgins, creoles and dialects

Pidgins develop in situations of language contact when speakers from two or more mutually unintelligible language groups develop a grammatically simple system of communication that exhibits properties of the substrate languages (Wardhaugh, 2002). At the point of origin, pidgins are necessarily second languages. However, when a new generation learns a pidgin as a first language, the pidgin typically develops into a creole, which is a grammatically more complex language with properties not found in any of the parent languages (Wardhaugh, 2002). Depidginization and decreolization take place when pidgins and creoles come into renewed or closer contact with their original source language (Trudgill, 1996, cited in Kwary, n.d.).

A dialect is a particular form of a language that is peculiar to a specific region or social group. First Nation English dialects likely developed as lingua francas – common languages – following contact between English and Indigenous populations. They appear to represent a late stage in processes of depidginization and decreolization (Ball and Bernhardt, 2008; Craig, 1991; Flanigan, 1985, 1987). Dialects are shaped by cultural patterns of communication, phenomena related to contact and linguistic features of the primary or source language(s). A particular dialect is typically associated with speakers who variously share historical events, geography, ethnicity, socioeconomic status, education, first language background or other social factors. Based on research on English dialects among Native Americans (Leap, 1993), it is likely that English dialects among Indigenous peoples in North America share many features, possibly reflecting historical periods in which speakers of the different dialects found themselves forced to live together, for example, on shared reserve lands or in Indian residential schools (Ball and Bernhardt, 2008; Leap, 1993). Documents from these eras indicate widespread intertribal dissemination of pidgins or creoles (Craig, 1991). Over time, the various dialects may have increasingly converged with standard English, resulting in nonstandard English dialects that vary only slightly between communities and regions, and to only a minor but nevertheless significant degree from standard English. Flanigan (1985, 1987) describes this process with reference to Lakota English.

Dialects and social status

Because dialects of the same language have slightly different grammars, grammatical errors in one dialect might be correct in another. Linguists do not view any dialect of a language as inherently more correct than others; they often use the term variety instead of dialect to emphasize this equality (Ball and Bernhardt, 2008).[6] However, certain dialects (or varieties) are accorded greater social status by their association with groups that hold power in the dominant culture's social institutions, for example, royalty, colonial government bodies, universities and the upper class. A dominant culture's high-status dialect is often enforced within institutions and

6   Another term, *register*, has sometimes been used to refer to varieties such as Indigenous Englishes (e.g., Eagleson, 1982). However, linguists define *register* as referring to a variety that is associated with a specific occupation or activity, for example, legal, air traffic control or religious registers (Schiffman, 1997; Wardhaugh, 2002). Perhaps the most appropriate term for Indigenous varieties is ethnolect, that is, a language variety that is associated with a specific cultural group. An ethnolect is a social, rather than a regional, dialect (Wardhaugh, 2002).

formal discourse through standardization, whereby one set of grammar and usage rules is sanctioned by the groups with political power for use in education, government and mass media. Dialects associated with more marginalized or lower status social groups are often stigmatized within these institutions (Wardhaugh, 2002). However, developmentalists and linguists have discounted earlier assertions by some scholars (e.g., Bernstein, 1972) that dialect use reflects intelligence and that only standard dialects can support advanced cognitive development and academic performance. Stigmatized dialects may hold covert prestige (Trudgill, 1972) in a social group that lacks formal power in the dominant groups' institutions, such as rap music artists, street gangs, members of an ethnic neighbourhood, a rural community or a sexual minority group (Hawley, 2005). And many nonstandard varieties of English have become well known (Lee, 1998), including Cockney English, African American Vernacular English (AAVE), Hawai'i Creole English (HCE), Spanglish, Singlish (Singapore English) (Lim, 2004), Tanglish (Tamil English) and Manglish (Malaysian English). Most recently, Globish, a global pidgin English for trade and cultural exchange, has emerged (McCrum, 2010).

Dialects and the colonial project

A basic Canadian value is that, wherever children live and irrespective of their ethnicity or home language, programmes for promoting their optimal development should be accessible and linguistically and culturally appropriate (Canadian Centre for Justice, 2001). At the same time, centuries of colonial policies and values in education have excluded Indigenous histories, cultures and languages from public school pedagogy and curricula in Canada (Battiste, 2000; Philipson, 1992). Regardless of linguistic and developmental theory – and evidence that dialects are not substandard versions of the 'real' language – negative social attitudes about language difference can have negative social sequelae, including discrimination and social exclusion (Milroy and Milroy, 1999). Persistent low academic achievement and early school leaving among Indigenous and ethnolinguistic minority children are outcomes that are likely attributable, in part, to language-in-education policies that disregard, actively disparage or even pathologize the language or dialect with which children enter formal schooling (Ball, 2010). For example, some educators and speech-language pathologists, along with First Nation leaders, have suggested that First Nation children may be disproportionately diagnosed with speech-language impairments, which may stem in part from misinterpretations of features of children's home dialects as evidence of speech-language deficits or delays (Ball, Bernhardt, and Deby, 2006). In the American context, Keulen, Weddington and DeBose (1998) and Wolfram (1993) have made the same observation.

Smith (2010) reflects on the insistence of dominant English culture on a singular identity; as a person moves into higher levels of education and, by association, into higher socioeconomic brackets, individuals must sacrifice their lower status first dialect while wholly adopting the high-status standard dialect. Smith argues that this assimilative pressure is part of the colonial agenda, and asks why it could not be possible for individuals to have plural selves, with plural dialects, to be used flexibly to meet the communication needs and goals of varied situations. In a post-colonial world, would it not support optimal social adjustment to promote children's capacities for bi- or even multidialectism?

Bidialectism

In jurisdictions around the globe, many children's home language or dialect differs from the language(s) of instruction used in schools. Research confirms that children can learn both more than one language (Cummins, 2000; Lightbown, 2008) and more than one dialect of the same language (McConvell, 2008). Whether they successfully retain their home language (or dialect of a dominant language) depends on the interaction of several factors, including the extent and effectiveness of efforts from speakers of a different dialect of the language aimed at motivating the child to eliminate features of their first dialect and assimilate features of the dialect to which they are newly exposed, and the extent and effectiveness of efforts from speakers of their first dialect aimed at motivating the child to retain their first dialect fluency, while adding a second dialect. A child may consciously or unconsciously select which dialect of a language to speak, and which variants of phonemes, words or grammars to use. These selections may arise out of a desire to fit in or succeed in their home community, the preferences of their family, peer groups or linguistic community, or their educational context. For example, if a child lives in a community where a large number of speakers use [f] for [T], the child may use [f], unless for some reason that child encounters someone or some group who suggests (or taunts) that [f] is wrong or of low prestige. The child may start to use [T] for all words where it is used in the standard variety, or only in those social contexts where use of [T] avoids discrimination and ensures acceptance; that is, the child may become unidialectal (standard variety) or bidialectal. Within families, individual children may differ in their degree of bidialectalism (Bernhardt, Ball and Deby, 2007).

Illustrative observations of First Nation English dialects

Nonstandard dialects of a dominant language are distinguished from the standard dialect by a range of phonological, syntactic, lexical and discourse-based features. Some of these features are discussed below in relation to First Nation English dialects.

Phonetic, syntactic and morphological features

In the Canadian project conducted by Ball, Bernhardt and Deby (2007), language specialists working with First Nation children made similar observations about First Nation children's speech as have been made by investigators of Native American English dialects in the US. With reference to phonological features, for example, restrictions on syllable- and/ or word-final consonants in indigenous languages may be carried over into both First Nation and Native American English dialects (Flanigan, 1987; Leap, 1993).[7] A variety of phonological and phonetic characteristics of First Nation languages may affect First Nation English dialects, producing 'accents' that may be interpreted as mispronunciations of standard English.

Participants in the Canadian project frequently observed a number of syntactic, morphological and pragmatic features in First Nation English dialects that have also been reported in the literature on Native American English dialects, including morphosyntactic features such as a lack of nominal and verbal inflection, omission of pronouns and prepositions, nonstandard uses of tense and multiple negation. For example, First Nation children in elementary school were reported as using pronouns in nonstandard ways, such as using the nominative pronouns *he* and *she*, and the accusative pronouns *her* and *him*, as possessive forms, as in the following sentence reported by one participant: *Him bouncing that ball on him nose* (Ball et al., 2006: 101). Innovative plural pronoun forms such as *theirself* and *theirselves* have also been noted in First Nation children's speech. It is unclear whether variants such as these reflect dialect differences or delays in language development. Further examination of adult speech in the children's communities is necessary to explore this issue.[8]

7   In the American context, Leap observed that standard English *hunt* is often pronounced as *hun* in Isletan English (1993: 114). Flanigan (1987) reports similar patterns for Lakota English. In Cheyenne English, word-final /t/ is deleted or pronounced as /ʔ/ (Leap 1993: 114–115).

8   Research in the Canadian context by Mulder (1982) and Tarpent (1982) highlights the influence of the ancestral language in some innovative plural pronoun constructions. For instance, Tsimshian English *them* constructions, such as *Don't play with them John* and *Them Fred's having a party tonight* (Tarpent, 1982: 118), appear to have their source in the Tsimshian plural marker *dim*. In Tsimshian English, this marker is used to refer both to the specified individual and to others who are associated with that individual.

Lexicon

Participants in the Canadian project reported differences in vocabulary usage in the English of First Nation children as compared to non-Indigenous children. Speech-language specialists stressed the difficulty of assessing these children's vocabulary accurately, given the lack of assessment tools based on community norms that reflect the range of children's vocabulary. In particular, participants noted First Nation children's lack of words for spatial location, speculating that this absence might be due to usage norms in the child's Indigenous language. For example, some children may be inclined to say *It's there* or *It's over there*, possibly in combination with facial and other gestures, rather than use spatial vocabulary to describe the exact location of an object or event (Ball et al., 1996: 45). In many First Nation languages, explicit locations or times are less important in reporting experiences than the events being described. One project participant stated that some First Nation children with whom she has worked as a speech-language therapist were unable to follow oral directions consisting of three or more steps. It is unclear whether such comprehension issues reflect cultural differences in time marking or children's individual memory constraints (Ball et al., 2006). These examples are cited here to emphasize the possibility of both important language differences that have implications for teaching and learning, and the need for more investigation, in particular concerning cultural focus and use of spatial, time and sequence marking.

Discourse

Canadian project participants noted several features of First Nations discourse, including silence, listening, eye contact behaviours, turn taking and topic development in narratives (Ball et al., 2006). First Nation children may learn very different participation frameworks from those of non-Indigenous children. Participation frameworks are the expectations underlying who can acceptably say something, when, and about what. Project participants commented on the use of silence by First Nation children, which mainstream teachers may interpret as shyness or even lack of knowledge. Sharla Peltier, a First Nation speech therapist and educator, explained silence and a characteristically parsimonious use of language in cultural terms:

> We're taught [that] our voice is a sacred gift. And there is a lot of power in words: when we speak, we're taught that our words go around the world forever. So people who are traditional don't engage in idle chit-chat and talk about tiny little things, because they really do believe that their words are very, very sacred and important and powerful. (Ball et al., 2006: 48)

Peltier explained that First Nation children may be silent and/or may not engage in casual conversation about everyday matters (e.g., the weather) in an effort to be respectful to other people, particularly adults, whom they presume already have the information. As well, First Nation children may take a long time to respond to questions or to take a turn in conversation because they have been taught the importance of weighing their words carefully before speaking. This contrasts with European-heritage society in Canada, where interjections and short pauses between turns are the norm. In an effort to listen carefully to what is being said to them, First Nation children may not make eye contact with their interlocutors, a practice which may be misunderstood as not being able or willing to pay attention. Peltier noted that preschool children had been referred to her by paediatricians who thought the children might have symptoms of autism because they did not look at the speaker when spoken to (Ball et al., 2006). These and other discourse features observed by participants in the Canadian project are also reported in the literature on Native American English discourse (Basso, 1970; Damico, 1983; Leap, 1993; Liebe-Harkort, 1983; Neha, 2003; Phillips, 1983).

Storytelling

As Gutiérrez-Clellen and Quinn (1993, p. 4) describe, 'storytelling is a social event governed by cultural norms and values. These extralinguistic rules dictate appropriate narrative behaviour.' Peltier (2010) explains that storytelling is an important life skill valued in First Nations' traditional practices of oral histories and languages; insights into First Nation orality can be gained by understanding aspects of narratives generated by First Nation children. Since activities revolving around stories (e.g., storytelling, reading, writing) are key pedagogical components in preschool and primary education, this knowledge can guide educators in creating culturally sensitive and appropriate bridges between storytelling and literacy areas of the language arts curriculum (Peltier, 2010).

A study by Erasmus (1989) of narrative and the storytelling process among the Athabascan (Dené language group) illustrates differences in narrative and storytelling processes between some First Nations and non-Indigenous groups. Erasmus notes that because First Nation children use unfamiliar manners of narrative presentation such as rhetorical style, mainstream teachers often do not hear the logic in the telling:

> People from the dominant English-speaking culture often perceive the discourse of nonmainstream speakers to be incoherent, disconnected, rambling, illogical and untruthful. When a person's discourse is devalued, so too are the meanings, experiences and knowledge to which that discourse refers ... Thus, the 'ways with words' which are part of the Aboriginal child's lived cultural experience become an impediment to achievement in schools. (273)

Erasmus calls for teachers to 'learn to listen and listen to learn' (1989: 274) in order to understand, validate and build upon First Nation learners' culturally based capacities for storytelling. Similarly, First Nation scholars Piquemal (2003) and Simpson (2000) stress the importance of being aware of cultural rules regulating oral traditions when interpreting stories told by First Nation people.

Piquemal (2003), Mader (1996) and Pesco and Crago (1996) describe a common, circular structure in traditional First Nation narrative as a story unfolds (e.g., events within events and meaning piled upon meaning). Unlike Euro-Western stories, the form and structure of First Nation stories may not be tied to any particular timeline, main character or event, and may not have a clear ending or resolution. Similar observations have been offered by earlier scholars in the US. For example, Leap (1993) describes how, among the Ute, traditional stories are often retold to audiences who are already familiar with them; therefore elaborate scene-setting openings are unnecessary and usually absent. Ute storytellers rarely recount 'the whole story'; instead, they select a focal segment or segments as appropriate for the specific storytelling event. Connections among elements within the story are often implied, but not explicit, requiring the listener to make the connections themselves. This is further achieved by a nonlinear, nonchronological style of topic development – features that often cause European-heritage listeners to find the story confusing or pointless, or to see a child as having problems with story grammar. According to Scollon and Scollon (1981), the preference for not stating the obvious is conspicuous among the Dené in Alaska, where 'the best telling of a story is the briefest' (119). Detailed explanations of events or characters' motivations are assumed to be understood and are therefore left unstated. Such assumptions of shared knowledge perform the added function of increasing solidarity among participants (Brown and Levinson, 1987).

Many studies have evaluated European-heritage children's narratives with reference to components of meaning and structure and performative aspects that are considered important from the perspective of Western literacy (see Johnston, 1982), dominant cultural ideals about goals for children's early education (Peltier, 2010), and standardized approaches to measuring children's speech and language development (Petersen, Laing Gillam, and Gillam, 2008). Following an exhaustive search of current literature, Peltier (2010) found an absence of emic, or culturally localized, approaches to evaluating First Nation children's storytelling specifically, and their speech, language and literacy development in general. She commented on the attendant risks of underappreciating, misinterpreting and even pathologizing First Nation children's language-mediated productions.

Supporting bidialectal language learning

Little understanding exists of the extent to which Indigenous or ethnolinguistic minority children use nonstandard varieties of the school language, or the extent to which their language difference may contribute to their lack of sustained educational engagement and success relative to children whose first language is used in school. Children may be seen as intellectually deficient and develop low expectations for their own achievement (Adger et al., 2007). They may be extracted from the regular stream of instruction to receive learning assistance based on false positive diagnoses of learning disabilities or speech-language pathology. Children who are criticized and corrected for speaking in the dialect of their home and community may develop low self-esteem or oppositional attitudes toward school (Delpit, 2006) or the dominant culture (Ogbu, 1999). Those who fail to replace their home dialect with the dialect used in school may face ridicule by teachers and peers and discrimination when they become adults (Grogger, 2009; Purnell et al., 1999).

Parental attitudes and behaviours in regard to dialect

The primacy of a child's home environment in determining a wide array of child development outcomes, including education and lifelong learning, is well understood. Less understood is the role parental attitudes and behaviours play in children's bidialectal language learning. Little research has been conducted in Canada on the effects of parental beliefs and behaviours in regard to First Nation children's mono- or bidialectal language learning. In the Australian context, investigators have noted that some speakers of a nonstandard dialect may believe they speak a deficient version of the dominant language and encourage their children to speak 'better' (Kaldor, Eagleson, and Malcolm, 1982), for example, by adopting standard pronunciation. In their discussion of Aboriginal Australian English, Kaldor and Malcolm (1991) observe that parents may indirectly value the home dialect. They may want their children to learn standard English in school, but at the same time ascribe it a lower value than the home dialect in the home context. Some families may be concerned that education or treatment in standard English will contribute to the loss of the community dialect, language and culture. Others may wish to have their children learn standard English to navigate more readily in the mainstream, either some of the time (bicultural/bidialectal) or most of the time. Based on research findings, Baker (1992) cautions against the assumption that a parent's stated attitudes about their child's language acquisition necessarily relate to the parent's language behaviour with the child.

The growing field of research on cross-cultural differences in language acquisition reveals different beliefs, values and expectations about language development that appear to motivate different patterns of caregiver-child interactions across cultural and linguistic groups (e.g., Crago, 1990; Edwards, Gandini and Giovaninni, 1996; Heath, 1989; Johnston and Wong, 2002; Schieffelin and Ochs, 1986; van Kleeck, 1994; Watts Pappas and Bowen, 2007). Gardner and Lambert (1972) characterize parents' language attitudes as either instrumental, focusing on utilitarian goals, or integrative, focusing on social goals. Kemppainen, Ferrin, Ward and Hite (2004) identify four types of parental language and culture orientation: mother tongue-centric, bicultural, multicultural and majority language-centric. Of course, in many situations, parents have no choice about the language of instruction. In these situations, De Houwer's (1999) conceptualization of impact belief is helpful, referring to the extent to which parents' behaviour is motivated by a belief that they can exert direct control over their children's language use.

Just as children's individual differences in eagerness to learn, susceptibility to peer influence, self-esteem and sensory capacities, including hearing and vision, may significantly affect their speed of learning the standard dialect and their capacity or willingness to retain their first, nonstandard, dialect, parents' willingness to use the standard dialect is also a variable. In the Australian context, Eagleson (1982) observed that Aboriginal individuals who used the standard English dialect in informal situations among other Aboriginal community members could be condemned as snobbish and self-aggrandizing. This observation was also noted by First Nation participants in the Canadian project on First Nation English dialects, and in related research (Ball and Lewis, 2005; Ball, 2005).

Preparing educators and other practitioners to provide culturally safe programmes

There is an urgent need to develop new approaches in education, assessment and early intervention services to understand, support and assess Indigenous children's oral language. Speech-language pathologists and other specialists need to be able to distinguish between language difference (dialect) and language impairment to provide appropriate supports for language and literacy development for those children who need them. In Canada, a growing number of teachers and service practitioners have been seeking better preparation through pre- and in-service training so that they are more confident and effective in their work with First Nation children (Ball and Lewis, 2005).

Additionally, educational and health professionals need to be knowledgeable about the languages and language varieties in their region and respect the family's, child's and community's wishes regarding language use. The School of Audiology and Speech Sciences at the University of British Columbia, and several teacher education programmes in Canada, have taken steps to ensure that teachers and speech-language pathologists and audiologists receive pre- and in-service opportunities to learn about the general historical, social, cultural and linguistic contexts of Indigenous learners. Steps are also being taken in the province of British Columbia for primary health care providers to become more knowledgeable about Indigenous histories, cultures, languages and social conditions, and more aware of how their own cultural values, beliefs and practices may affect the ways they perceive, interpret and respond in interactions with Indigenous people.

The relationship between language, culture, well-being and educational achievement is complex. It is generally understood that respect for a child's self-concept, family and community is foundational for a child to feel safe and socially included at school (Ogbu, 1999; Peltier, 2009; Sterzuk, 2008). Other key components in preparing educators and other practitioners to provide programmes for Indigenous and ethnolinguistic minority children are explored below.

Awareness raising

Strengthening the perceived validity of nonstandard language requires public education about the equality of dialects in an effort to teach tolerance (Trudgill, 1995). Efforts have been made in this regard in Australia, where language activists argue that bidialectal awareness must be cultivated among all members of society, not just among Indigenous people (Kaldor and Malcolm, 1991; Simpson and Wigglesworth, 2008). Lack of general awareness and education can be felt acutely by Indigenous people, as evidenced by one woman's words:

> Well they garra [gotta] djidan [sit down] an' prepared to learn. How come we prepared to sit down and learn about their ways and culture, from li'l kid up to y'know ... Whatrong, the kaan kamdan [come down] to our level too; learn; sidan an' learn these things, learn about our way of life. Or are they too superior? Health sister ought to be learning about our traditions and ways; and the teacher should be learning about customs and language and the way people live. Teacher should go down and look at the situation; where that kid come from, y'know, what type of lifestyle the kid is living. It's got to be both ways, cooperation, you know. (Thies, 1986, cited in Kaldor and Malcolm, 1991: 78)

Some high school programmes have been developed to teach Australian students about dialect diversity (Eades and Siegel, 1999). Non-teaching professionals in the education system have also been targeted for awareness raising. For example, the Australian professional organization for speech-language pathologists has developed a pamphlet for clinicians working with very young Aboriginal children (Speech Pathology Australia, n.d.). Outside the education system, training has been improved in some situations where non-Aboriginal workers interact frequently with Aboriginal clients, for example, doctors, parks officers, museum workers, social workers, employment service providers and other public service sectors (Eades and Siegel 1999). The legal system has been a particular focus, which is especially important given the serious consequences of dialect misunderstanding in trials of Aboriginal defendants (Eades, 1996, 2000). Following a particularly notorious case, the Queensland Law Society funded and published a handbook on Aboriginal English for legal professionals (Eades, 1992), and legal organizations have sponsored workshops on the topic.

Cultural sensitivity and cultural safety

One of the most crucial steps to the development of culturally sensitive programmes is for educators and other practitioners to recognize their own invisible cultural biases and implicit cultural curricula (López, 2005; McIntosh, 2002). Personal blinders may hinder their receptivity and responsiveness to children who come to school speaking a nonstandard dialect of the language of instruction and lead to misinterpretations and an overly prescriptive approach to correcting children's speech productions. In Canada, efforts to encourage children to express themselves in their nonstandard dialect and introduce the standard dialect later, once the children have adapted to the school environment, are being made under the increasingly well-accepted rubric of cultural safety for Indigenous and other ethnolinguistic minority groups (Ball, 2008; Smye and Brown, 2002).

Cultural safety is a concept that originated in Aotearoa/New Zealand in a training programme for Maori nurses (Papps and Ramsden, 1996). It refers to service recipients' experiences of having their cultural identity and culturally based values, goals and preferences respectfully acknowledged by a service practitioner. Cultural safety depends in part on the practitioner being culturally self-aware and willing to acknowledge different cultural outlooks and forms of interactions as valid and not inherently more or less worthy of consideration (Ball, 2008). As Eades (1991), Harkins (1990) and Malcolm (1999) point out with reference to Australia, non-Indigenous teachers may assume a worldview that is not shared by Indigenous children, with a resulting mismatch in general expectations about communications that can leave both teachers and students feeling frustrated and confused. Addressing this situation requires changes in attitudes and understandings, as well as in curriculum and methodology.

Culturally and linguistically sensitive assessment strategies

Implementing principles of cultural sensitivity is challenging. In regard to language assessment, a lack of valid methods for assessing speakers of nonstandard dialects can result in both over- and underidentification of language impairment (Ball and Lewis, 2005). Further, very little is known about how to implement language intervention in First Nation communities in ways that resonate with community and family communication and cultural patterns. The vast majority of screening, assessment and intervention programmes are based on standard English and mainstream North American culture (Laing and Kamhi, 2003; Peltier, 2010; Stockman, 2000; Taylor and Pane, 1983; Washington, 1996). To address these barriers, both the Canadian and American professional associations for speech and language pathologists have developed position statements and policies to promote sensitivity to cultural and linguistic differences and to recruit prospective practitioners from diverse ethnic and linguistic backgrounds into professional training programmes (e.g., Canadian Association of Speech-Language Pathology and Audiology, <http://www.caslpa.ca>; American Speech-Language Hearing Association, <http://www.asha. org>). The Canadian Association for Speech and Language Pathology and Audiology has used their annual national conference as a forum to introduce professional development opportunities for diagnosticians and therapists to educate themselves about historical and contemporary factors that affect oral language trajectories of many Indigenous children, and to become aware of the need to differentiate between oral language differences, delays and deficits. A similar effort has been made by the Australian professional organization for speech-language pathologists (Speech Pathology Australia, n.d.).

All of these efforts are elementary and general in nature, in part to keep pace with the degree of readiness of professionals and the public alike. Needed reforms are impeded by a lack of linguistic and educational research on Indigenous dialects, processes that support bidialectism, and strategies to ensure unbiased interpretations of Indigenous children's speech and language performances.

Education policies to support children who speak nonstandard English dialects

Effective education policies regarding support for teaching and learning in various languages and dialects must be informed by a careful reading, not only of the research, but also of the social ecology in which the child is an active participant, to avoid inadvertently co-opting the child into language practices that could alienate them from their primary social group and to counter the prevailing tendency for educators to presume and impose what is in a child's best interest, irrespective of parents' preferences or understandings of the options and likely outcomes available to them. With respect to First Nation children in Canada, educators and other practitioners need to learn all they can about the First Nation communities and cultures in their local practice environment, for example, by attending community events or talking with Elders and other community members, as well as with community-based practitioners such as family support workers and public health nurses. Practitioners need to recognize that in no country are all Indigenous peoples exactly the same, that a variety of cultures and languages may distinguish Indigenous learners and their families from one another, and that parents may exhibit a spectrum of language socialization practices, attitudes, goals, concerns and degrees of readiness regarding the use of nonstandard and standard dialects of the dominant language. This point has also been emphasized by Eades (1991) with reference to the heterogeneity among Australian Aboriginal cultures and families. The individual educator or other practitioner does not have to wait for research to be done before making changes in practice that reflect cross-cultural sensitivity. Teachers and learning specialists can form partnerships with community members from various cultural and linguistic groups to develop useful, sensitive methodologies.

A first step that schools and other institutional settings (e.g., health care, recreation programmes) can take is to acknowledge the validity of children's particular English dialect. This acknowledgement can promote children's sense of being capable learners and of belonging in the mainstream school setting. Other recommendations for teachers and practitioners found in the literature, especially from Australia (Galloway, 2008;

Gould, 2008; Jones and Nangari, 2008; Moses and Wigglesworth, 2008), and offered by participants in the Canadian project (Ball, Bernhardt, and Deby; 2007; Peltier, 2010) include the following: (1) employ Indigenous teacher assistants who speak both the children's nonstandard dialect and the standard dialect; (2) provide opportunities for peer play before engaging in conversation, assessment or structured language arts activities or interventions; (3) start with language reception and comprehension tasks rather than language production tasks; (4) avoid correcting children's language production while they are storytelling or engaging in other spontaneous and creative speech; and (5) avoid teacher domination of classroom discussion; instead use a preponderance of peer-to-peer discourse and guided participation of less skilled learners by more skilled learners.

Several scholars note that Indigenous children whose home language is a nonstandard variant of English need some kind of bridging or transition support to prepare them to succeed in school (Philpott, 2004; Simpson and Wigglesworth, 2008; Walton, 1993). Most promising in this regard are efforts to help Indigenous children add a second English dialect – in the words of Smith (2010), to be allowed the complicated gift of being many-voiced rather than merely replacing their home dialect. This additive, rather than subtractive, approach can support children's cultural identity and pride in their family and community origins. Efforts in the United States, Australia and Canada are explored below.

A 'linguistically informed' approach in the US

African-American students in the US have long been misdiagnosed as having language impairment, erroneously labelled as handicapped, and inappropriately placed in limited English proficiency classes (Baugh, 1993; Wolfram, 1983, 1993). While no national policy exists, some highly visible efforts have been made to acknowledge African-American Vernacular English (AAVE), most notoriously an attempt by the Oakland Unified School District in California to recognize and teach AAVE as a distinct language (Morgan, 1999). This effort was an explosive failure, sparking the acrimonious 'Ebonics debate' (Perry and Delpit, 1998; Keulen et al., 1998).

Rickford (1999: 331) refers to 'massive educational failure' in supporting the academic success of African-American learners, citing evidence that attempts to stamp out or ignore AAVE have been unsuccessful as strategies for teaching standard English to AAVE-speaking children. Correction tends to have a detrimental effect by damaging student's self-esteem, decreasing their interest in reading, and even increasing their use of nonstandard forms.

However, Rickford (1999) cites examples of what he calls a 'linguistically informed' approach in which language arts programmes validate AAVE in the classroom. In some jurisdictions, teachers are educated about AAVE and trained to distinguish between errors that are due to dialect difference and those due to reading difficulty. They are then better equipped to give appropriate feedback and decide when such feedback is necessary. Another method, contrastive analysis, focuses on raising students' awareness of dialect differences and code switching; it has been used successfully in programmes in Tennessee, Chicago and Atlanta (Rickford, 1999). Some programmes advocate teaching African-American children to read and write in AAVE using dialect readers and then gradually transitioning to standard American English. In this way, the task of literacy acquisition is separated from the task of learning the standard. This approach, which Rickford calls 'using the vernacular to teach the standard' (p. 340) has been shown to produce dramatically better results than submersion in the students' non-native variety. Rather than a panacea, dialect readers should be considered one of many possible resources for bidialectal education (Rickford and Rickford, 1995).

'Two-way' bidialectal education in Australia

Pioneering work has been done in Australia on English as a Second Dialect, where Aboriginal English dialects have been recognized as valid at the federal level (Malcolm et al., 1999).[9] A 'two-way' bidialectal approach (Harris,

---

9   Kaldor and Malcolm (1991) comment that a continuum of Australian Aboriginal English exists, with a creole at one end and an almost standard variety at the other.

1990; Malcolm, 2001) recognizes the bidialectal and bicultural realities of many Aboriginal learners. Both Aboriginal and mainstream dialects, cultural practices and worldviews are incorporated into the classroom, in proportions that the community sees fit.

The success of a bidialectal approach depends on appropriate teacher training, curricula and methodologies, and the inclusion of more Aboriginal and ethnic minority teachers and teaching assistants in the education system. Researchers of nonstandard English dialects in North America can learn from the Australian experience (e.g., Berry and Hudson, 1997; Cahill, 2000; Eades, 1995; McRae, 1994; Simpson and Wigglesworth, 2008). The ways in which Australian educators have addressed Aboriginal students' norms of silence, directness and inhibition about being singled out may be relevant in other Indigenous learning contexts and could stimulate development of culturally appropriate curricula. It may also be worthwhile to examine Australian approaches to teacher education, especially regarding how to support teachers in doing ad hoc dialect research and assessment relevant to their community.

Standard English as a Second Dialect (SESD) programmes in Canada

Several provinces in Canada now have policies and funding to support school-based Standard English as a Second Dialect (SESD) programmes. Not much is known about these programmes, with the exception of a little research attention in British Columbia. A policy framework in this province provides substantial supplementary funding to school districts to support students who speak variations of English that differ significantly from the English used in the broader Canadian society and in school (British Columbia Ministry of Education, 2009). Over the past decade, the number

---

They note that Australian Aboriginal English typically arises from exposure to educational situations. In contrast, creoles develop in the absence of formal training. Because creoles are more clearly differentiated from standard English and have distinctive phonemic writing systems, they are often more readily accepted as separate grammatical systems, and therefore enjoy a relatively higher status than Australian Aboriginal.

of school districts to access this funding has increased rapidly. About 9% of primary school students in BC are identified by their parent or guardian as Aboriginal, and most of the students who benefit from this funding are Aboriginal, although the policy is not restricted to Aboriginal learners. The programme's goal is to improve learners' literacy skills. Criteria for a district to receive SESD funding are broad. The district must conduct an annual assessment of proficiency in standard English and design an annual instruction plan that lists specific services each student in an SESD programme will receive to improve their proficiency. Districts are expected to provide services using culturally relevant resources. An English as a Second Language specialist must participate in planning and delivering the programme (British Columbia Ministry of Education, 1999). Flexibility is provided for districts to use the funds in a variety of ways. A qualitative study conducted in five school districts in British Columbia showed that districts vary considerably in their definition of Standard English as a Second Dialect, assessment methods, personnel involved and approaches to dialect training (Campbell, 2011).

A systematic study to determine learning gains attributable to participation in SESD programmes was conducted by Battisti, Friesen and Krauth (2009). Although they did not conduct an analysis of pedagogical components used in SESD programmes, information they gathered indicated that strategies included specific pedagogical strategies for vocabulary development, specialized oral language instruction on a weekly basis, acquiring reading materials with Aboriginal content, and integrating strategies for oral language development into regular literacy programmes. Early findings indicate that the SESD funding has been highly effective at improving the reading skills of Aboriginal students, as measured by a foundation skills assessment exam administered to all students in grades 4 and 7. This benefit is concentrated among students in the lower end of the distribution of reading test scores gains (Battisti, Friesen, and Krauth, 2009).

These findings suggest the promise of initiatives to improve Aboriginal learners' language skills. However, without programme ethnographies or other analysis of what the teachers do to secure students' success, it is not known whether teachers are helping children to add a second dialect or merely replacing their home dialect with the school dialect. Nevertheless, as a first step in evaluating the effectiveness of initiatives that recognize and somehow build on Indigenous learners' existing oral language, it warrants attention. It should also be noted that in British Columbia, a lack of consensus exists among Indigenous scholars about whether code switching should be encouraged. Some scholars argue that the goal should be policy support and public investment in Indigenous-language-mediated instruction. Other scholars argue that leaving their 'village English' behind and becoming singularly versed in standard English allows students to improve their chances for success in mainstream education, employment and civil society. Still others advocate a vision of plural identities and multilingualism that includes learning to use more than one dialect of the dominant language and to code switch from one to another depending on one's purpose in varying social situations.

Conclusion

Accommodations in a linguistically diverse society are often in the direction of the dominant cultural standard. However, this process reduces the heterogeneity among social groups that derives from our diverse histories and ecologies, just as the distinctive calls of the ravens in various parts of British Columbia may identify them with their respective places of origin within the region. The relentless pressure to relinquish the vestiges of one's distinctive origins in order to access the resources and privileges of the dominant social group with its dominant cultural education perpetuates processes of discrimination and minoritization associated with colonialism, hastens the process of assimilation, and promotes linguistic and cultural loss. Educators and other practitioners can help to sustain linguistic and cultural pluralism, even within individuals, through pedagogical, assessment and intervention practices that honour and support each family's and community's goals for children's speech and language development and educational success.

To support such linguistic and cultural pluralism, documentation is urgently needed of the linguistic, educational and cultural significance of nonstandard dialects of English in Canada and around the globe. Research with Indigenous community members on Indigenous dialects of English could be particularly useful as a complementary enterprise to language revitalization projects underway across Canada, the US, Australia, Aotearoa/ New Zealand and elsewhere. Additionally, research is crucial to help teachers and speech-language specialists to identify children's true language deficits in order to know when intervention is needed, what it should entail, and how it should proceed. Research is also needed that will guide educators in developing effective, culturally safe educational programmes for nonstandard dialect speakers. Much can be learned in this latter respect from the innovative work in Australia over the past decade to support Aboriginal children to learn 'two ways.'

The practical goal of improving supports for children's optimal development must always be measured in relation to communities' own goals for the same (Ball, 2005). Culturally safe, decolonizing approaches to research emphasize central roles for Indigenous community representatives in defining and conducting the research, with clear written agreements regarding the conduct of a research project, including ethical principles that will guide the project, methods, data ownership, researchers' accountability, project control, outputs and dissemination of findings (Apffel-Marglin and Marglin, 1996; Ball, 2005; Ball and Janyst, 2008; Canadian Institutes for Health Research, 2007; Mutua and Swadener, 2004; Smith, 1999). As a Lil'wat First Nation grandmother, Marie Leo, expressed in an interview about Indigenous goals for children's language and literacy (Ball and Lewis, 2005):

> We are like Argyle socks, all intertwined and diamond. Our children have to cross over and back like the threads in those socks. To know how to do that they need to be able to listen to the voices of our ancestors which they can hear in our stories, telling them how to move in this world. They need to listen and learn from the voices of their friends who nowadays are from every part of the world living in this land people call Canada. And they need to listen and learn from the words of their teachers and textbooks. That's how they'll come to know how to live in the world still to come. One voice, one way to listen, one way to speak, is not enough for our

children. To know who they are and where they are going, they need to be able to hear many voices, listen to many peoples' stories, and learn to speak with many different people about how they are moving forward and intertwining with the things and people – the other diamonds – that are part of their world.

Acknowledgments

The authors thank the First Nation Peoples of Canada and participants in the Canadian project on First Nation English dialects for their insights, ingenuity and perseverance.

References

Adger, C. (1997). *Issues and implications of English dialects for teaching English as a second language* [TESOL Professional Paper #3]. <http://www.tesol.edu/pubs/profpapers/adger1.html>.

American Speech-Language-Hearing Association (ASHA) (1985). Position Statement: Clinical Management of Communicatively Handicapped Minority Language Populations. *Asha, 27* (6), 1–6.

Apffel-Marglin, F. and Marglin, S. (1996). *Decolonizing knowledge: From development to dialogue.* New York: Clarendon.

Baker, C. (1992). *Attitudes and language.* Clevedon: Multilingual Matters.

Ball, J. (2005). 'Nothing about us without us': Restorative research partnerships involving Indigenous children and communities in Canada. In A. Farrell (ed.), *Ethical research with children* (pp. 81–96). Berkshire: Open University Press/McGraw Hill Education.

Ball, J. (2008). Promoting equity and dignity for Aboriginal children in Canada. *Institute for Research on Public Policy, Choices, 14* (7), 1–30.

Ball, J. (2010). *Enhancing learning of children from diverse language backgrounds: Mother tongue-based bilingual or multilingual education in early childhood and early primary school years.* Paris: UNESCO. <http://www.unesco.org/en/languages-in-education/publications/>

Ball, J., Bernhardt, B. and Deby, J. (2006). *First Nations English dialects: Exploratory project proceedings.* Unpublished monograph, University of Victoria and University of British Columbia.

Ball, J. and Bernhard, B.M. (2008). First Nations English dialects in Canada: Implications for speech-language pathology. *Clinical Linguistics and Phonetics, 22,* 570–588.

Ball, J. and Janyst, P. (2008). Enacting research ethics in partnerships with Indigenous communities in Canada: 'Do it in a good way.' *Journal of Empirical Research on Human Research Ethics, 3* (2), 33–52.

Ball, J. and Lewis, M. (2005). Using Indigenous parents' goals for children's language to guide speech-language practice and policy. Paper presented at the World Indigenous Peoples' Conference on Education, Hamilton, Aotearoa/New Zealand, 27 November–1 December. <http://www.ecdip.org/reports/>

Basso, K. (1970). To give up on words: Silence among the Western Apache. *Southwest Journal of Anthropology,* 26(3), 213–239.

Battiste, M. (2000). Maintaining Aboriginal identity, language, and culture in modern society. In M. Battiste (ed.). *Reclaiming Indigenous voice and vision,* 192–208. Vancouver: UBC Press.

Battisti, M., Friesen, J. and Krauth, B. (2009). *Non-standard English at school: Can targeted funding improve student achievement?* Working Paper, Centre for Education Research and Policy, Simon Fraser University. <http://www.sfu.ca/cerp/research/esd.pdf>

Baugh, J. (1993). Linguistics, education, and the law: Educational reform for African-American language minority students. In S. Mufwene, J. Rickford, G. Baily and J. Baugh (eds), *African-American English: Structure, history and us,* 282–301. New York: Routledge.

Bernhardt, B.M., Ball, J. and Deby, J. (2007). Cross-cultural interaction and children's speech acquisition. In S. McLeod (ed.). *The international guide to speech acquisition,* 101–106. Clifton Park, NJ: Thompson Delmar.

Bernstein, B. (1971). *Classes, codes and control.* London: Routledge and Paul.

Berry, R. and Hudson, J. (1997). *Making the jump: A resource book for teachers of Aboriginal students.* Broome, Australia: Catholic Education Office, Kimberley Region.

Bougie, E. (2010). *Family, community, and Aboriginal language among young First Nations children living off reserve in Canada.* Catalogue No. 11–008-X, Canadian Social Trends. Ottawa: Statistics Canada.

218   JESSICA BALL AND BARBARA MAY HANFORD BERNHARDT

British Columbia Ministry of Education (1999). *ESL: A guide for ESL specialists 1999.* <http://www.bced.gov.bc.ca/esl/policy/special.pdf>

British Columbia Ministry of Education (2009). *English as a Second Language Policy and Guidelines.* <http://www.bced.gov.bc.ca/esl/policy/guidelines.pdf>

Brown, P. and Levinson, S. (1987). *Politeness: Some universals in language usage.* Cambridge: Cambridge University Press.

Cahill, R. (2000). *Deadly ways to learn.* East Perth, Australia: Deadly Ways to Learn Consortium.

Campbell, H. (2011). *A qualitative study of selected Standard English as a Second Dialect school-based programs in British Columbia.* Unpublished Masters of Science Thesis, School of Audiology and Speech Sciences, University of British Columbia.

Canadian Association of Speech-Language Pathologists and Audiologists (CASLPA) (2002). CASLPA Position Paper on Speech-Language Pathology and Audiology in the Multicultural, Multilingual Context. <http://www.caslpa.ca/english/resources/multicult.asp>

Canadian Institutes for Health Research (2007). *CIHR Guidelines for health research involving Aboriginal people.* Ottawa: Author. <http://www.cihr-irsc.gc.ca/e/documents/ethics_aboriginal_guidelines_e.pdf/> (accessed 16 June 2007).

Canadian Centre for Justice (2001). *Aboriginal peoples in Canada.* Statistics Profile Series. Ottawa: Minister of Industry.

Canadian Heritage (2005). *Towards a new beginning: a foundation report for a strategy to revitalize First Nation, Inuit, and Métis languages and cultures.* Report to the Minister of Canadian Heritage by The Task Force on Aboriginal Languages and Cultures, June 2005. Ottawa. Cat. No. CH4–96/2005.

Crago, M.B. (1990). Development of communicative competence in Inuit children: Implications for speech-language pathology. *Journal of Childhood Communication Disorders,* 13, 73–83.

Craig, B. (1991). American Indian English. *English World-Wide,* 12(1), 25–61.

Crystal, D. (2000). *Language death.* Cambridge: Cambridge University Press.

Cummins, J. (2000). *Language, power and pedagogy.* Clevedon: Multilingual Matters.

Damico, J. (1983). *Functional language proficiency.* Unpublished manuscript, American Indian Bilingual Education Centre, Albuquerque.

De Houwer, A. (1999). Environmental factors in early bilingual development: The role of parental beliefs and attitudes. In E. Guus and L. Verhoeven (eds), *Bilingualism and migration,* 75–95. New York: Mouton de Gruyter.

Delpit, L. (2006). *Other people's children: Cultural conflict in the classroom.* New York: The New Press.

Dixon, R.M.W. (1997). *The rise and fall of languages*. Cambridge: Cambridge University Press.

Dyson, G. (2006). George Dyson. In J. Brockman (ed.). *What we believe but cannot prove: Today's leading thinkers on science in the age of certainty*, 136. New York: Harper Perennial.

Eades, D. (1991). Communicative strategies in Aboriginal English. In S. Romaine (ed.), *Language in Australia*, 84–93. Cambridge: Cambridge University Press.

Eades, D. (1992). *Aboriginal English and the law: Communicating with Aboriginal English speaking clients: A handbook for legal practitioners*. Brisbane: Queensland Law Society.

Eades, D. (1995). *Aboriginal English*. North Sydney: Board of Studies, NSW.

Eades, D. (1996). Legal recognition of cultural differences in communication: The case of Robyn Kina. *Language and Communication, 16*(3), 215–227.

Eades, D. (2000). I don't think it's an answer to the question: Silencing aboriginal witnesses in court. *Language in Society, 29*(2), 161–95.

Eades, D. and Siegel, J. (1999). Changing attitudes towards Australian creoles and Aboriginal English. In J. Rickford and S. Romaine (eds), *Creole genesis, attitudes and discourse: Studies celebrating Charlene J. Sato*, 265–277. Philadelphia: John Benjamins.

Eagleson, R. (1982). *Aboriginal English in an urban setting. English and the Aboriginal Child*. Canberra: Curriculum Development Centre.

Edwards, C.P., Gandini, L. and Giovaninni, D. (1996). The contrasting developmental timetables of parents and preschool teachers in two cultural communities. In S. Harkness and C.M. Super (eds). *Parents' cultural belief systems: Their origins, expressions, and consequences*, 270–288. New York: The Guilford Press.

Erasmus, C. (1989). Ways with stories: Listening to the stories Aboriginal people tell. *Language Arts, 66*(3), 267–275.

Fettes, M. and Norton, R. (2000). Voices of winter: Aboriginal languages and public policy in Canada. In M. Brant Castellano, L. Davis and L. Lahache (eds), *Aboriginal education: Fulfilling the promise*, 29–54. Vancouver: University of British Columbia Press.

First Nations Child and Family Caring Society of Canada. (2005). *A chance to make a difference for this generation of First Nations children and young people: The UNCRC and the lived experience of First Nations children in the child welfare system of Canada*. Submission to the Standing Senate Committee on Human Rights, 7 February 2005. <http://www.fncfcs.com/docs/CommitteeOnHumanRightsFeb2005.pdf? (accessed 2 February 2006).

First People's Cultural Foundation. (2007). <http://www.fpcf.ca/>

First Voices. (2007). <http://www.fpcf.ca/language-index.html>

Fishman, J.A. (2001). 300-plus years of heritage language education in the U.S. In J.K. Peyton, D.A. Ranard and S. McGinnis (eds), *Heritage languages in America: Preserving a national resource*, 81–97. Washington, DC: Center for Applied Linguistics.

Flanigan, B. (1985). American Indian English and error analysis: The case of Lakota English. *English World-Wide*, 6(2), 217–236.

Flanigan, B. (1987). Language variation among Native Americans: Observations on Lakota English. *Journal of English Linguistics, 20*(2), 181–199.

Gardner, R. and Lambert, W. (1972). *Attitudes and motivation in second-language learning.* Rowley, MA: Newbury House.

Grogger, J. (2009). *Speech patterns and racial wage inequality.* Harris School Working Paper No. 08.13. University of Chicago.

Gutiérrez-Clellen, V.F., Peña, E. and Quinn, R. (1995). Accommodating cultural differences in narrative style: A multicultural perspective. *Topics in Language Disorders, 15*(4), 54–67.

Harkins, J. (1990). Shame and shyness in the aboriginal classroom: a case for practical semantics. *Australian Journal of Linguistics, 10*, 293–306.

Harris, S. (1990). *Two-way Aboriginal schooling: Education and cultural survival.* Canberra, Australia: Aboriginal Studies Press.

Hawley, J.C. (2005). Lavender ain't white: Emerging queer self-expression in its broader context. In A.J. López (ed.), *Postcolonial whiteness: A critical reader on race and empire*, 53–78. Albany, NY: State University of New York Press.

Heath, S.B. (1989). The learner as cultural member. In M. Rice and R. Schiefelbusch (eds), *The teachability of language*, 333–350. Baltimore, MD: Paul Brookes.

Johnston, J.R. (1982). A new look at communication problems in older language-disordered children. *Language, Speech, and Hearing Services in Schools, 13*, 144–155.

Johnston, J.R. and Wong, M-Y.A. (2002). Cultural differences in beliefs and practices concerning talk to children. *Journal of Speech, Language, and Hearing Research, 45*, 1–11.

Kaldor, S., Eagleson, R. and Malcolm, I. (1982). The teacher's task. In R. Eagleson, S. Kaldor and I. Malcolm (eds), *English and the Aboriginal child*, 193–217. Canberra, Australia: Curriculum Development Centre.

Kaldor, S. and Malcolm, I. (1991). Aboriginal English – An overview. In S. Romaine (ed.), *Language in Australia*, 67–83. Cambridge: Cambridge University Press.

Kemp.painen, R., Ferrin, S.E., Ward, C.J. and Hite, J.M. (2004). 'One should not forget one's mother tongue': Russian-speaking parents' choice of language of instruction in Estonia. *Bilingual Research Journal, 28*(2), 207–229.

Keulen, J.E. van, Weddinton, G.T. and DeBose, C.E. (1998). *Speech, language, learning, and the African American child.* Boston: Allyn and Bacon.

Kwary, D.A. (n.d.). *From pre-pidgin to post-creole*. <http://www.kwary.net>

Laing, S.P. and Kahmi, A. (2003). Alternative assessment of language and literacy in culturally and linguistically diverse populations. *Language, Speech, and Hearing Services in Schools*, 34, 44–55.

Lawrence, B. (2004). '*Real' Indians and others: Mixed-blood urban Native peoples and Indigenous nationhood*. Vancouver, BC: UBC Press.

Leap, W. (1993). *American Indian English*. Salt Lake City: University of Utah Press.

Lee, S.K. (1998). *Manglish: Malaysian English*. Kuala Lumpur: Times Books International.

Liebe-Harkort, M.L. (1983). A note on the English spoken by Apaches. *International Journal of American Linguistics*, 49(2), 207–208.

Lightbown, P. (2008). Easy as pie? Children learning languages. *Concordia Working Papers in Applied Linguistics*, 1, 1–25.

Lim, L. (2004). *Singapore English: A grammatical description*. Philadelphia, PA: John Benjamins.

López, A.J. (2005). Whiteness after empire. In A.J. Lopez (ed.). *Postcolonial whiteness: A critical reader on race and empire*, 1–30. Albany, NY: State University of New York Press.

Mader, C. (1996). *Reverence for the ordinary: A reciprocal inquiry into stories of local knowledge and teacher education on a traditional Cree reserve*. Doctoral dissertation, Department of Elementary Education, University of Alberta, Edmonton, November 1996.

Malcolm, I. (2001). Two-way English and the bicultural experience. In B. Moore (ed.), *Who's centric now?: The present state of post-colonial Englishes*, 219–240. New York: Oxford University Press.

Malcolm, I., Haig, Y., Konigsberg, P., Rochecouste, J., Collard, G., Hill, A. and Cahill, R. (1999). *Towards more user-friendly education for speakers of Aboriginal English*. Perth: Centre for Applied Language and Literacy Research.

McConvell, P. (2008). Language mixing and language shift in Indigenous Australia. In J. Simpson and G. Wigglesworth (eds), *Children's language and multilingualism: Indigenous language use at home and school*, 237–260. London: Continuum.

McRae, D. (1994). *Langwij comes to school: Promoting literacy among speakers of Aboriginal English and Australian Creoles*. Canberra: Department of Employment, Education and Training.

McCrum, R. (2010). *Globish: How the English language became the world's language*. New York: Norton.

McIntosh, P. (2002). White privilege: Unpacking the invisible knapsack. In P.S. Rothenberg (ed.), *White privilege: Essential readings on the other side of racism*, 97–102. New York: Worth Publishers.

Miller, J.R. (1996). Shingwauk's vision: A history of Native residential schools. Toronto, ON: University of Toronto Press. Royal Commission on Aboriginal Peoples (1996). *Report of the Royal Commission on Aboriginal Peoples: Vol. 3. Gathering Strength*. Ottawa, ON: Canada Communication Group.

Milroy, J. and Milroy, L. (1999). *Authority in language*. New York: Routledge.

Morgan, M. (1999). US Language planning and policies for social dialect speakers. In T. Huebner and K. Davis (eds), *Sociopolitical perspectives on language policy and planning in the USA*, 173–191). Philadelphia: John Benjamins.

Moseley, C. (ed.). (2010). *Atlas of the world's languages in danger*. Paris: UNESCO.

Mulder, J. (1982). The Tsimshian English dialect: The result of language interference. In H. Guillermo Bartelt, S. Penfield-Jasper and B. Hoffer (eds), *Essays in Native American English*, 95–112. San Antonio, TX: Trinity University Press.

Mutua, K. and Swadener, B.B. (2004). *Decolonizing research in cross-cultural contexts: Critical personal narratives*. Albany, NY: SUNY Press.

Neha, V. (2003). Home again: A Native American SLP's experiences teaching in a Navaho reservation school. *The ASHA Leader Online*. <http://www.asha.org/about/publications/leader-online/archives/2003/q1/030218fa.htm> (accessed 6 October 2004).

Norris, M.J. (2007). Aboriginal languages in Canada: Trends and perspectives on maintenance and revitalization. In J. White, D. Beavon and S. Wingert (eds). *Aboriginal policy research: Moving forward, making a difference*, 197–228. Vol.3. Toronto: Thompson Educational Publishing.

Norris, M.J. and Jantzen, L. (2002). *From generation to generation: Survival and maintenance of Canada's Aboriginal language within families, communities and cities*. Ottawa, ON: Indian and Northern Affairs Canada.

Ogbu, J. (1999). Beyond language: Ebonics, proper English, and identity in a Black-American speech community. *American Educational Research Journal (Summer)* vol. 36 (2).

Papps, E. and Ramsden, I. (1996). Cultural safety in nursing: The New Zealand experience. *International Journal for Quality in Health Care, 8* (5), 491–497.

Peltier, S. (2009). *First Nations English dialects in young children: Assessment issues and supportive interventions*. Canadian Language and Literacy Research Network.

Peltier, S. (2010). *Valuing children's storytelling from an Anishinaabe orality perspective*. Unpublished Master of Education Thesis, Nipissing University, North Bay, Ontario. <http://www.ecdip.org/reports/>

Perry, T. and Delpit, L. (1998). *The real Ebonics debate: Power, language, and the education of African-American children*. Boston: Beacon Press.

Pesco, D. and Crago, M. (1996). 'We went home, told the whole story to our friends': Narratives by children in an Algonquin community. *Journal of Narrative and Life History, 6*, 293–321.

Petersen, D.B., Laing Gillam, S. and Gillam, R. (2008). Emerging procedures in narrative assessment: The index of narrative complexity. *Topics in Language Disorders, 28*(2), 115–130.

Phillips, S. (1983). *The invisible culture: Communication in classroom and community on the Warm Springs Indian Reservation*. New York: Longman.

Philipson, R. (1992). *Linguistic imperialism*. Oxford: Oxford University Press.

Philpott, D. (2004). *An educational profile of the learning needs of Innu youth*. Memorial University, NFLD. <http://www.turtleisland.org/discussion/viewtopic.php> (accessed 18 January 2007).

Piquemal, N. (2003). From Native North American oral traditions to Western literacy: Storytelling in education. *Alberta Journal of Educational Research, 29*(2), 113–122.

Purnell, T., Idsardi, W. and Baugh, J. (1999). Perceptual and phonetic experiments on American English dialect identification. *Journal of Language and Social Psychology, 18*(1), 10–30.

Rickford, J. (1999). *African American vernacular English*. Malden, MA: Blackwell.

Rickford, J. and Rickford, A. (1995). Dialect readers revisited. *Linguistics and Education, 7*(2), 107–128.

Royal Commission on Aboriginal Peoples (1996). *Gathering strength: Report on the Royal Commission on Aboriginal Peoples, 13*. Ottawa: Canada Communication Group Publishing.

Salée, D. (2006). Quality of life of Aboriginal people in Canada: An analysis of current research. *Institute for Research on Public Policy Choices, 12* (6), 1–30.

Schieffelin, B.B. and Ochs, E. (eds) (1986). *Language socialization across cultures*. New York: Cambridge University Press.

Schiffman, H. (1997). *Linguistic register*. <http://ccat.sas.upenn.edu/~haroldfs/messeas/regrep/node2.html> (accessed 4 September 2004).

Scollon, R. and Scollon, R. (1981). *Narrative, literacy and face in interethnic communication*. Norwood, NJ: Ablex.

Simpson, L. (2000). Stories, dreams, and ceremonies: Anishinaabe ways of learning. *Tribal College Journal, 11*(4), 26–30.

Simpson, J. and Wigglesworth, G. (eds) (2008). *Children's language and multilingualism: Indigenous language use at home and school*. London: Continuum International Publishing Group.

Smith, L.T. (1999). *Decolonizing methodologies: Research and Indigenous peoples.* New York: Zed Books.

Smith, Z. (2010). Speaking in tongues. In C. Hitchens (ed.). *The best American essays,* 179–194. New York: Houghton, Mifflin, Harcourt.

Smye, V. and Brown, A. (2002). 'Cultural safety' and the analysis of health policy affecting Aboriginal people. *Nurse Researcher, 9* (3), 42–56.

Speech Pathology Australia. *Speech Pathologists working in Early Intervention Programs with Aboriginal Australians.* Fact Sheet 2.4.

Statistics Canada. (2006). *Census of the population 2006.* Ottawa, ON: Statistics Canada.

Sterzuk, A. (2008). Whose English counts? Indigenous English in Saskatchewan schools. *McGill Journal of Education, 43,* 9–20.

Stockman, I. (1996). The promises and pitfalls of language sample analysis as an assessment tool for linguistic minority children. *Language, Speech, and Hearing Services in Schools,* 27, 355–366.

Stockman, I. (2000). The new Peabody Picture Vocabulary Test-III: An illusion of unbiased assessment. *Language, Speech, and Hearing Services in Schools,* 31, 340–353.

Tarpent, M.-L. (1982). A Tsimshian English expression: 'Them Fred'. In H.G. Bartelt, S. Penfield-Jasper and B. Hoffer (eds), *Essays in Native American English,* 113–121. San Antonio, TX: Trinity University Press.

Taylor, O. and Pane, K. (1983). Culturally valid testing: A proactive approach. *Topics in Language Disorders,* 3, 8–20.

Trudgill, P. (1972). Sex, covert prestige and linguistic change in the urban British English of Norwich. *Language in Society, 1,* 179–195.

Trudgill, P. (1995). *Sociolinguistics: An introduction to language and society.* Harmondsworth: Penguin.

van Kleeck, A. (1994). Potential cultural bias in training parents as conversational partners with their children who have delays in language development. *American Journal of Speech-Language Pathology, 3,* 67–78.

Walton, C. (1993). Aboriginal education in Northern Australia: A case study of literacy policies and practices. In P. Freebody and A.R. Welch (eds), *Knowledge, culture and power: international perspectives on literacy as policy and practice.* Pittsburgh, PA: University of Pittsburgh Press.

Wardhaugh, R. (2002). *An introduction to sociolinguistics.* Malden, MA: Blackwell.

Washington, J. (1996). Issues in assessing the language abilities of African American children. In A. Kamhi, K. Pollock and J. Harris (eds), *Communication development and disorders in African American children: Research, assessment, and intervention,* 35–54. Baltimore, MD: Brookes.

Watts Pappas, N. and Bowen, C. (2007). Speech acquisition and the family. In S. McLeod (ed.), *The international guide to speech acquisition*, 86–90. Clifton Park, NY: Thomson Delmar Learning.

Wolfram, W. (1983). Unmarked tense in American Indian English. *American Speech*, 59(1), 31–50.

Wolfram, W. (1993). Research to practice: A proactive role for speech-language pathologists in sociolinguistic education. *Language, Speech and Hearing Services in School, 24*, 181–185.

IAN G. MALCOLM AND ADRIANO TRUSCOTT

10 English Without Shame: Two-Way Aboriginal Classrooms in Australia

Introduction

In Australian school classrooms language and literacy practices have often given priority to standard Australian English (SAE) and marginalized or excluded the use of Aboriginal English, the ethnolect which has been maintained for communication within Aboriginal communities. In these circumstances, communication in classrooms is, for many Aboriginal students, associated with a sense of unwelcome conspicuousness sometimes referred to as being (or feeling, or getting) 'shame'. Shame on the part of students may be associated with self-consciousness, lack of engagement and inappropriate and non-compliant behaviours in the school setting.

Two-way bidialectal education attempts to reduce shame by recognizing Aboriginal English as a part of classroom communication and learning. This chapter outlines the principles and practices associated with two-way bidialectal education as practised in Western Australia, and examines its implementation in three diverse schools: fringe metropolitan, fringe rural and rural/remote. The key roles of the school principal, teachers and Aboriginal staff are illustrated as are the impediments to the success of the programme and observations are made on the potential benefits, and limitations, of such a programme.

Shame and education

When asked to reflect on their experience of being in school, Aboriginal Australians often refer to 'shame' or 'big shame'. Typical comments are: 'I was shame. I said nothing', 'I would have felt very shame if I'd done something silly' (Arthur, 1996: 108); '... lot of kids, they frighten' to ask the tutor ... or the teacher ... They frightened. They might feel shame' (Malcolm and Rochecouste, 1998: 65); 'Aboriginal students feel shyness, shame, and do not want to give the wrong answer' (WAAETC, 2003: 55); 'Kids will pull out if it's hard to keep up. The expectations may be too high and they feel shame if they can't keep up – fear of failure' (WAAETC, 2003: 30); 'We get big shame because we think the other people are greater than us, they know more than us, scared that we may say something wrong ...' (Kaldor and Malcolm, 1982: 99).

The word 'shame' is used in English to refer to an Aboriginal concept which is concerned not so much with individual guilt as with social irregularity. It can be experienced by being given unwelcome prominence as much for positive as for negative reasons. As Arthur (1996: 107) notes: 'Shame functions as a form of social control, whereby the force of the emotion affects people's behaviour, such that they are less likely to transgress rules of social behaviour. Aboriginal society is one that values social cohesion, the highly socialised person above the individual achiever ...'. In traditional Aboriginal society, as Meggitt (1965: 190–191) has observed, the term translated 'shame' may be used to refer to one's behaviour towards 'the mother-in-law as with that towards circumcisers, subincisers and ritual friends' and is built in to the terminology of the kinship system which provides the organizing principle for inter-personal relationships.

In the context of the school, Aboriginal students are faced with a situation where the old social rules cannot be relied upon. As one student, interviewed at university, put it: 'When you are at school you have to change to suit Wadjela [non-Aboriginal] ways' (Malcolm, Rochecouste and Hayes, 2002: 19). When, however, the student is unsure as to what ways apply, a decision has to be made as to whether to risk shame by operating according to known rules, or to withdraw from communication altogether. The latter is often seen as the preferable course. An Aboriginal contributor to a consultation on post-compulsory education put it: 'Most teachers don't realise that a lot of Aboriginal kids are perfectionists and they deeply do not like making mistakes – or at least making mistakes in front of others. So often they would rather sit there and not start, not do anything. Many teachers interpret this as rebellion, but it is not that at all. The kids just are supremely *not* confident' (WAAETC, 2003: 17). This choice of action is reflected in comments by a number of Aboriginal university students on their school experience: 'So you were a Nyungar [South-West Aboriginal] kid, you sat at the back at school, you kept your mouth shut;' '... if you didn't fully understand, you sort of sat behind and missed out. You were afraid to ask, you know, if you asked the teacher you were dumb;' 'I pulled out of school early. I s'pose the teachers in the class didn't spend much time with Nyungar kids. I don't know whether tha's 'cause the Nyungar kids never asked ... or they not got Nyungar kids putting their hands up in a classroom full of white kids ... So I never learned much;' 'I was the only black kid in the whole school ... I spent most of my days crying on the desk, just sitting in the back, the back of the room crying. The teacher never even noticed I was there' (Malcolm and Rochecouste, 1998: 64–65).

It is shame, to an Aboriginal student, to be discriminated from the group, to be individually focused on, whether by being shown to be lacking in knowledge or skill, or by being credited with higher achievement than the group. While in a context where all or most present are Aboriginal it is shame to behave differently from the group (for example, by speaking 'flash' like a non-Aboriginal Australian), the sense of shame is also generalized to contexts where non-Aboriginal conventions apply (like most classrooms), and where the sense of not coming up to expectations can be related to what one Aboriginal has described as 'the historical memory of Aboriginal people not achieving well' (WAAETC, 2003: 56). It is shame to fall short of the expectations of the group, whether Aboriginal or non-Aboriginal, and expectations of language use are a particular area of focus in this regard.

Englishes in opposition

Two varieties of English took root in Australia after the British occupation of the continent in the late eighteenth century, one in the immigrant
community and one in the Aboriginal community. Australian English
is a dialect directly related to British English (Collins and Peters, 2008:
357) and reflecting the impact of regional and social varieties which were
dominant in the settler population, as well as influential aspects of the
Australian environment. Being the language of administration and education, it is most widely used in a standardized variety (SAE), while many of
its speakers can also switch into a non-standard variety when appropriate.
Aboriginal English has a quite different ancestry. It resulted not from the
direct adoption of settler English but from the generation of a new form
of communication with significant conceptual and grammatical continuity with Aboriginal languages and with the distinctive employment of
vocabulary drawn from regional and social varieties of eighteenth-century
English as well as other contact varieties from maritime sources. Processes of
pidginization and, in some places, creolization, preceded the development
towards English in Aboriginal contexts, and evidence of these processes
remains embedded in the dialect.

    Like Australian English, Aboriginal English has undergone significant
levelling across the continent so that, although local names like Koori
English or Nyungar English may be used, its speakers from widely separated areas readily identify with and understand one another. At the same
time, there is, across the continent among Aboriginal people, a general
non-identification with SAE, which (in Aboriginal contexts) is often dis-
paragingly referred to as 'high' or 'flash' or 'proper' English, even though
most Aboriginal English speakers will attempt to approximate to it in
non-Aboriginal contexts. One way in which switching into SAE has been
described is as putting on a mask (Eagleson, Kaldor and Malcolm, 1982:
241). The relation between their own English and that of the majority
culture reflects what Ogbu (1978, cited in Siegel, 2010: 170) has called an
'oppositional social identity' on the part of Aboriginal Australians. Non-

Aboriginal Australians, in their turn, are frequently disparaging about Aboriginal English, seeing it not as a dialect in its own right but as a corrupt form of their own English. Accordingly, many teachers have seen it as their role to 'correct' the English of Aboriginal students, or to override it by ignoring it and using only SAE. At the level of educational planning it is common for the term 'English' to be used without qualification to refer to SAE, leading not only to an absence of provision for the particular needs of Aboriginal English speakers but also to a sense on their part that the cultural continuity for which their dialect stands is being excluded from the educational process.

The combined effect of the consciousness of 'shame' among Aboriginal students and of the oppositional relationship between SAE and Aboriginal English is to make the school experience for many Aboriginal students one of discomfort (Grey, 1974: 14–16). Such students may respond to this experience by lack of engagement (whether by non-attendance or by distractedness within the classroom), non-compliance, such as silence, looking down, covering the mouth or inaudibility in response to questioning, failure to comply with assessment requirements (by non-attendance on the testing day or complying minimally with requirements) and occasionally by emotional outbursts and swearing at the teacher. Some Aboriginal students accept the view that there is something wrong with their English and that they will never be able to succeed at school. In responding this way, Australian Aboriginal students are comparable to many other marginalized groups in educational settings in other parts of the world. (For some comparative data, see, e.g., Malcolm, 1989.)

Approaches to managing dialect

The two dialects that co-exist in classrooms where Aboriginal students are present can continue in an oppositional relationship if the educational goal is seen as subordinating one to the other in the interests of achieving mono-cultural outcomes. The entire linguistic focus of the classroom can be on the right use of SAE and its literacy. This has face validity, in that it might seem that students who are unfamiliar with SAE need greater exposure to it. It is also relatively easy to implement since there is a lack of teacher competence, and of learning materials, in Aboriginal English. The cost of this approach is, however, that by discriminating against Aboriginal people and their dialect it inevitably invokes 'shame' and all its negative consequences. The alternative is to find a way to bring these opposing Englishes into a productive relationship to the end that their interrelationships and contrasts might be recognized and used and that Aboriginal students might be oriented towards bidialectal competence and biliteracy.

On the basis of a research association with Edith Cowan University, the Western Australian Department of Education has over a number of years been developing principles for the implementation of two-way bidialectal education (see, e.g., Malcolm, 1995; Malcolm et al, 1999; Malcolm and Königsberg, 2007). This marks a paradigm shift, in that it recognizes that language use is expressive of relationships and it seeks to found its English language programme on cross-cultural relationships of mutual respect, rather than on the unspoken assumption that all communication must favour one group over the other. The approach is two-way in that both Aboriginal and non-Aboriginal staff work on it together, and in that it envisages that both Aboriginal and non-Aboriginal students will be engaged in learning from one another and from their respective dialects. It is bidialectal, in that it recognizes Aboriginal students' need for communicative competence and literacy in both Aboriginal English and SAE; it also recognizes non-Aboriginal students' need for at least passive communicative competence in Aboriginal English (for the sake of mutual comprehension, cross-cultural understanding and respect) in addition to literacy in SAE.

Table 1 (pp. 234–235) summarizes the aims and dimensions of two-way bidialectal education and the ways in which it is intended to engage schools/ principals, teachers, Aboriginal staff members and students. It envisages a school in which both Aboriginal and non-Aboriginal students are present and in which the staffing will include Aboriginal and non-Aboriginal educators. Aboriginal staff, in Western Australia, are most commonly appointed in an ancillary capacity as Aboriginal and Islander Education Officers

(AIEOs) and teachers are, in most cases, non-Aboriginal. All dimensions of two-way bidialectal education are applied simultaneously and are mutually reinforcing, though Relationship Building is fundamental and ever present. The practical outworking shown here is by no means exhaustive and its application will depend on the disposition of those involved.

The first dimension of two-way bidialectal education is relationship building. It is recognized that Aboriginal and non-Aboriginal Australians retain different dialects because they belong to different and only partially-overlapping speech communities. The two cultural groups need to be motivated to communicate with one another. The school needs to become a domain which is friendly to both dialects. It needs to be the location of events with which Aboriginal community members will identify, a place where one will not be conspicuous by speaking one's own dialect. The Principal has a major role in relationship building in that s/he needs to show interest in getting to know and learning from the local community members. This can be done through visits, in company with an Aboriginal staff member, and through inviting Aboriginal community members into the school, with the opportunity, when they are ready, to share their cultural knowledge. The Principal is also responsible for ensuring that non-Aboriginal teaching staff (many of whom may have had no prior contact with Aboriginal people) are sensitized to Aboriginal culture, and that the campus, by its art works and artefacts, as well as its educational resources, reflects an interest in Aboriginal culture.

Where the Principal sets the policy of bicultural and bidialectal respect at the school level, the teacher does so at the classroom level, ensuring that the planning of units of study and the selection of associated resources are done in collaboration with Aboriginal staff members and that the class procedures favour working in cross-cultural groups and allowing for appropriate use of both dialects.

Where the teacher is non-Aboriginal, the Aboriginal staff member works together with her/him to raise awareness of cultural sensitivities affecting the students' attendance, learning or behaviour and the way in which they may respond to learning materials. The students develop an expectation of working, where feasible, in bicultural pairs and groups and learning from one another.

Table 1. A framework for two-way bidialectal education: dimensions of two-way bidialectal education linked with practical outworking

	Aim	School/Principal	Teacher	Aboriginal Staff	Students
Relationship Building	To motivate communication	(a) Community Contact • reciprocal visitation • cross-generation relationships (b) School Policy • cross cultural sensitivity • use of Aboriginal English (c) Staff development • enculturation of staff (d) Bicultural school environment	(a) Empowerment of Aboriginal staff • shared planning • appropriate class role (b) Openness to appropriate use of Aboriginal English (home language – HL) (c) Class Policy • mutual respect building • mutual cultural learning • mutual dialect acceptance (d) Classroom environment	(a) Community Contact with Principal • independently (b) Providing input to teacher • on student communication • on cultural sensitivities • on learning materials (c) Providing input and counselling to students	(a) Reciprocal respectful relationship building (b) Reciprocal cultural learning (c) Working in bicultural pairs and groups (d) Equal access to empowerment through election of school councillors
Mutual Comprehension Building	To facilitate communication	(a) Staffing • appointing sufficient Aboriginal staff • providing appropriate bicultural staff induction (b) Staff development • performance management (c) Resourcing • allocating time • funding resources	(a) Classroom Organization (b) Organizing learning in small groups and pairs (c) Exploiting bidialectal competence of Aboriginal staff (d) Mutual sociolinguistic enabling (e) Developing cross-dialectal listening skills	(a) Providing interpretation and translation to teacher (b) Providing interpretation to students as needed (c) Assisting in modifying learning materials (d) Assisting in classroom enculturation of students (e) Counselling disaffected students	(a) Assisting culturally different students with mutual expression and understanding (b) Learning from culturally diverse materials (c) Acquiring cross-dialectal listening and comprehension skills

Repertoire Building	To expand communication	(a) Mandating recognition of prior English learning in literacy instruction (b) Incorporating bidialectal competencies in school assessment policy (c) Promotion of bias-free ways of referring to HL	(a) Designated HL time (b) Bidialectal learning resources (developed or modified) (c) Bidialectal learning strategies (d) Multi-modal communicative support (e) Celebrating bidialectalism	(a) Modelling Aboriginal English (b) Modelling code-switching (c) Alerting teachers to cross-dialectal conceptual mismatches	(a) Aboriginal students developing active bidialectal skills including biliteracy and code switching (b) Non-Aboriginal students developing passive bidialectal skills
Skill Building	To enhance learning	(a) Providing literacy materials for home use (b) Providing time for modification of SAE learning materials (c) Ongoing professional development for all (d) Rewarding biliteracy	(a) Bridging from established HL literacy to SAE literacy (b) Exploit teaching of dimensions of dialect contrast (c) Biliteracy learning resources (d) Systematic recording of SAE progress (using tools such as the ESL/ESD Progress map) (e) Bidialectal assessment	(a) Assisting with bidialectal assessment (b) Ongoing feedback to teachers on student learning problems (c) Ongoing feedback to community on student progress	(a) Peer feedback in pairs or groups (b) Using appropriate home literacy materials (c) Setting progressive achievement goals

The second dimension of two-way bidialectal education is mutual comprehension building. The key to facilitating cross-cultural communication is in having bicultural staff members who can mediate when communication breaks down. Where AIEOs are part of the staffing profile of the school, the Principal is responsible for ensuring that these Aboriginal staff are working in the most strategically advantageous way so that all teachers with Aboriginal students have access to them and for encouraging non-Aboriginal teachers to acquire a passive knowledge of Aboriginal English. The teacher is responsible for organizing the classroom so that Aboriginal students are in the communicative hub rather than on the fringes, and for modelling cross-dialectal listening so that potential miscommunications can be anticipated and avoided. The Aboriginal staff members will constantly serve as interpreters to both teacher and students and will assist the teacher, where necessary, in modifying learning materials and instructions to make them comprehensible to Aboriginal students. The Aboriginal staff member is the key to alleviating the 'discomfort' experienced by students who find the classroom environment challenging. Progressively, students themselves will be able to assume an interpretive role for one another in cross-cultural learning.

The third dimension in this kind of education is repertoire building. The intention is not only to cope with dialectal diversity in the classroom but to make it a part of the means and content of learning. Just as additive bilingualism has been an objective in bilingual education (Cummins, 2001: 230) so additive bidialectalism (or additive second dialect acquisition) has been advocated in bidialectal situations (Siegel, 2010: 66; McCaffery and Harvey, 2009: 3). The objective is, rather than to reduce the dialectal variation of Aboriginal speakers, to confirm and extend it. For this, it is essential that the school require the recognition of the relevance of the first learned dialect to the acquisition of literacy. Students need to acquire literacy in their first dialect, then transfer their literacy skills to the second dialect. (For comprehensive evidence of the effectiveness of such an approach, see Siegel, 1997, 1999, 2010). Some schools will elect to allow for timetabled periods for the use of the home dialect so that it will be celebrated and used for learning rather than being squeezed out, and the bidialectal skills of Aboriginal staff members should be duly recognized and modelled so that students will gain confidence in code-switching and biliteracy.

The fourth dimension is skill building in SAE to enhance its usefulness to the student as a tool for further learning. High standards should be set for all students in SAE but it should be recognized that learning a second dialect poses particular difficulties (discussed in some detail in Siegel, 2010) and therefore some students need more support than others in achieving these standards. For many learners, existing materials for students learning through SAE may need to be modified. Differences between dialects need to be made explicit and learning needs to be focused on areas of dialect divergence. It is especially important that assessment, in keeping with the bidialectal nature of the programme, recognizes student achievement in both dialects, while providing student and teacher with diagnostic guidance for the ongoing improvement of skills in the second dialect (Some of the pitfalls, and opportunities, are discussed in Malcolm, 2011).

Case studies of three schools

The test of the validity of two-way bidialectal educational approaches needs to be seen in how, and to what effect, they can be worked out in detail in actual school settings. For this it is necessary to have documentation of what occurs in schools where at least some of the staff have undergone appropriate professional development. It needs to be shown how closely, if at all, practice can line up with the principles that have been put forward, and whether any obstacles to the practices that have been advocated can be overcome.

Before referring to individual schools, some comments need to be made about the context of state education in the location where this investigation took place. While classrooms (and their occupants) are inevitably subject to a host of pressures (national to local socio-political ones, for example) from various sources that cannot be detailed here, it is necessary, nevertheless, to consider particular current national level developments. There are major national policy statements that recognize Aboriginal English and bicultural learning (ACARA, 2010 (see below); MCEETYA, 2006; MCEECDYA,

2010). The Aboriginal and Torres Strait Islander Education Action Plan (2010–2014) recognizes the predominance of Aboriginal English as a home language,[1] the importance of acknowledging Aboriginal English in education and how SAE language and literacy development requires using and developing pedagogies that are linguistically and culturally appropriate. At the same time, as in other nations, new system accountabilities are exerting considerable pressures on schools (Lingard, 2009). Programme delivery that is not seen as directly related to student achievement in SAE literacy (that can be evidenced by improved national testing scores) may not be prioritized (see Simpson, McConvell and Caffrey, 2009 for the closing of bilingual programmes; and Graham, 2010 for the impact of testing on schooling). These system pressures can be exacerbated by a low level of awareness/knowledge about Aboriginal English at the general community and school level (due to the oppositional relationship between Aboriginal English and SAE in the community, and high teacher turnover).

These system level factors were raised in all three sites and reveal a paradoxical and unique situation: there are multiple levels of acceptance, awareness and advocacy around Aboriginal English from across the nation and within systems and the school. This results in a lack of consensus as to what English and language programmes involving Aboriginal students should be like.

Visits were made by the authors in 2010 to three schools to document the implementation of programmes of two-way bidialectal education and to gain detailed information from principals, teachers, Aboriginal staff, students and community members on the initiatives that were being taken and their effectiveness. Three schools of significant Aboriginal enrolment but in diverse locations were selected for this study: one a primary (elementary) school in outer-metropolitan Perth, one a primary school on the outskirts of a major regional rural centre, and one in a rural-remote district high school. The authors obtained data in each case by observing the learning

---

[1]   It is important to note that Aboriginal students will speak Aboriginal English and or a creole or Indigenous language. This chapter is centred however on students who speak Aboriginal English as their dominant language.

environment, both in the campus as a whole and in individual classrooms, interviewing principals, non-Aboriginal teachers and Aboriginal staff members (AIEOs and teachers), observing lessons and school events, and, where possible, talking with students, parents and community members. Learning materials and student work samples were copied or photographed. Five on-site visits were made, preceded by teleconferencing with teachers and principals. In order to give an impressionistic profile of each school/class visited as a place of bidialectal learning, relevant observations made at each school will be recorded here using the categories introduced in Table 1.

'School 1', the fringe metropolitan school

School 1 is a primary school located in an outlying suburb of Perth, the capital city of Western Australia. The school has a population of 138 of whom 40 per cent are Aboriginal. There are seven classes, eleven non-Aboriginal teachers and three Aboriginal and Islander Education Officers (two of whom are also qualified teachers).

Dimension 1: relationship building

(a) Community contact
- Two years prior to our visit the Principal, accompanied by an Aboriginal staff member, began visiting homes of Aboriginal students to engage them in the school's programme; since then, the school programme has been the subject of discussion at community level.
- The school has an on-campus Community Learning Centre where Aboriginal adults come to study the Nyungar language, taught by one of the Aboriginal staff of the school. The same teacher teaches Nyungar language in the regular school programme.
- Parents and grandparents are encouraged to monitor students' progress and students at pre-primary level have been given take-home literacy backpacks designed with Aboriginal motifs by an Aboriginal staff member.

- This is the preferred school for many Aboriginal families and some parents who have shifted from the district drive a considerable distance every day because they want continuity of family members' learning there.

(b) Bicultural school environment
- The outside walls of the school buildings have been painted in Aboriginal designs.
- From Year 1, it has become customary for many students to include Aboriginal flags in their art work.

(c) Appropriate use of Aboriginal English
- Aboriginal English is used for 1–2 hours on certain days in sessions designated for 'home talk' – these days have a positive link with Aboriginal students' attendance.
- Students' access to home talk strengthens the home-school link, e.g. one student commented to the AIEO, 'I been to your house.'
- Home talk sessions are used to elicit students' prior knowledge.
- Use of Aboriginal English in class interaction increases the number of student initiated exchanges.
- Aboriginal English is used to praise student performance (e.g. 'This is deadly!').
- Teachers not yet familiar with two-way approaches have been invited to observe home talk sessions to see that students they thought silent do communicate.
- When students leave the language room the teacher farewells them individually in Aboriginal English, strengthening the sense of implied relationship.

(d) Emphasis on relationships
- Some Year 1 students feel free to call the AIEO 'auntie'.
- The AIEO's approach to students having problems is 'having them for a Milo'.
- 'Our Tree of Kindness' poster in Year 1 celebrates students' positive social behaviours.
- Aboriginal and non-Aboriginal staff are expected to participate together in professional development.

(e) Empowerment of Aboriginal people
- Current Head Boy and Head Girl of the school (on the vote of all students) are Aboriginal and were in the Home Talk Group two years ago.
- The Nyungar language teacher experienced empowerment as non-Aboriginal staff members began sitting in on her lessons.
- The empowerment of one Aboriginal staff member as teacher of Nyungar language led to other Aboriginal staff taking initiatives (e.g. making home literacy packs which are decorated by the pre-primary students).

Dimension 2: mutual comprehension building

(a) Classroom organization
- There is a designated language room with activity centres and pictures where Nyungar, Aboriginal English and SAE are focused on.

(b) Active role of Aboriginal staff
- The AIEO/Nyungar language teacher models Aboriginal English and code-switching.
- The AIEO/Nyungar language teacher elicits Aboriginal English and Nyungar during home talk sessions.
- The AIEO is on call in the classroom and helps students in need.

(c) Teacher openness to student dialect
- Teachers gave evidence of having increased their awareness of Aboriginal English by seeking clarification of basic words used by students both in class and around the school.

(d) Use of small groups and pairs
- Learning normally takes place in small groups and pairs.
- Student sharing (in speech and in writing) in small groups is uninhibited (e.g. 'Someone bin died'; 'Er mum had a baby'; 'Tomorrow I am going to prisn to see my dad').

e) Developing cross-dialectal listening skills
- Students engage in 'campfire news', sitting around an artificial camp fire. Students who were part of the news event can join in with the news teller. This activity reflects Aboriginal story telling practices and therefore becomes a more authentic and comfortable task for Aboriginal students, and non-Aboriginal students are exposed to alternative ways of story telling.

Dimension 3: repertoire building

(a) Multi-modal communication support
- Student learning materials and approaches encourage the coordination of graphic and written communication.
- Year 1 students use their drawings as a basis for talking to the class.

(b) Designated Aboriginal English time
- Timetabling of Home Talk sessions (see above).
- Awareness of Home Talk/School Talk distinction is increasingly apparent in students as they move beyond Year 1.

(c) Bidialectal learning resources
- 8 Laminated Big Books based on student compositions in home talk are used by Aboriginal and non-Aboriginal students.
- A Home Talk – SAE Dictionary has been developed and is used to elicit talk.

(d) Promotion of inclusive language
- Teachers are specifically advised to avoid use of the word 'mistakes' to refer to dialect features.

Dimension 4: skill building in SAE

(a) Enhanced expectations for Aboriginal students
- Given cultural and linguistic affirmation, Aboriginal students are expected to meet the standards set.

(b) Initial literacy via Aboriginal English
- In home talk sessions, the AIEO teaches students to sound out words to spell them.
- Home talk is used to get students talking, then, as talk flows, they are helped to try to turn it into writing.

(c) Appropriate use of SAE learning resources
- Use of resources giving systematic focus on phonological awareness was claimed to have dramatically raised students' skills in this area.
- Intensive SAE learning resources are used in activity centres, between which groups circulate, supervised, in the language room. Activities focus on such features of SAE as opposites, possessive adjectives, listening to instructions and plurals.
- To help students identify word boundaries, they may be asked to use blocks to identify the separate words while an utterance is being made.
- Resources on wall include 'syllable snake' poster showing (on its bends) 2–5 syllable words, a felt board with spaces for insertion of words (including students' names) beginning with each letter of the alphabet, and bilingual English/Nyungar word lists.
- Pictures are exploited to practise verb forms (e.g. 'what is he doing?/ going to do?' etc.).
- Student literacy is supported by cards (alphabet picture cards, day of the week cards, colours cards, blends and digraphs cards).

(d) Systematic recording of SAE progress
- The ESL/ESD Progress Map (Department of Education, Western Australia 2010) is used to record progress.

(e) Peer-assisted learning
- Senior Aboriginal students lead small groups from pre-primary in phonological awareness exercises.

'School 2', the rural fringe primary school

School 2 is a rural primary school, with 60 per cent Aboriginal enrolment.
The school has approximately thirty-eight teachers (some part-time), twelve
Aboriginal/Islander Education Officers and twelve Education Assistants.
In this school, we observed a Year 6/7 class.

Dimension 1: building relationships

(a) Community contact
  • Community visitation is carried out by a teacher with an AIEO.
  • The school has educated the parents of many of its students, which
    strengthens the attachment of the parents to the school (An AIEO
    commented: 'A lot of blackfellas like this school.')
  • The school provides a bus to facilitate attendance by Aboriginal
    students.

(b) Appropriate use of Aboriginal English
  • The AIEOs regularly use Aboriginal English to praise student effort
    (e.g. 'Solid!').
  • The AIEOs use Aboriginal English when assisting individual
    students.
  • The AIEOs employ counselling to defuse tension ('sitting down
    and having a talk with him').
  • There are bidialectal captions under student art work displayed in
    the school.

(c) Emphasis on relationships
  • It is important to Aboriginal families that the relatives (cousins,
    uncles, aunts, parents) of students attend/attended the school.
  • The AIEOs visit homes when students are absent.

(d) Empowerment of Aboriginal people
  • The AIEOs take the initiative to provide cultural background in
    lessons.
  • Aboriginal students are comfortable to say it is inappropriate for
    Aboriginal staff to use only SAE in addressing them ('You jus tryna
    talk like a whitefella, Miss.').

- An Aboriginal parent protested at the denigration of her child's dialect by a teacher: 'But that's how we talk!'

(e) Sensitivity to Aboriginal perceptions
- Because she knows students identify loud speech with hostility, the teacher is always softly spoken.
- Because she knows students are intimidated by negative expressions of emotion, the teacher avoids showing her emotions when students do not cooperate.
- An AIEO gives reassurance to students who claim they are lacking in skills (Her comment: 'They're shame. They're not ignorant.')

Dimension 2: mutual comprehension building

(a) Classroom organization
- In the first week the teacher establishes student patterns of mutual accountability.
- The physical configuration of the classroom is designed to facilitate two-way learning.

(b) Teacher openness to student dialect
- Teachers are asked in their appraisal if they are aware of Aboriginal English.
- The teacher is honest about her limitations as an exponent of the students' dialect and seeks students' help when she does not understand.
- Teachers show evidence of listening to their students' use of dialect to learn from it.
- Aboriginal students are comfortable in using their dialect to contribute to news sessions, while AIEO responds in SAE.

(c) Use of small groups and pairs
- Bicultural peer communication is widely employed to structure the class in a way which reduces teacher-centredness.

(d) Active role of Aboriginal staff
- The AIEO helps some first year students in understanding basic concepts such as 'word' and 'letter'.

- The AIEOs are active in interpreting to both teacher and students.
- The AIEOs perform a role of socializing Aboriginal students in the school context.

(e) Peer-assisted learning
- Students are paired with 'buddies' from the buddy class in Year 1.

Dimension 3: repertoire building

(a) Multi-modal communication support
- Students are encouraged to accompany writing with graphics.
- The AIEOs provide support for the cultural component of learning with art work and models.

(b) Bidialectal learning resources
- SAE core words (*100 Most Used Words*) are given dialect-sensitive expansion by the teacher.
- Learning materials include stories in Aboriginal English.
- Home talk/school talk phrase list is compiled by an Aboriginal staff member.

(c) Bidialectal learning strategies
- Students retell in Aboriginal English a story heard in SAE, thus enabling cross-dialectal interference to be detected.
- Non-Aboriginal students are exposed to Aboriginal English in the classroom.
- Students engage in peer editing and reflection in cross-cultural pairs.
- Students engage in bidialectal role play.
- Students carry out code-switching exercises.

Dimension 4: skill building in Standard Australian English

(a) Enhanced expectations for Aboriginal students
- The AIEO counsels students who think they lack skill.

(b) Initial literacy via Aboriginal English
- Aboriginal English literacy is used as a bridge to SAE literacy.
- Story retelling initial literacy exercise: Students hear story in SAE – draw pictures to depict narration – caption pictures in Aboriginal English words – with AIEO change captions to sentences in Aboriginal English.

(c) Modification of monodialectal SAE learning resources
- Existing SAE literacy materials (*Literacy Scope and Sequence*) are given a bidialectal dimension.
- Students are given an Aboriginal English translation of national language testing material instructions during test practice sessions.

(d) Development of appropriate SAE learning strategies
- Colour coding is used to highlight grammatical features in SAE sentences.
- Students are rewarded for demonstrating SAE competence (e.g. in being able to recognize and produce rhyming words).
- Card game involving the words 'Do you have a ...' is used to help students to switch from 'Do you gotta ...'

'School 3', the rural-remote district high school

School 3 is a district high school in an outer-agricultural area of cultural significance to Aboriginal people. The school population is 95 per cent Aboriginal. The staff includes an Aboriginal principal and an Aboriginal teacher, as well as four other teachers, three of whom have had little prior contact with Aboriginal people. There are five classes and three Aboriginal/Islander Education Officers. Students at the school range from pre-primary to Year 12.

District high schools exist principally in rural/remote areas where student numbers are not substantial enough to justify having separate primary and secondary schools. Also, the catchment area of the school tends to be broad relative to non-district high schools. Often a result of such low numbers is multi-aged classrooms, thus increasing the need of the teacher to differentiate the curricula and teaching practices.

In School 3, we observed a senior class consisting of students aged from thirteen to seventeen years old.

Dimension 1: building relationships

(a) Bicultural school environment
- Classrooms and main areas of the school are labelled in Wajarri (the local Aboriginal language).

(b) Appropriate use of Aboriginal English
- Aboriginal staff members use Aboriginal English to praise effort.
- The Aboriginal teacher is able to reduce confrontation and makes communication more 'low key' through the use of Aboriginal English.
- The Aboriginal teacher sometimes adds humour to classroom communication with Aboriginal English.

(c) Enculturation of non-Aboriginal staff
- The Aboriginal cultural awareness training is conducted using a purpose designed audio-visual package.

Dimension 2: mutual comprehension building

(a) Active role of Aboriginal staff
- The Aboriginal principal inducts new teachers.
- The Aboriginal principal vets texts for cultural appropriateness.
- The Aboriginal teacher is able to access local concepts used by the students (e.g. 'carloads' = an impending fight).

(b) Teacher openness to student dialect
- The Aboriginal teacher practises the use of Aboriginal English 'to keep the students comfortable'.

Dimension 3: repertoire building

(a) Multi-modal communication support
- Pictures are used to elicit narration.

- Student artistic expression is used to express and respond to learning.

(b) Bidialectal learning resources
- The bidialectal training resource *Solid English* is available and used for teacher development.

(c) Bidialectal learning strategies
- Students are given pictures of an Aboriginal story and invited to order them in the way that best suits their intended narration in Aboriginal English. This sequencing activity is followed by discussion of the interpretations.
- Code-switching is associated with school policy on inter-personal respect and is promoted as part of a behaviour coaching programme.

Dimension 4: skill building in Standard Australian English

(a) Computer support
- Senior students use the computer as a resource for developing SAE written expression.
- Some students who require additional practice in word recognition skills log onto computer-based literacy support where words are highlighted as they are spoken.

Discussion

It is necessary to recognize, in the first instance, the importance of teacher competence in the implementation of bidialectal programmes. This includes a 'working knowledge' of students' backgrounds to 'assist teachers in their cross-cultural conversations and capacity to make these students feel welcomed and develop a sense of belonging' (McDonald, 2010: 38). To develop as teachers of a multicultural classroom in the schools we observed, teachers had recognized the need for reflection, honesty and reinvention.

1) Reflection, i.e. the importance of thinking about how SAE is used, its status compared to other dialects.
2) Honesty, i.e. being able to confront one's beliefs about the aim of English language literacy and education in general.
3) Reinvention, i.e. being able to modify their own practice to cater better for dialect difference.

It is recognized that these elements of good bidialectal practice are common to good teaching practice in general. However it is clear that, in addition to the above, knowledge of second dialect acquisition and minority education (social justice) are also required in a bidialectal model.

The three schools observed are at different stages of the implementation of bidialectal educational approaches and are clearly responding to different needs, challenges and opportunities associated with their different local situations. Specific comparisons between the schools would be unhelpful in the light of the fact that the classrooms observed at each school were operating at different levels and the teachers and Aboriginal staff had different levels of experience, different local resources and different length of exposure to bidialectal practices.

The data gathered show that schools with heavy Aboriginal enrolment can take effective action to build relationships between Aboriginal and non-Aboriginal members of the school and wider community. It was apparent that in some cases relationships with the community had been confirmed by home visits by non-Aboriginal staff accompanied by Aboriginal staff; Aboriginal English had been effectively brought into the discourse of the school; the physical environment of the school had become visibly inclusive of Aboriginal culture; Aboriginal staff and students had experienced empowerment through being entrusted with responsible roles and some practices adopted show a clear attempt to show respect for Aboriginal perceptions. There was evidence that a school ambience could be created in which cross-cultural communication and learning were enabled. The 'discomfort' which often characterizes Aboriginal involvement in communication at school had been at least in part allayed, as shown by the readiness of students to communicate in kin terms and to volunteer personal information with one another and the teachers. Aboriginal staff members often showed the way in easing communication, as, for example, in dealing with student disciplinary issues by having a chat with the student concerned. This is not to say that the building of relationships was complete or uniform across the schools. There was still evidence that, even where schools had a majority of Aboriginal students, some classes did not have regular access to Aboriginal staff members and that in all schools some teachers and AIEOs were mutually wary as to how to relate to one another. Some students were more secure in their identity, either as Aboriginal or as non-Aboriginal, than others, and this was reflected in the ways in which they responded to bidialectal educational strategies.

On the second dimension, mutual comprehension building, there was evidence of progress in each of the schools. Aboriginal staff in each school served as cross-dialectal interpreters and teachers showed a receptive attitude to student contributions made in Aboriginal English, readily recognizing, in the case of non-Aboriginal teachers, their need not to take students' meanings for granted but to explore dialect-related differences. Where learning in small groups or pairs was planned for, the flow of interaction was enhanced; where, on the other hand, teacher-centred approaches were used, students responded in many cases with the typical 'shame' reactions.

There was evidence in all schools of positive steps towards repertoire building. Teachers in all classes observed recognized the interrelatedness, to Aboriginal students, of the graphic and verbal modes in their communication, using one to support the other. It was clear that fluency and literacy in SAE was not expected independently of, or prior to, fluency and literacy in Aboriginal English. Classes observed in two schools had time and place designated for home language use and both also had developed learning resources to strengthen awareness of home talk/school talk differences. Schools were at different levels in developing a range of bidialectal learning strategies designed to extend the repertoire of both Aboriginal and non-Aboriginal students. There was also some recognition of the need to ensure that, in teacher language, dialect features were not incorrectly labelled as errors.

The fourth dimension of two-way bidialectal education, skill building in SAE, was being pursued systematically in the lower grades in the schools observed, where Aboriginal English literacy was being used as the first step towards literacy in SAE and where Aboriginal students were being encouraged, especially by Aboriginal staff, to meet high expectations. There was a recognition of the need to make selective use of SAE learning resources, modifying them where necessary for bidialectal learners, and the capacity of more advanced learners to help beginners was recognized, with allowance being made for senior students to coach Year 1 partners or 'buddies' at given times. The plotting of student progress on a [standard] English as a Second Dialect progress map (Department of Education, Western Australia, 2010) was also carried out.

To introduce two-way bidialectal approaches into a school is clearly to make heavy demands on the school at the level of its senior administration, teaching staff and support staff. It is, however, in the perspective of those included in this study, a desirable and achievable, though long-term, objective. It is possible to motivate communication between culturally divergent groups and to redefine the roles of Aboriginal and non-Aboriginal staff members so that education may become a much more two-way endeavour and so that, with Aboriginal empowerment, new energies can be unleashed to create a positive learning community within which no group will feel subordinated.

Limitations

This study has, however, shown that the potential for the effective delivery of two-way bidialectal education is clearly limited by a number of factors.

One factor is time. It takes time for teachers, most of whom are monodialectal English speakers, to recognize the legitimacy and nature of a nonstandard dialect and its relevance to the learning of those who speak it. Typically teachers now committed to dialect-sensitive education described their experience as 'a long journey'. One told us, 'It's taken me four years to get my head around it.' It takes time, also, for the culture of a school to change. One school, for example, found it necessary to focus on one grade per year in implementing two-way bidialectal education. This rate of change is not going to produce the kind of quick turnaround in student results which is most likely to impress governments and funding authorities. There is no short cut to implementing this kind of educational change. It is possible, however, to maximize the good use of time by embedding appropriate practices into the policy and strategic plans of the school, to provide prompt induction to new staff and to encourage experienced staff to serve as mentors to newcomers.

A second highly significant factor is staff continuity. Schools with large Aboriginal enrolments are not easy to staff. They are often in less-favoured places of residence and make heavy demands on the teacher. Appointees to these schools are often new graduates or teachers recruited from overseas. Although many of these are excellent teachers, it takes time for them to adjust to the needs of Aboriginal students, as well as for the students to adjust to them, and after a year (or less) they may move on. One school in the year of our visits had retained two teachers from the previous year and gained six new ones. The inexperience of new teachers often contrasts markedly with that of the Aboriginal staff, whose presence in the school has usually been long-term. The principal remarked of one teacher in a year 5–7 class with an AIEO, '[he] can't release control'. Often inexperienced teachers do not know how to relate to, or work effectively with, AIEOs. Consequently Aboriginal staff may feel underutilized and disempowered, which will have a negative effect on their motivation as well as on how they are perceived by students.

Two-way bidialectal education also faces difficulties as a result of student perceptions, or misperceptions. In two of the schools we visited the focus on the needs and dialect of Aboriginal students had caused some reaction on the part of a small number of non-Aboriginal students who felt disadvantaged by not being Aboriginal, and even, in some cases, wanted to claim Aboriginality. It is important that the education be genuinely two-way, giving all students a sense of pride in their own heritage as well as a sense of increasing biculturalism. There are also problems if bidialectal education assumes more sociolinguistic awareness than is reasonable among very young students, who may be bewildered by talk about dialect, and, on the other hand, if it takes too little account of the sociolinguistic insights which may be brought into the programme by students in adolescent years.

Community participation, or at the very least, contact is fundamental for the implementation of bidialectal approaches but is not unproblematic. Divisions within the community may impact on the school and, in some cases, Aboriginal staff of the school may not be recognized by the local community. The strengthening of community relationships becomes more difficult if staff are living outside of the town in which the school is located.

A final factor which emerged was that of the need for structuring to underlie efforts at two-way bidialectal education. The fact that the students' home language is being recognized does not imply that there is any less attention to the way in which the discourse of the classroom is planned for and organized. The amount of structure imposed by the teacher on the learning situation varied greatly between classes we observed. In classes with high accountability where students were required, for example, to set themselves daily goals, to take responsibility for one another's learning, to work in approved pairs or groups, to complete work on task sheets prepared by the teacher and to plot and record their progress the students were more focused and able to work independently, than in low accountability classrooms. While this might seem unsurprising, it is nevertheless essential to reduce the need for the kind of teacher-centred whole-of-class activity which readily induces 'shame'.

Implications

These limitations reveal certain areas of consideration in enhancing delivery of a two-way bidialectal programme. One area is embedding bidialectal practice in school policy and planning. Such an administrative process could ensure increased awareness and, if possible, common practice across the school and over time, thus marginally negating the effects of high teacher turnover. Developing a bidialectal programme through the school policy would provide opportunities to reaffirm the role of Aboriginal staff, whose presence may often be undervalued and/or misunderstood. Opportunities to reaffirm their role could include lesson and curriculum planning, modelling bidialectalism and resource development. This final aspect is important to ensure opportunities for staff and students to reflect on, comparing and visually displaying the different dialects in the classroom. Enriching the print environment like this with both dialects is a means of fostering code-switching skills and cross-cultural understanding, as well as a sense of ownership and pride with respect to the students. Though it is acknowledged that this is often a challenge for schools, it could be seen from School 1, for example, that creating and maintaining opportunities for family/carer/community inclusion in the school has a positive impact on the success of the bidialectal programme.

With respect to practicability of bidialectal education, it is necessary to recognize the unique demands on teachers, especially in times of high school accountability measures (ACTA, 2010). However the benefits from modifying sometimes just a few elements of practice and policies can help ensure effective bidialectal/bicultural practice.

Furthermore the linguistic/dialectal reflection that is necessary for all involved (to different, but overlapping extents) is not only necessary for the effective implementation of these programmes, but it could, in the future, be argued as mandatory for all schools. The current draft of the new Australian Curriculum: English makes explicit reference to the importance of considering additional dialects.

> Students will be taught that there are many languages and dialects spoken in Australia including Aboriginal English and SAE and that these languages may have different writing systems and oral traditions. Students will be taught to develop critical understandings about social, historical and cultural contexts, aesthetic qualities, and the perspectives associated with different uses of language and textual features. (Preamble, ACARA, 2010)

In addition, for example, in Year 1, students will be required to know about the 'community languages and dialects used in the classroom including those of Aboriginal and Torres Strait Islander peoples from the local

256 IAN G. MALCOLM AND ADRIANO TRUSCOTT

area' (ibid: Year 1 section). Indeed, in Year 3, students will be even required to compare dialects.

As recognition of the importance of dialect difference increases, so will the need for effective bidialectal programmes become more apparent.

Conclusion

This chapter has attempted to argue, on the basis of linguistic evidence, that the education of Aboriginal students should be sensitive to the bidialectal situation they find themselves in in Australia and should lead them towards literacy skills in SAE by way of Aboriginal English. Having set forth this ideal and a model for its implementation, it has attempted to determine its feasibility by examining attempts to implement it in diverse schools.

We conclude that it is possible, though challenging, to implement programmes of this kind. Time, continuity of staff, sensitivity in implementation, community engagement and careful structuring at the school and classroom level are all important variables. The success of the programme will not be observed in the short term in dramatic improvements in grades (sometimes identified, unilaterally and over-simplistically, as 'outcomes') but in the progressive development of enduring and interacting bidialectal communities in which there will be no room for shame on either side.

References

Australian Council of TESOL Associations (ACTA), Applied Linguistics Association of Australia (ALAA) and Australian Linguistics Society (ALS) (2010). Joint Submission to the Senate Education, Employment and Workplace Relations Committee Inquiry into the administration and reporting of NAPLAN testing.

Australian Curriculum, Assessment and Reporting Authority (2010). *Australian Curriculum: English K-10. Draft Consultation version 1.1.0.* <http://www.australiancurriculum.edu.au/Home>, accessed 24 November 2010.

Arthur, J.M. (1996). *Aboriginal English: A Cultural Study.* Melbourne: Oxford University Press.

Collins, P. and Peters, P. (2008). Australian English: morphology and syntax. In K. Burridge and B. Kortmann (eds), *Varieties of English 3: The Pacific and Australia*, 341–361. Berlin: Mouton de Gruyter.

Cummins, J. (2001). From multicultural to anti-racist education: an analysis of programmes and policies in Ontario. In C. Baker and N.H. Hornberger (eds), *An Introductory Reader to the Writings of Jim Cummins*, 215–239. Clevedon: Multilingual Matters.

Department of Education, Western Australia (2010). *The ESL/ESD Progress Map.* East Perth: Department of Education, Western Australia.

Eagleson, R.D., Kaldor, S. and Malcolm, I.G. (1982). *English and the Aboriginal Child.* Canberra: Curriculum Development Centre.

Graham, J. (2010). The Naplan Debate. Editorial: The Trouble with My School. In *Professional Voice* 8 (1). The Australian Education Union: Victoria.

Grey, A. (1974). Towards understanding Aboriginal children. In *Aboriginal Children in the Classroom.* Taree: Department of Education, New South Wales.

Kaldor, S. and Malcolm, I.G. (1982). Aboriginal English in country and remote areas: a Western Australian perspective. In R.D. Eagleson, S. Kaldor and I.G. Malcolm, *English and the Aboriginal Child*, 75–112. Canberra: Curriculum Development Centre.

Lingard, B. (2009). Testing times: The need for new intelligent accountabilities for schooling. *QTU Professional Magazine*, 24 November 2009: 13–19.

Malcolm, I.G. (1989). Invisible culture in the classroom: minority pupils and the principle of adaptation. In O. Garcia and R. Otheguy (eds), *English Across Cultures, Cultures Across English: A Reader in Cross-cultural Communication*, 117–135. Berlin: Mouton de Gruyter.

Malcolm, I.G. (1995). *Language and Communication Enhancement for Two-Way Education.* Perth: Edith Cowan University in association with the Education Department of Western Australia.

Malcolm, I.G. (2011). Issues in assessing Indigenous speakers of English in Australia. *Language Assessment Quarterly* 8 (2): 190–199.

Malcolm, I.G, Haig, Y., Königsberg, P., Rochecouste, J., Collard, G., Hill, A. and Cahill, R. (1999). *Towards More User-Friendly Education for Speakers of Aboriginal English.* Mount Lawley; Centre for Applied Language and Literacy Research, Edith Cowan University, and Education Department of Western Australia.

Malcolm, I.G. and Königsberg, P. (2007). Bridging the language gap in education. In G. Leitner and I.G. Malcolm (eds), *The Habitat of Australia's Aboriginal Languages: Past, Present and* Future, 266–297. Berlin: Mouton de Gruyter.

Malcolm, I.G. and Rochecouste, J. (1998). *Australian Aboriginal Students in Higher Education.* Perth: Centre for Applied Language Research, Edith Cowan University.

Malcolm, I.G., Rochecouste, J. and Hayes, G. (2002). *The Application of Indigenous Skills to University Teaching and Learning.* Mount Lawley: Centre for Applied Language and Literacy Research, in association with Kurongkurl Katitjin School of Indigenous Australian Studies, Edith Cowan University.

McCaffery, J. and Harvey, N. (2009). *Engaging learners: Making Links.* An unpublished paper presented to EDPROFST 226 & EDPROFST 701 Block Courses July 2010, Faculty of Education, University of Auckland.

McDonald, T. (2010). *Classroom Management: engaging students in learning.* South Melbourne, Victoria: Oxford.

Meggitt, M.J. (1965). *Desert People.* Chicago: University of Chicago Press.

MCEECDYA (Ministerial Council for Education, Early Childhood Development and Youth Affairs) (2010). *Aboriginal and Torres Strait Islander Education Action Plan (2010–2014).* Victoria: MCEECDYA.

MCEETYA (Ministerial Council on Education, Training and Youth Affairs) (2006). *Australian directions in Indigenous education, 2005–2008.* Carlton South, Victoria: MCEETYA.

Siegel, J. (1997). Using a pidgin language in formal education: help or hindrance? *Applied Linguistics* 18 (1), 86–100.

Siegel, J. (1999). Stigmatized and standardized varieties in the classroom: interference or separation? *TEOSOL Quarterly* 33 (4), 701–728.

Siegel, J. (2010). *Second Dialect Acquisition.* Cambridge: Cambridge University Press.

Simpson, J., McConvell, P. and Caffery, J. (2009). *Gaps in Australia's Indigenous Language Policy: Dismantling bilingual education in the Northern Territory.* AIATSIS Research Discussion Paper 24.

Western Australian Aboriginal Education and Training Council (WAAETC) (2003). *Consultation Related to Post-Compulsory Schooling of Aboriginal Students in Western Australia.* Perth: Curriculum Council.

JEFF SIEGEL

11 Educational Approaches for Speakers of Pidgin and Creole Languages

Introduction

Pidgin and creole languages develop out of a need for communication among people who do not share a common language – for example, among trading partners or plantation labourers from diverse geographic origins. Most of the words in the vocabulary of the new language come from one of the languages of the people in contact, called the 'lexifier' (or sometimes the 'superstrate') – usually the language of the group with the most power or prestige. However, the meanings and functions of the words, as well as the way they are pronounced and put together (i.e. the grammatical rules) of the pidgin or creole, are different to those of the lexifier.

Once developed, a pidgin language usually continues to be learned as only an auxiliary language and used when necessary for intergroup communication. Its total vocabulary is small, and it has little if any grammatical words and endings – for instance, to indicate past tense or plural. An example is Chinese Pidgin English, once an important trade language in southern China and Hong Kong. But in some cases, the use of a pidgin is extended in a multilingual community as it becomes the everyday lingua franca. As a result, the language expands over time in its vocabulary and grammar, and becomes what is fittingly called an 'expanded pidgin'. Examples are Nigerian Pidgin and Melanesian Pidgin. Each of the three dialects of Melanesian Pidgin (Tok Pisin in Papua New Guinea, Bislama in Vanuatu and Pijin in Solomon Islands) has its own writing system, and is used widely not only for communication between people who have different mother tongues but also in radio broadcasting, parliamentary debates and religious contexts.

In some contexts people in a mixed community shift to an expanding or expanded pidgin as their primary language, which they speak to their children. Thus, children growing up in this context acquire the expanded pidgin as their mother tongue (or first language). This language is referred to as a 'creole'. Like any other vernacular language, a creole has a large vocabulary and a complex set of grammatical rules, and is not at all restricted in use, having a complete range of informal functions. This context was common on Caribbean plantations, resulting in the English-lexified and French-lexified creoles that are still spoken there – for example, Jamaican Creole and Haitian Creole.

There are currently over fifty different expanded pidgins or creoles spoken by an estimated 123 million people (based primarily on figures in Gordon, 2005). More than 100 million people speak expanded pidgins, with Nigerian Pidgin being the largest (an estimated 80 million speakers). Nigerian Pidgin and the other widely spoken expanded pidgins, Cameroon Pidgin (16 million speakers) and Melanesian Pidgin (4 million), are all lexified by English.

More than 23 million people speak creoles, approximately 10 million lexified by French, 6.5 million by English, 4.7 million by African languages (especially Kongo and Ngbandi), 1.5 million by Portuguese or Spanish, and 0.4 million by other languages, including Malay, Hindi and Arabic. Haitian Creole (French-lexified) is the largest (with approximately 7.4 million speakers), followed by Jamaican Creole (English-lexified, 3.2 million). Expanded pidgins or creoles are spoken in at least fifty countries or territories, mostly former European colonies in the Caribbean region, Africa, the south-western Pacific and the western Indian Ocean. Millions of speakers of these languages have also migrated to the US, Canada, Britain, France and the Netherlands. For example, it is estimated that there are as many as 1 million speakers of Haitian Creole in the US (Berotte Joseph, 2010).

Immigrants speaking an expanded pidgin or creole (hereafter abbreviated as P/C) are of course minorities in their adopted countries. Some P/C speaking communities are also a minority in the country where they originated – for example, those speaking Gullah and Louisiana Creole in the US and Kriol in Australia. In other places, P/C speakers are the majority in a particular state or territory, but a minority in the country as a whole – for example, in Hawai'i in the US. However, in most places where a P/C is spoken, its speakers make up a majority of the population as a whole – for example in Papua New Guinea, Vanuatu and Solomon Islands in the Pacific; Mauritius, Réunion and the Seychelles in the Indian Ocean; Cape Verde, Guinea-Bissau, Sierra Leone, Nigeria and the Central African Republic in Africa; and Belize, Suriname, Guyana, Haiti, Jamaica, Trinidad and Tobago, St Lucia, Dominica, Guadeloupe, Netherlands Antilles and Aruba in the Caribbean region.

Nevertheless, in nearly all of these places, the P/C is an important marker of social identity. However, it is spoken only in informal contexts –at the market or among family and friends – while a different language is used for formal contexts, including the education system. This language is most often the standard form of a European language – French, English, Portuguese or Dutch – usually the former colonial language that has been chosen as the official language even after independence. P/C-speaking children generally have to acquire literacy not in their own language but in the standard European language that is officially used in the formal education system. Thus in their first few years of school, they have to acquire both a second language (L2) and literacy. Craig (1999) called this the 'lexifier L2' situation.

Very often P/C-speaking students are expected to acquire the L2 without any special programmes to help them do so. Rather, students are treated as if they are poor speakers of the standard language rather than L2 learners, and the teaching of literacy is done as if their first language (L1) does not exist – what Craig (2001: 66) refers to in English-lexifier creole contexts as the 'English-as-the-mother-tongue tradition'. The linguistic features of the students' creole L1s are seen as 'bad habits' that must be replaced with the 'good habits' of the standard.

This chapter is about the approaches that do exist specifically to help P/C-speaking students acquire initial literacy and the standard language of the education system. It begins by outlining the reasons for the historical lack of use of P/Cs in formal education. Then it describes four different educational approaches aimed at P/C speakers and their results. The chapter concludes with some suggested explanations for the results.

Why P/Cs have historically had a limited role in formal education

Studies show that P/Cs are seen positively by their speakers as a marker of solidarity and local social identity, and valued in the private domains of family and friendship. But unlike other languages, P/Cs are rarely valued in public formal domains such as education and in these contexts they are often characterized by negative attitudes and low prestige (see, for example, Winford, 1994; Mühleisen, 2002).

There are several possible reasons for the low prestige of P/Cs. First, it may be attributed to their history. Each P/C-speaking country or territory was formerly the colony of a European power. Those in control and those with economic advantage spoke the European language. The P/C speakers who later became the educated and well-off elite were those who acquired this language. When they became leaders, they supported the European language remaining as the official language. Thus, as the language of the former colonial power and the current leaders, the European language is seen as the key to upward mobility and economic success. In contrast, the P/C, as a language of former slaves or indentured labourers, is often associated with repression and powerlessness.

In addition, as the new languages of relatively recently formed speech communities, P/Cs suffer from comparison to the official languages. European languages have long historical traditions and bodies of literature, whereas P/Cs do not (Alleyne, 1994). Also, European languages are clearly standardized in both writing system and grammar, and have many dictionaries and grammar books, whereas most P/Cs do not have a widely recognized standard grammar or writing system, although many dictionaries and grammatical descriptions have been written by linguists.

Most significantly, however, P/Cs are often not considered to be legitimate languages, but rather deviant and corrupt forms of their lexifiers, and therefore not suitable for the education system (see, for example, Kephart, 1992, regarding Carriacou; Mann, 1996, regarding Nigeria; and Rajah-Carrim, 2007, regarding Mauritius). This is especially true in situations where a P/C coexists with the standard form of its lexifier which is the official language – for example, Hawai'i Creole and standard American English. This view is reinforced by the fact that, at least superficially, the P/C and the standard share the same lexicon. It is thought that the P/C does not have its own grammatical rules, and consequently, the way it is spoken is considered to be the result of performance errors rather than language differences. This lack of autonomy is exacerbated in countries like Jamaica and Guyana where a P/C and the standard form of its lexifier are both commonly used and there seems to be no clear dividing line between them (what is called a 'creole continuum').

However, with more understanding that P/Cs are legitimate languages, with their increased use in literature and the media, and with more realization of their importance to local identity, attitudes have begun to become more positive in some places, such as Hawai'i, Jamaica and other Caribbean countries (see Romaine, 1999; Mühleisen, 2002; Devonish, 2007). Nevertheless, this has not translated into widespread use or acceptance of P/Cs in formal education. Some educators, administrators and even linguists still argue that using P/C in education would be both impractical and a waste of time, as well as being detrimental to students. These arguments have to do with issues such as lack of standardization, no recognition of benefits and fear of interference with acquisition of the standard form of the European official language, since learning of this standard is the ultimate goal of the education system everywhere P/Cs are spoken.

Teaching approaches for P/C speakers

Some teaching programmes or approaches for P/C speakers in the formal education system do make use of the students' home languages. These have been categorized as instrumental, accommodation and awareness (Siegel, 1999, 2007). For speakers of English-lexifier creoles who are immigrants in English-speaking countries, we can also add the ESL (English as a Second Language) approach. Each of these approaches is described in the following subsections.

Instrumental approaches

The instrumental approach uses the students' expanded pidgin or creole as a medium of instruction to teach initial literacy and sometimes content subjects such as mathematics, science and health. Instrumental programmes are similar to transitional bilingual programmes in that a language well-known by the children (L1) is initially used while they are learning the language of the educational system (L2). Such an approach is most suitable in situations where the L1 is clearly distinguished from the L2 and where all students in the classroom are speakers of the L1.

P/Cs as official languages of education

Of the many countries where a P/C is the L1 of the vast majority of the population, only three have officially designated this language as the medium of instruction for the early years of primary school, and therefore as the medium for acquiring initial literacy. These are the Seychelles, Haiti and Curaçao and Bonaire in the Netherlands Antilles.

In the Seychelles, Seselwa (a French-lexified creole) has been the medium of instruction in kindergarten and early primary since 1981, after which English becomes the language of education. In an early study, Ravel and Thomas (1985) compared grade 3 students in 1983, the last grade 3 to be taught in English with grade 3 students in 1984, the first to be taught in Seselwa. The findings were that the creole-educated students performed better than the English-educated students, not only on standardized tests but also in school subjects, namely English and mathematics. Bickerton (1988) reported the results of a similar study done two years later which showed the creole-educated students achieving higher scores in French, mathematics, science and social studies. He concluded: 'The prediction by the enemies of creole, that education in creole would lower scores in English and French, has failed to be borne out.' (Bickerton, 1988: 3). More recently Leste, Valentin and Hoareau (2005) reported on a large scale study of the achievement of grade 6 students in twenty-four schools. It was found that students average scores in reading in English were above the standardized means.

A reform of education in Haiti was declared in 1979 making Haitian Creole (French-lexified) the medium of instruction for the first five years of primary school. French is supposed to be learned during this period to become the language of instruction along with Creole in grade 6. However, after ten years (1989) only 16.2 per cent of all classrooms had implemented the new curriculum (Locher, 2010: 179). Ten years later, the education ministry reported that all schools were using the reform curriculum, but in reality, this was not being done exhaustively, with many schools missing Creole textbooks, and a great deal of teaching still occurring in French (Dejean, 2010; Locher, 2010).

The most recent detailed evaluation of the reform was done in the 1987, as described by Locher (2010). In tests in mathematics, French and general studies, students in grades 4 and 6 in reformed schools performed significantly worse than those in traditional schools. However, the tests concentrated on traditional skills such as memorization rather than goals of the reform such as critical thinking and self-confidence. Also, by grade 6, students in reformed schools were not that far behind those in traditional schools in competency in French, contradicting predictions that instruction in Creole would be detrimental to acquisition of French. The authors of the study did not attribute the poor results in reformed schools to the use of the students' mother tongue, Creole, but rather to the structural failure of the Haitian state to properly manage the schools (Locher, 2010: 180). The reform has actually brought some benefits: a greater demand for education and literacy (in Creole) among the majority of students.[1]

In the Netherlands Antilles, Papiamentu (a creole lexified by both Spanish and Portuguese) has been supported by the government as the language of instruction in the early grades of most primary schools on Curaçao and Bonaire, changing to Dutch in grade 4 or 5 (Dijkhoff and Pereira, 2010).[2] No detailed evaluations have been carried out, but some

---

1   See Trouillot-Lévy (2010) for a case-study of a successful private school using Haitian Creole as the medium of instruction.

2   There was also a plan to make Papiamentu the language of instruction in nearby Aruba, which has separate political status. However, this has not been implemented (see Dijkhoff and Pereira, 2010).

indications can be seen in the results in the first primary school in the Netherlands Antilles that instituted Papiamentu as the language of instruction, the Kolegio Erasmo, established in 1987. Between 2001 and 2008, 84.1 per cent of primary students went on to higher levels. In the four-year high school, established in 1997, 95.3 per cent passed their exams in 2002 and 90.3 in 2003, well above the national average of between 60 and 70 per cent (Dijkhoff and Pereira, 2010: 253).

The only other country where a P/C spoken by a majority of the population is officially accepted and widely used to teach literacy in formal education is Papua New Guinea (PNG). For the first three years of school (Elementary), the language of instruction is chosen by the community. English is introduced in the second or third year of Elementary School and becomes the medium of instruction in the following six years of school (Primary). Although recent figures are not available, it has been reported that many communities, especially in urban areas, have chosen Tok Pisin (the PNG dialect of English-lexified Melanesian Pidgin) for their schools (Ray, 1996). Also, at least in one rural area, in the Sepik Province, there were at least twenty-six Elementary Schools using Tok Pisin (Wiruk, 2000).

Before the PNG reform began, there was a community-run preschool programme in the Ambunti district of the Sepik Province that taught initial literacy and numeracy to children through the medium of Tok Pisin before they began formal education in the standard English-medium primary schools. This was called the Tok Pisin Prep-School Program. From 1989 to 1995 I conducted an evaluation of the programme (Siegel, 1992, 1997), mainly to investigate the validity of claims that use of Tok Pisin in the classroom would be detrimental to students' later acquisition of English in primary school because of interference. However, interviews revealed overwhelming satisfaction with the programme among both teachers and parents, and teachers reported that there were no special problems of interference. In fact, the students who had learned initial literacy in Tok Pisin were said to learn standard English more easily than the other students. The statistical analysis of data on academic achievement showed that children who had been involved in the prep-school programme scored significantly higher in term tests than those who had not been involved. These results included English, where those who learned initial literacy in Tok Pisin actually scored higher, not lower, than those students who learned literacy only in standard English. Furthermore, the prep-school children showed significantly higher academic achievement in English across time (i.e. in upper grades as well).

Over the years there have been a few experimental studies and pilot projects involving the use of majority creole languages in teaching initial literacy.

In Guinea-Bissau (Africa), the language of education is standard Portuguese, but the vast majority of the population speak Crioulo (or Kriyol), a Portuguese-lexified creole. Children come to school without a knowledge of the language of instruction, and most teachers also have difficulty with the language. In 1986, the Ministry of Education started an experimental programme which included using Crioulo to teach literacy and content subjects in the first two years of primary education, followed by transition to standard Portuguese. Benson (1994, 2004) conducted a detailed evaluation of the programme during the 1992/93 school year. Performance of students involved in the programme was measured in Crioulo, Portuguese, mathematics and creativity, and compared to that of students involved in other programmes. The results, however, showed that except for a predictably better performance in Crioulo, there was no statistically significant difference between students involved in the programmes and those not involved. The programme could possibly have been more effective if the 1992/93 school year had not been curtailed by a high level of political unrest and strikes by teachers (who were not receiving their salaries), and if the transition to standard Portuguese had occurred after more than only two years of schooling in creole. (A longer period of three to five years is usually recommended for bilingual programmes.) Nevertheless, the evaluation demonstrated various advantages of the programme. First, the learning of literacy in Crioulo and its use in teaching topics such as health and agriculture enabled students to understand their lessons. Second, more students spoke in class, and there was less reliance on rote learning. It was clear that education in the creole L1 did not hurt the students, as they performed comparably if not better than those in other programmes. Taking into account the positive results, Benson concluded that the 'waste of time' argument was not borne out by any of the assessment results.

In St Lucia (Caribbean), Kwéyòl (French-lexified) is spoken by the majority, but English is the language of education. An experimental study was conducted by Simmons-McDonald (2006, 2010). Three grade 5 and 6 children reading at the beginning level were taught literacy in Kwéyòl in addition to English. The results were that at the end of the study, after only three terms, all three children had not only learned to read Kwéyòl, but also increased their reading levels in English – two to grade 1 level, and one to grade 3 level. Thus, the study revealed a positive transfer of reading abilities from the first language to the second language – i.e. from the creole to the official language of education.

In Jamaica, a Bilingual Education Project was approved by the government and implemented in 2004 in three pilot public schools (Devonish and Carpenter, 2007). The project involves full and equal use of Jamaican Creole (English-lexified) alongside standard Jamaican English in all aspects of formal education from grades 1 to 4. This is a significant departure from the usual practice of teaching students as if English was their mother tongue. Carpenter and Devonish (2010) describe an evaluative study of students in grade 3 in one of the pilot schools. The students were given the usual Jamaican Language Arts Diagnostic Test in English, as well as a specially-designed equivalent test in Jamaican Creole. Predictably, scores were higher in Jamaican Creole than in English. However, the scores in English of students in the bilingual school compared to the scores of students in monolingual English schools would not have been predicted by educators. The mean scores for the bilingual school students was actually higher, thus demonstrating as in other studies that using the students' creole mother tongue in formal education does not have a negative effect on learning the educational standard.

P/Cs in bilingual (and trilingual) programmes for minorities

Instrumental programmes have existed and still exist for P/C-speaking minorities where the students' L1 is used as the medium of instruction for the first few years of primary school.

In the Northern Territory of Australia, a bilingual programme began at Barunga School in 1977 for Aboriginal speakers of Kriol (English-lexified).

Kriol was used for teaching reading and writing from grade 1 until a change to English in grade 4 or 5. After then, Kriol was restricted to subjects about cultural heritage (see Siegel, 1993). A thorough evaluation of this programme was done by Murtagh (1982). The purpose of his study was 'to find out whether or not a bilingual programme which uses Creole and English as languages of instruction facilitates the learning of both Standard English and Creole' (15). Murtagh compared several measures of oral language proficiency in Kriol and English of students in the first three grades at two different schools: the Kriol/English bilingual school at Barunga and an English-only school at Beswick Reserve, where the children are also Kriol speakers. The overall results were that students at the bilingual school scored significantly better than those at the monolingual school, especially in grade 3. Despite such results, this bilingual programme, along with others, was terminated by the Northern Territory government at the end of 1998.

A bilingual programme has existed since the 1980s in north-eastern Brazil among two Amerindian groups, the Karipúna and Galibi-Marwono who speak Kheuól (Amazonian French Creole) (Ferreira, 2010). This is a three-year transitional programme in which children learn initial literacy in the creole but then shift to Portuguese, the main educational language. There have been no formal or informal evaluations of the educational effects of this programme.

Two pilot projects or experimental programmes are also underway. In the Caribbean islands of San Andres, Providence and Santa Catalina, which are part of Colombia, an experimental 'trilingual' programme was started in 1999, using the local creole (referred to as 'Islander English'), standard English and Spanish (Morren, 2001). The creole is used as the medium of education in the two pre-primary years of school and grade 1. Oral English is introduced in grade 1, and oral Spanish (the official and national language) in grade 2. English is used for reading and writing and to teach some subjects from grade 2. Spanish is similarly used from grade 3. By grade 4 all subjects are taught in English or Spanish. The results of an Islander English diagnostic reading inventory administered to children after they completed grade 1 indicated that the programme had been successful in teaching the various skills needed to become a successful reader (Morren, 2004, 2010).

A pilot programme also started in 2007 in Nicaragua for speakers of Kriol (English-lexified) in five schools on the Caribbean Coast (Koskinen, 2010). Kriol is initially the language of instruction and Spanish and English are taught as second languages. An informal evaluation of the programme after the first year found that children participated more actively and learned to read more quickly, at first in Kriol and then in Spanish.

Instrumental approaches for immigrants

There are millions of creole-speaking immigrants in countries in North America and Europe. With regard to the use of their languages education, most available information concerns the United States.

In the 1980s, bilingual programmes were established in Massachusetts, New York and Florida for immigrant children speaking creoles that have a lexifier other than English, especially Cape Verde Creole (Portuguese-lexified) (Gonsalves, 1996) and Haitian Creole (French-lexified) (Zéphir, 1997).

Again, very little research has been done to evaluate bilingual programmes. One example is a study by Burtoff (1985) conducted in New York City involving illiterate Haitian Creole-speaking immigrants. Two groups were compared: the control group, who received instruction only in English as a second language (ESL) for twenty-four weeks, and the experimental group, who received instruction in ESL for twelve weeks and in Haitian Creole (HC) literacy for twelve weeks. There were some problems with the research design and the low number of subjects, but the statistical results revealed that the HC literacy group developed ESL literacy skills greater than those of the ESL-only group, despite having half the amount of instruction.

However, the number of bilingual programmes for creole speakers has decreased significantly. In Massachusetts the bilingual education law was overturned by voters and scrapped by the state government in 2003 (de Jong-Lambert, 2003). And in New York and Florida, there are now fewer programmes. For example, even though there are over 30,000 Haitian children in New York City public schools, there is currently only one bilingual programme (Berotte Joseph, 2010: 241).

Summary

All of the evaluations of programmes and pilot projects using the instrumental approach showed positive benefits to students in terms of participation in the formal education system and acquisition of literacy in both the expanded pidgin or creole (L1) and the official language of education (L2). Nevertheless, nearly all programmes have faced difficulties because of lack of support from parents, teachers and administrators who are still not convinced about the advantages of such programmes, and also because of problems of resources and management.

ESL approaches

The situation with regard to immigrant children speaking English-lexified creoles is very different. As pointed out by Winer (2006: 109–110), Caribbean Creole-speaking children in North America are dealt with in one of three ways: mainstreaming, special education or ESL programmes. In mainstreaming, they are put in classes along with other students who already know the varieties close to the standard. Coelho (1988: 144) described the situation in Canada when this occurs:

> Divergence from Standard English usage by Caribbean students is usually not regarded with the same tolerance as errors made by students who are learning English as a Second Language, because Caribbean students are generally not regarded as language learners. They are regarded as English speakers who are careless with the language.

In the US, Pratt-Johnson (1993) and Winer (1993) reported that teachers' lack of familiarity with Caribbean creoles and culture has led to difficulties in communication in the classroom, and to creole-speaking children being put in special education, remedial or even speech therapy classes.

Educators who recognize the legitimacy of creole-speaking students' language often place them into ESL programmes along with speakers of Japanese, Russian, etc. But this causes other problems. First of all, creole speakers usually see themselves as speakers of English (Nero, 1997, 2001), and as Winer (2006: 110) noted: 'They are astonished and resentful at being treated in this fashion.' Second, beginning and intermediate ESL classes are not really appropriate because creole speakers have a large vocabulary and a good receptive knowledge of English compared to other learners. Third, many creole-speaking students are eventually outperformed, especially in formal writing, by other ESL students who started out with much less English. This is frequently due to a lack of recognition of how certain standard English structures differ from those of the creole, and the persistence of negative transfer (Calchar, 2004; Winer, 2006).

Calchar (2004, 2005) conducted two research studies to compare patterns of acquisition of standard English by speakers of English-lexified creoles from the Caribbean who had been living in Florida for two years or less. She concluded (2004: 163) that these students 'have difficulties building a separate mental representation for standard English because of the blurred boundaries between standard and creole-English and their habit of constantly shifting back and forth between these varieties'. Since such difficulties do not occur for the usual ESL students, creole-speaking students do not fit into either mainstream or ESL programmes that reflect the usual dichotomy between native and non-native speakers of English. Thus, Calchar (2005: 324) stressed the need for 'a specialized curriculum that addresses the specific writing needs of English-based creole speakers, who are neither native nor non-native speakers of English'. Such a curriculum would help learners perceive the differences between the creole and the educational standard.

Accommodation approach

In the accommodation approach (Wiley, 1996: 127), also referred to as the integrative approach (Roberts, 1994), the P/C is not a medium of instruction or subject of study, but it is accepted to some extent in the classroom. This may occur in several different ways. In the early years of school, students may be free to use their home varieties of language, without correction, for speaking. In addition, teachers may utilize their students' own interactional patterns and stories for teaching the standard. At the higher levels, literature and music from students' communities may be accommodated into the curriculum.

One of the most well-known accommodation programmes was in Hawai'i. The Kamehameha Early Education Program (KEEP) was started in the 1970s for ethnic Hawaiian children, mostly speakers of Hawai'i Creole. In teaching reading, the programme made use of discourse modes and participation structures similar to those in a speech event found in Hawai'i Creole called *talk-story*. At least a dozen studies (e.g. Speidel, 1987) showed increased reading achievement and development of spoken SAE as a result of using these HC patterns of interaction in the classroom. (See Boggs, 1985, for a detailed description of the programme and other references to evaluative research on it.)

Two other studies of the accommodation approach also were done in Hawai'i. Day (1989) describes an experimental programme involving Hawai'i Creole-speaking children in kindergarten up to grade 4. In this programme, teachers were first made aware of the history of creole languages and the logic of vernaculars such as HC. The teachers accepted Hawai'i Creole as a valid linguistic variety, and did not react negatively to students using it in class. The study showed a significant increase over time in the scores of the students involved in the programme on standardized tests of abilities in both Hawai'i Creole and standard English. Rynkofs (1993, 2008) gives an ethnographic account of one teacher's programme of writing workshops for Hawai'i Creole-speaking students in grade 2. The children were allowed to speak and write in any variety, and early versions of their work included many Hawai'i Creole features. But through a process of modelling and recasting in the workshops, rather than correction, the students became more proficient in written standard English.

In the English-speaking Caribbean, accommodation has involved increased acceptance of creole languages in schools, mainly in literature and creative writing. Winer (1990) reported that in Trinidad and Tobago, the Ministry of Education's 1975 syllabus called for the recognition of 'the vernacular', i.e. Trinidad Creole (TC), 'as a real language and as a legitimate vehicle for oral and written expression' (245). Educators were asked to accept the students' spoken and written 'dialect' in school work and examinations. Although there were initially adverse reactions to this syllabus in the community, Winer concluded:

> This attitude no longer generally holds ... TC has a measure of officially sanctioned and even required educational use, and is widely available in written form ... Although few would advocate the use of TC as the primary educational medium, even in primary education, there is a widely recognized need, from teachers and community, for its use in education as complementary, additive, and transitional to standard English. (245)

Still in the Caribbean, Christie (2003: 46) reports that according to the recent Reform of Secondary Education in Jamaica, 'students should be allowed to express themselves freely, employing whatever variety makes them comfortable in the classroom and outside'. However, it is questionable whether accommodation has actually gone this far in most classroom contexts.

Accommodation is also one possible component of the awareness approach, described in the following section.

Awareness approach

In the awareness approach for P/C-speaking students (Hudson, 1984; Siegel, 1993, 1999), their first language is seen as a resource that can be used for learning the standard educational language and for education in general, rather than as an impediment. It has some similarities with 'language awareness', popular in Britain in the 1980s and 1990s (e.g. Hawkins, 1987; James and Garrett, 1991), and a great deal in common with 'dialect awareness' in the US (Adger, 1994; Wolfram, 1998, 2009), although the approach described here is more focused on acquisition.

Teaching programmes using the awareness approach have at least two of the following three components. In the accommodation component, students' P/C is accepted in the classroom in various ways, as described in the preceding section. In the sociolinguistic component, students learn about variation in language and the many different varieties that exist, such as types of dialects, pidgins and creoles. They also find out about the socio-historical processes that lead to a particular variety becoming accepted as the standard. As students are studying the world around them, this component of the approach is sometimes more like social studies than language arts. In the contrastive component, students learn about the rule-governed nature and linguistic characteristics of their own varieties and see how they differ from those of the varieties of other students and from the standard. This is sometimes called contrastive analysis (Rickford, 1999, 2002; Wolfram and Schilling-Estes, 1998).[3]

In the remainder of this section, I talk first about promoting awareness among teachers and the community, and then describe awareness programmes with different P/Cs that have been evaluated in some way, as well as some experimental studies.

Promoting awareness among teachers and the community

The first step in implementing an awareness approach for P/C-speaking students is often educating the teachers themselves, and giving them some ideas about classroom activities. Some useful materials have been written for teachers in particular locations – for example in Canada for teaching Caribbean immigrants (Coelho, 1988, 1991), and in the Caribbean itself (Craig, 1999). (See Siegel, 1999, for other references.)

In Australia a professional development course for teachers, *Fostering English Language in Kimberley Schools* (FELIKS), was created with the aim of training educators about Kriol (and also Aboriginal English) so that they can more effectively teach Aboriginal students who speak these varieties. The FELIKS course starts by showing participants that Kriol is a valid language (and Aboriginal English is a valid dialect of English) – not 'poor English'. It goes on to illustrate some of the systematic semantic, phonological and grammatical differences between each of these varieties

---

3   This should not be confused with the Contrastive Analysis that was used for foreign language teaching in the 1950s and 1960s.

and standard Australian English and the potential for miscommunication when these differences are not understood. Participants also learn about some basic sociolinguistic terms such as pidgin, creole and speech continuum. The course emphasizes the importance of students having control of both standard Australian English and Kriol (or Aboriginal English). Teachers come to understand that each of these varieties can be used appropriately in different contexts, and that children need to be able to switch between them if they want to participate in both Aboriginal and non-Aboriginal Australian society. FELIKS has been published as a kit (Catholic Education Office, 1994) which contains all the material needed for running a two-day (seven-session) course. It includes a manual for presenters, audio and videotapes, overhead transparencies, participants' booklets and handouts for group activities and games. A resource book for teachers based on the FELIKS materials has also been published (Berry and Hudson, 1997).

In Hawai'i, an organization has been in existence since 1998 that promotes awareness among teachers and the general community about Hawai'i Creole, locally known as 'Pidgin'. Its name is 'Da Pidgin Coup' (all puns intended). In 1999, members wrote a position paper for educators and the general public titled 'Pidgin and Education'. It presented information about the complex relationship between Pidgin and standard English, and about the equally complex issues surrounding the use of Pidgin in education. The paper can be seen on the web at www.hawaii.edu/sls/pidgin.html.[4] Some members of Da Pidgin Coup have been also running awareness workshops for teachers at various venues, including teachers' conferences (see Siegel, 2007; Higgins, 2010). Although no official awareness programmes are currently running in Hawai'i schools, there were some in the past, as described in the next subsection.

---

4   At the time of writing this chapter, the position paper was being revised and
     updated.

Awareness programmes, past and present

The Hawai'i English Programme, which ran from 1968 to 1983, used the awareness approach in several ways. First, it had some exercises comparing features of Hawai'i Creole to standard English. Second, it included some stories written in the creole and children were sometimes given the choice to read either these or others in standard English. Third, there was a unit on dialects that looked at dialect diversity outside Hawai'i, as well as containing activities to encourage students to view Hawai'i Creole as a legitimate form of language with its own dialectal diversity (Rogers, 1996). However, because of negative attitudes toward the use of an unstandardized variety such as Hawai'i Creole in formal education, these components of the programme were not widely covered by teachers (Eades et al., 2006: 158).

Project Holopono, which was implemented in Hawai'i from 1984 to 1988, was a programme involving approximately 300 students of limited English proficiency in grades 4 to 6 in eight schools. Half of these students were Hawai'i Creole speakers. The programme included some awareness activities, such as studying literature containing Hawai'i Creole and contrasting features of the creole and standard American English. The evaluation of the final year of the project showed an increase in oral proficiency in standard English among 84 per cent of the students (Actouka and Lai, 1989).

Another Hawai'i programme, Project Akamai, ran from 1989 to 1993. It involved more than 600 Hawai'i Creole speakers in grades 9 and 10 in eleven schools. It also included the use of literature in Hawai'i Creole and some contrastive activities. An evaluation of the final year of the project reported increases of between 35 and 40 per cent on tests of standard American English and oral language skills (Afaga and Lai, 1994).

In Britain, the awareness approach was also used by the Afro-Caribbean Language and Literacy Project in Further and Adult Education, aimed primarily at Caribbean creole-speaking immigrants. It was established by the Language and Literacy Unit of the Inner London Education Authority (ILEA) in 1984, and culminated in the publishing of a book of language materials for teachers and students: *Language and Power* (ILEA Afro-Caribbean Language and Literacy Project in Further and Adult Education,

1990). The programme, as described in the book, actually goes beyond most other awareness programmes in emphasizing the students' own expertise (see Chapter 9), as can be seen in this extract:

> The book is based on the belief that a key part of the language curriculum for all students should be an outline of the social and political factors which helped to determine the development of Standard English. It is also necessary to make available to both students and teachers as much information as possible about languages in general and about the history and development of Caribbean Creole languages in particular. This includes an understanding of their grammatical structure, pronunciation patterns, vocabulary and idiom. The students themselves can contribute a great deal of this information, and their confidence will grow when their expertise in this area is acknowledged. Students' own knowledge and understanding of different languages and language varieties are an invaluable resource for language teaching. It is in this context that progress on the language issue in the multilingual classroom can be achieved, not just for students of Afro-Caribbean origin, but for students of all races and backgrounds. (v)

Unfortunately, this programme was never evaluated.

The most successful and longest running use of the awareness approach is in the US: the Caribbean Academic Program (CAP) at Evanston Township High School near Chicago. This is a programme for Creole-speaking high school students who have migrated to the area from the Caribbean. Both standard English and various Caribbean English-lexified Creoles are used in the classroom for speaking, reading and writing, and issues concerning these languages and standard English are discussed (Fischer, 1992a; Menacker, 1998). A study was done on the progress of the students involved in the programme. In the 1991/92 school year, 73 per cent of the fifty-one CAP students were placed in the lowest of the four levels (or tracks) in the school based on academic ability; none of them were in the two highest levels. But after one year in the programme, only 7 per cent remained in the lowest level; 81 per cent had moved up at least one level; 24 per cent had moved up two or more levels; 26 per cent were in the two highest levels (Fischer, 1992b).

A couple of studies of experimental programmes using aspects of the awareness approach have also been reported. In the Caribbean, Elsasser and Irvine (1987) described a programme integrating the study of the local Creole and standard English in a college writing programme in the US Virgin Islands. They reported that the programme did not interfere with the learning of the standard, and it led to increased interest in language in general, and to a greater 'understanding of the role of grammatical conventions, standardized spelling, and the rhetorical possibilities of both languages' (143).

Decker (2000) gave an account of an experimental study carried out over thirteen weeks in a grade 3 classroom in Belize. Four grammatical areas were identified which differ in Belize Kriol (English-lexified) and standard English: plural marking on nouns, past time reference, present time reference and subject-verb agreement. The teacher discussed with the students, in Kriol, how these features function in Kriol, and students were asked to write in Kriol using these features. The teacher then moved on to describe, again in Kriol, how the corresponding features function in standard English, and then gradually switched to discussing this with the students in English. Students were then engaged in various story-telling, writing and translation activities using these features in both languages. Although there were some methodological problems with the study, the results on the basis of a pre-test and post-test were that the students involved showed statistically significant improvement in performance in these areas of standard English.

Summary

The few evaluations that have been done on the accommodation and awareness approaches, like those on the instrumental approach, have demonstrated that the use of the students' P/C in the classroom had none of the detrimental effects feared by parents and educators. On the contrary, the approaches in general led to higher scores in tests measuring reading, writing or oral skills in the standard language of education and in some cases to increases in overall academic achievement. Other benefits included greater interest and motivation, and higher rates of participation. Some of the reasons for these results are discussed in the following section.

Explaining the results

As shown by the evaluations described in the preceding sections, instrumental, accommodation and awareness approaches – all of which make use of the students' P/C in the classroom – are successful in achieving higher scores in tests measuring reading and writing skills, and in some cases in leading to improvements in students' participation and overall academic achievement. Here I present several possible explanations for these results.

Ability to separate varieties and notice differences

As mentioned in the section 'ESL approaches' above, in situations where there is not a clear distinction between a creole and its lexifier, it is difficult for learners to separate the two varieties. However, in the study of the Kriol/ standard Australian English bilingual instrumental programme in Australia (as already described under the heading 'P/Cs in bilingual (and trilingual) programs for minorities'), Murtagh (1982) attributed the higher language proficiency of the bilingual programme students to their 'progressively greater success at separating the two languages', as a consequence of 'the two languages being taught as separate entities in the classroom'.

Craig (1966, 1988) has also observed that because of the superficial similarities between the P/C and the lexifier, the learner in traditional teaching is often unaware of some of the differences that do exist. He (1966: 58) notes, 'the learner fails to perceive the new target element in the teaching situation'. In second language acquisition (SLA) theory, Schmidt's 'noticing hypothesis' (1990, 1993) stipulates that attention to target language forms is necessary for acquisition; these forms will not be acquired unless they are noticed. However, it appears that using the P/C in educational programmes makes learners aware of differences between it and the standard educational language that they may not otherwise notice. This may occur in instrumental programmes as a result of the juxtaposition of the two varieties or in the contrastive component of the awareness approach.

Easier acquisition of reading and academic skills

A well-known principle in education is that it is easier for children to acquire literacy in a variety of language that is familiar to them. Also widely recognized is that literacy skills can be transferred from one language to another (Cummins, 1981; Snow, 1990; Thomas and Collier, 2002). These principles would also seem to apply to P/C contexts. That is, it would be easier for children to acquire literacy in their L1 than in the L2, especially when there are some significant linguistic differences between the two, but once acquired, literacy skills can easily be transferred to the L2. In the case of the instrumental programmes described in sections entitled 'P/Cs as official languages of education' and 'P/Cs in bilingual (and trilingual) programs for minorities', the higher scores on tests of reading were most likely a consequence of these principles being put into practice.

Furthermore, according to the 'interdependency principle' or 'common underlying proficiency generalization' proposed by Cummins (1988, 2001), the combination of linguistic knowledge and literacy skills necessary for academic work, which he originally called 'cognitive/academic language proficiency' (CALP), is common across languages and once acquired in one language or dialect, it can be transferred to another. Since CALP is easier to acquire in the L1 than in the L2, it appears that students in programmes where the P/C was used in the classroom had a better opportunity to acquire these skills and then transfer them to general academic work in the standard language of education.

Greater awareness and more positive attitudes among teachers

As we saw above, teachers of speakers of P/Cs, especially minority and immigrant students, may be unaware of the problems their students face with regard to learning the main language of education. As a result, they may interpret 'errors' students make in the standard as carelessness or laziness, rather than a reflection of vernacular norms, and develop negative attitudes towards these students. Teachers may also equate the lack of knowledge of the educational standard as a lack of intelligence, and this can lead to lower expectations and the self-fulfilling prophecy of poorer student performance. Even if teachers recognize that their students come to school speaking another dialect, a lack of awareness of the legitimacy of this form of speech can result in their denigrating or rejecting it, and as Au (2008: 66) pointed out, 'rejecting students' home language is tantamount to rejecting the students themselves'. Such negative attitudes may be internalized by the students, affecting their own self-image, or rejected by the students, causing them to withdraw from participation in the education system. In both cases, the consequence is poor school performance.

But because of the fundamental nature of instrumental, accommodation and awareness approaches, and the knowledge and training needed to implement them, teachers involved will know that language variation and diversity are 'normal'. They will also become aware of the legitimacy and complex rule-governed nature of their students' P/Cs and how they differ from the standard. Therefore, as they understand the reasons for some of their students' 'errors', they develop more positive attitudes and higher expectations, which is reflected in student performance. These factors, as well as more tolerance of the use of the P/C in the classroom, have other flow-on effects, as described below.

Greater cognitive development among students

It is obvious that children's self-expression is facilitated if they are allowed to speak in a familiar language (e.g. UNESCO, 1968: 690). Thus, children are clearly disadvantaged when they are not free to express themselves in their own variety of language (Thomas and Collier, 2002) – the situation in formal education for many speakers of P/Cs. One important factor is that self-expression may be a prerequisite for cognitive development (Feldman et al., 1977). For example, in a study of cognitive development and school achievement in a Hawai'i Creole-speaking community, Feldman, Stone and

Renderer (1990) found that students who did not perform well in high school had not developed 'transfer ability'. Here transfer refers to the discovery or recognition by a learner that abstract reasoning processes learned with regard to materials in one context can be applied to different materials in a new context. For this to occur, new materials must be talked about, described and encoded propositionally. The problem in Hawai'i was that some students did not feel comfortable expressing themselves in the language of formal education, standard American English, and their own language, Hawai'i Creole, is conventionally not used in formal education.

Thus, one possible reason for the overall positive results in all three kinds of approaches using P/Cs is that students were allowed to express themselves in their own varieties, thus better facilitating cognitive development.

Increased motivation and self-esteem among students

Most theories of SLA agree that the individual factors of learner motivation, attitudes, self-confidence, and anxiety have some effect on L2 attainment. For example, Skutnabb-Kangas (1988: 29) observed that when the child's home language is valued in the educational setting, it leads to low anxiety, high motivation and high self-confidence, three factors which are closely related to successful educational programmes.

Another factor relates to the importance of a P/C as a marker of social identity. As Tamura (1996: 439–440) points out for Hawai'i Creole speakers:

> [U]sing nonstandard English [i.e. Hawai'i Creole] symbolizes their solidarity within a social group. Such peer-group loyalty is especially strong among youths. As an intermediate school girl noted, 'If we speak good English, our friends usually say, "Oh you're trying to be hybolic (acting superior by using big words) yeah?!"'

The problem is that many educators believe that students must choose one variety or the other – ignoring the possibility of bilingualism in the P/C and the educational standard. For example, in 1999 Mitsugi Nakashima, Chairman of the Hawai'i State Board of Education, made the following statement (*Honolulu Advertiser*, 29 September 1999) with regard to Pidgin (i.e. Hawai'i Creole):

> If your thinking is not in standard English, it's hard for you to write in standard English. If you speak pidgin, you think pidgin, you write pidgin ... We ought to have classrooms where standard English is the norm.

Because of this view, many students feel they have to make a choice, and fear that learning and using the educational standard means abandoning their own language and thus risking being ostracised from their social group.

The use of the P/C in the classroom would reduce some of this anxiety by demonstrating that both it and the standard have a role in society. Also, according to Clément's (1980) Social Context Model of SLA, such use of the L1 (here the P/C) would be expected to reduce fear of assimilation and thus increase motivation to learn the L2, here the standard language of education. Again in Hawai'i, Reynolds (1999: 310) observes:

> My own experience has revealed that when I am not trying to snatch away the language of my students, they do not feel that they have to hang onto it so tightly. Instead, the more we talk and plan and practice with both HCE [Hawai'i Creole English] and ASE [American Standard English], the more interested we all become in both languages ...

Conclusion

It is clear that students learn best when their own way of speaking is valued and included in the educational process. Thus, although it may seem counter-intuitive to use an undervalued pidgin or creole in the educational process, such practices have many educational benefits – including helping students to acquire the more valued standard language used at the higher levels of formal education.

References

Actouka, M. and Lai, M.K. (1989). *Project Holopono, Evaluation Report, 1987–1988*. Honolulu: Curriculum Research and Development Group, College of Education, University of Hawai'i.

Adger, C.T. (1994). *Enhancing the Delivery of Services to Black Special Education Students from Non-standard English Backgrounds: Final Report*. University of Maryland, Institute for the Study of Exceptional Children and Youth (ERIC Document no. ED 370 377).

Afaga, L.B. and Lai, M.K. (1994). *Project Akamai, Evaluation Report, 1992–93, Year Four*. Honolulu: Curriculum Research and Development Group, College of Education, University of Hawai'i.

Alleyne, M.C. (1994). Problems of standardization of creole languages. In M. Morgan (ed.), *The Social Construction of Identity in Creole Situations*, 7–18. Los Angeles: Center for Afro-American Studies, UCLA.

Au, K.H. (2008). If can, can: Hawai'i Creole and reading achievement. *Educational Perspectives* 41: 66–76.

Benson, C. (1994). *Teaching Beginning Literacy in the 'Mother Tongue': A Study of the Experimental Crioulo/Portuguese Primary Project in Guinea-Bissau*. PhD dissertation. University of California at Los Angeles.

Benson, C. (2004). Trilingualism in Guinea-Bissau and the question of instructional language. In C. Hoffmann and J. Ytsma (eds), *Trilingualism in Family School and Community*, 166–184. Clevedon: Multilingual Matters.

Berotte Joseph, C.M. (2010). Haitians in the US: Language, politics, and education. In A.K. Spears and C.M. Berotte Joseph (eds), *The Haitian Creole Language: History, Structure, Use, and Education*, 229–247. Lanham, MD: Lexington.

Berry, R. and Hudson, J. (1997). *Making the Jump: A Resource Book for Teachers of Aboriginal Students*. Broome: Catholic Education Office, Kimberley Region.

Bickerton, D. (1988). Instead of the cult of personality ... *The Carrier Pidgin* 16: 2–3.

Boggs, S.T. (1985). *Speaking, Relating, and Learning: A Study of Hawaiian Children at Home and at School*. Norwood, NJ: Ablex Publishing.

Burtoff, M. (1985). *Haitian Creole Literacy Evaluation Study: Final Report*. Washington, DC: Center for Applied Linguistics.

Calchar, A. (2004). The construction of Creole-speaking students' linguistic profile and contradictions in ESL literacy programs. *TESOL Quarterly* 38: 153–165.

Calchar, A. (2005). Creole-English speakers' treatment of tense-aspect morphology in interlanguage written discourse. *Language Learning* 55: 275–334.

Carpenter, K. and Devonish, H. (2010). Swimming against the tide: Jamaican Creole in education. In Migge, B. Léglise, I. and Bartens, A. (eds), *Creoles in Education: An Appraisal of Current Programs and Projects*, 167–181. Amsterdam/Philadelphia: Benjamins.

Catholic Education Office (Kimberley Region) (1994). *FELIKS: Fostering English Language in Kimberley Schools*. Broome: Catholic Education Commission of Western Australia.

Christie, P. (2003). *Language in Jamaica*. Kingston: Arawak.

Clément, R. (1980). Ethnicity, contact and communicative competence in a second language. In H. Giles, W.P. Robinson and P.M. Smith (eds), *Language: Social Psychological Perspectives*, 147–154. Oxford: Pergamon.

Coelho, E. (1988). *Caribbean Students in Canadian Schools, Book 1*. Toronto: Carib-Can Publishers.

Coelho, E. (1991). *Caribbean Students in Canadian Schools, Book 2*. Toronto: Pippin Publishing.

Craig, D.R. (1966). Teaching English to Jamaican Creole speakers: A model of a multi-dialect situation. *Language Learning* 16: 49–61.

Craig, D.R. (1988). Creole English and education in Jamaica. In C.B. Paulston (ed.), *International Handbook of Bilingualism and Bilingual Education*, 297–312. New York: Greenwood.

Craig, D.R. (1999). *Teaching Language and Literacy: Policies and Procedures for Vernacular Situations*. Georgetown, Guyana: Education and Development Services.

Craig, D.R. (2001). Language education revisited in the Commonwealth Caribbean. In P. Christie (ed.), *Due Respect: Papers on English and English-related Creoles in the Caribbean in Honour of Professor Robert Le Page*, 61–76. Kingston: University of West Indies Press.

Cummins, J. (1981). The role of primary language development in promoting educational success for language minority students. In California State Department of Education (ed.), *Schooling and Language Minority Students: A Theoretical Framework*, 3–49. Los Angeles: National Evaluation, Dissemination and Assessment Center.

Cummins, J. (1988). Second language acquisition within bilingual education programs. In L.M. Beebe (ed.), *Issues in Second Language Acquisition: Multiple Perspectives*, 145–166. New York: Newbury House.

Cummins, J. (2001). *Language, Power and Pedagogy: Bilingual Children in the Crossfire*. Clevedon: Multilingual Matters.

Da Pidgin Coup (1999). Pidgin and Education: A Position Paper: University of Hawai'i (available at <http://www.hawaii.edu/sls/pidgin.html>).

Day, R.R. (1989). The acquisition and maintenance of language by minority children. *Language Learning* 29: 295–303.

de Jong-Lambert, C. (2003). From the islands to the classroom and back. *The Christian Science Monitor*, 15 April 2003. <http://www.csmonitor.com/2003/0415/p13s02-lecs.html>, accessed 15 December 2003. Reprinted in *Pidgins and Creoles in Education (PACE) Newsletter* 14, 8–11.

Decker, K. (2000). The use of Belize Kriol to improve English proficiency. Paper presented at the 5th International Creole Workshop, Florida International University.

Dejean, Y. (2010). Creole and education in Haiti. In A.K. Spears and C.M. Berotte Joseph (eds), *The Haitian Creole Language: History, Structure, Use, and Education*, 199–216. Lanham, MD: Lexington.

Devonish, H.S. (2007). *Language and Liberation: Creole Language and Politics in the Caribbean* (2nd edition). Kingston: Arawak.

Devonish, H.S. and Carpenter, K. (2007). *Full Bilingual Education in a Creole Language Situation: The Jamaican Bilingual Primary Education Project.* St Augustine, Trinidad & Tobago: Society for Caribbean Linguistics (Occasional Paper No. 35).

Dijkhoff, M. and Pereira, J. (2010). Language and education in Aruba, Bonaire and Curaçao. In Migge, B. Léglise, I. and Bartens, A. (eds), *Creoles in Education: An Appraisal of Current Programs and Projects*, 237–272. Amsterdam/Philadelphia: Benjamins.

Eades, D., Jacobs, S., Hargrove, E. and Menacker, T. (2006). Pidgin, local identity, and schooling in Hawai'i. In S.J. Nero (ed.), *Dialects, Englishes, Creoles, and Education*, 149–163. Mahwah, NJ: Erlbaum.

Elsasser, N. and Irvine, P. (1987). English and Creole: The dialectics of choice in a college writing program. In I. Shor (ed.), *Freire for the Classroom: A Sourcebook for Literacy Teaching*, 129–149. Portsmouth, MA: Boynton/Cook.

Feldman, C.F., Addison Stone, C., Wertsch, J.V. and Strizich, M. (1977). Standard and nonstandard dialect competencies of Hawaiian Creole English speakers. *TESOL Quarterly* 11: 41–50.

Feldman, C.F., Addison Stone, C. and Renderer, B. (1990). Stage, transfer, and academic achievement in dialect-speaking Hawaiian adolescents. *Child Development* 61: 472–484.

Ferreira, J-A.S. (2010). Bilingual education among the Karipúna and Galibi-Marwono. In Migge, B. Léglise, I. and Bartens, A. (eds), *Creoles in Education: An*

Appraisal of Current Programs and Projects, 211–236. Amsterdam/Philadelphia: Benjamins.

Fischer, K. (1992a). Educating speakers of Caribbean English in the United States. In J. Siegel (ed.), *Pidgins, Creoles and Nonstandard Dialects in Education*, 99–123. Melbourne: Applied Linguistics Association of Australia (Occasional Paper no. 12).

Fischer, K. (1992b). Report. *Pidgins and Creoles in Education (PACE) Newsletter* 3: 1.

Gonsalves, G.E. (1996). Language policy and education reform: The case of Cape Verdean. In C.E. Walsh (ed.), *Education Reform and Social Change: Multicultural Voices, Struggles and Visions*, 31–36. Mahwah, NJ: Lawrence Erlbaum.

Gordon, R.G. (2005). *Ethnologue: Languages of the World*. Dallas: Summer Institute of Linguistics International.

Hawkins, E. (1987). *Awareness of Language: An Introduction* (revised edition). Cambridge: Cambridge University Press.

Higgins, C. (2010). Raising critical language awareness in Hawai'i: Da Pidgin Coup. In Migge, B. Léglise, I. and Bartens, A. (eds), *Creoles in Education: An Appraisal of Current Programs and Projects*, 31–54. Amsterdam/Philadelphia: Benjamins.

Hudson, J. (1984). Kriol or English: An unanswered question in the Kimberleys. Paper presented at the 54th ANZAAS Conference, Canberra.

ILEA Afro-Caribbean Language and Literacy Project in Further and Adult Education (1990). *Language and Power*. London: Harcourt Brace Jovanovich.

James, C. and Garrett, P. (eds) (1991). *Language Awareness in the Classroom*. London: Longman.

Kephart, R.F. (1992). Reading creole English does not destroy your brain cells! In J. Siegel (ed.), *Pidgins, Creoles and Nonstandard Dialects in Education*, 67–86. Melbourne: Applied Linguistics Association of Australia (Occasional Paper no. 12).

Koskinen, A. (2010). Kriol in Canribbean Nicaragua schools. In Migge, B. Léglise, I. and Bartens, A. (eds), *Creoles in Education: An Appraisal of Current Programs and Projects*, 133–165. Amsterdam/Philadelphia: Benjamins.

Leste, A., Valentin, J. and Hoareau, F. (2005). The SACMEQ II Project in Seychelles: A Study of the Conditions of Schooling and the Quality of Education. Harare and Mahé: Southern and Eastern Africa Consortium for Monitoring Educational Quality (SACMEQ) and Seychelles Ministry for Education and Youth.

Locher, U. (2010). Education in Haiti. In A.K. Spears and C.M. Berotte Joseph (eds), *The Haitian Creole Language: History, Structure, Use, and Education*, 177–197. Lanham, MD: Lexington.

Mann, C.C. (1996). Anglo-Nigerian Pidgin in Nigerian education: A survey of policy, practice and attitudes. In T. Hickey and J. Williams (eds), *Language, Education and Society in a Changing World*, 93–106. Clevedon: Multilingual Matters.

Menacker, T. (1998). A visit to CAP. *Pidgins and Creoles in Education (PACE) Newsletter* 9: 3–4.

Migge, B., Léglise, I. and Bartens, A. (eds) (2010). *Creoles in Education: An Appraisal of Current Programs and Projects*. Amsterdam/Philadelphia: Benjamins.

Morren, R.C. (2001). Creole-based trilingual education in the Caribbean archipelago of San Andres, Providence and Santa Catalina. *Journal of Multilingual and Multicultural Development* 22: 227–241.

Morren, R.C. (2004). Linguistic results of a Creole reading inventory. Paper presented at the Conference of the Society for Caribbean Linguistics and the Society for Pidgin and Creole Linguistics, Curaçao.

Morren, R.C. (2010). Trilingual education: On the islands of San Andres, Providence and Santa Catalina. In Migge, B. Léglise, I. and Bartens, A. (eds), *Creoles in Education: An Appraisal of Current Programs and Projects*, 297–322. Amsterdam/Philadelphia: Benjamins.

Mühleisen, S. (2002). *Creole Discourse: Exploring Prestige Formation and Change across Caribbean English-lexicon Creoles*. Amsterdam/Philadelphia: Benjamins.

Murtagh, E.J. (1982). Creole and English as languages of instruction in bilingual education with Aboriginal Australians: Some research findings. *International Journal of the Sociology of Language* 36, 15–33.

Nero, S.J. (1997). English is my native language ... or so I believe. *TESOL Quarterly* 31, 585–592.

Nero, S.J. (2001). *Englishes in Contact: Anglophone Caribbean Students in an Urban College*. Cresskill, NJ: Hampton.

Nero, S.J. (2006). Language identity and education of Caribbean English speakers. *World Englishes* 25: 501–511.

Pratt-Johnson, Y. (1993). Curriculum for Jamaican Creole-speaking students in New York City. *World Englishes* 12: 257–264.

Rajah-Carrim, A. (2007). Mauritian Creole and language attitudes in the education system of multiethnic and multilingual Mauritius. *Journal of Multilingual and Multicultural Development* 28: 51–71.

Ravel, J-L. and Thomas, P. (1985). *État de la réforme de l'enseignement aux Seychelles (1981–1985)*. Paris: Ministère des Relations Extérieures, Coopération et Développement.

Ray, C. (1996). Report: Papua New Guinea. *Pidgins and Creoles in Education (PACE) Newsletter* 7: 3.

290 JEFF SIEGEL

Reynolds, S.B. (1999). Mutual intelligibility? Comprehension problems between American Standard English and Hawai'i Creole English in Hawai'i's public schools. In J.R. Rickford and S. Romaine (eds), *Creole Genesis, Attitudes and Discourse: Studies Celebrating Charlene J. Sato*, 303–319. Amsterdam/Philadelphia: Benjamins.

Rickford, J.R. (1999). *African American Vernacular English: Features, Evolution, Educational Implications*. Oxford: Blackwell.

Rickford, J.R. (2002). Linguistics, education, and the Ebonics firestorm. In J.E. Alatis, H.E. Hamilton and A-H. Tan (eds), *Linguistics, Language and the Professions (Georgetown University Roundtable on Languages and Linguistics, 2000)*, 25–45. Washington, DC: Georgetown University Press.

Roberts, P.A. (1994). Integrating Creole into Caribbean classrooms. *Journal of Multilingual and Multicultural Development* 15: 47–62.

Rogers, T.S. (1996). Poisoning pidgins in the park: The study and status of Hawaiian Creole. In J.E. Alatis, C.A. Straehle, M. Ronkin and B. Gallenberger (eds), *Linguistics, Language Acquisition and Language Variation: Current Trends and Future Prospects Georgetown University Roundtable on Languages and Linguistics, 1996*, 221–235. Washington, DC: Georgetown University Press.

Romaine, S. (1999). Changing attitudes to Hawai'i Creole English: Fo' find one good job, you gotta know how fo' talk like one haole. In J.R. Rickford and S. Romaine (eds), *Creole Genesis, Attitudes and Discourse: Studies Celebrating Charlene J. Sato*, 287–301. Amsterdam/Philadelphia: Benjamins.

Rynkofs, J.T. (1993). *Culturally Responsive Talk Between a Second Grade Teacher and Hawaiian Children during Writing Workshop*. PhD dissertation. University of New Hampshire.

Rynkofs, J.T. (2008). Culturally responsive talk between a second grade teacher and native Hawaiian children during a 'writing workshop'. *Educational Perspectives* 41: 44–54.

Schmidt, R. (1990). The role of consciousness in second language learning. *Applied Linguistics* 11: 129–158.

Schmidt, R. (1993). Awareness and second language acquisition. *Annual Review of Applied Linguistics* 13: 206–226.

Siegel, J. (1992). Teaching initial literacy in a pidgin language: A preliminary evaluation. In J. Siegel (ed.), *Pidgins, Creoles and Nonstandard Dialects in Education*, 53–65. Melbourne: Applied Linguistics Association of Australia (Occasional Paper no. 12).

Siegel, J. (1993). Pidgins and creoles in education in Australia and the Southwest Pacific. In F. Byrne and J. Holm (eds), *Atlantic Meets Pacific: A Global View of Pidginization and Creolization*, 299–308. Amsterdam: Benjamins.

Siegel, J. (1997). Using a pidgin language in formal education: Help or hindrance? *Applied Linguistics* 18: 86–100.

Siegel, J. (1999). Creoles and minority dialects in education: An overview. *Journal of Multilingual and Multicultural Development* 20: 508–531.

Siegel, J. (2007). Creoles and minority dialects in education: An update. *Language and Education* 21: 66–86.

Simmons-McDonald, H. (2006). Vernacular instruction and bi-literacy development in French Creole speakers. In H. Simmons-McDonald and I. Robertson (eds), *Exploring the Boundaries of Caribbean Creole Languages*, 118–146. Kingston: University of West Indies Press.

Simmons-McDonald, H. (2010). Introducing French Creole as a language of instruction in St Lucia. In Migge, B. Léglise, I. and Bartens, A. (eds), *Creoles in Education: An Appraisal of Current Programs and Projects*, 183–209. Amsterdam/Philadelphia: Benjamins.

Skutnabb-Kangas, T. (1988). Multilingualism and the education of minority children. In T. Skutnabb-Kangas and J. Cummins (eds), *Minority Education: From Shame to Struggle*, 9–44. Clevedon: Multilingual Matters.

Snow, C.E. (1990). Rationales for native language instruction: Evidence from research. In A.M. Padilla, H.H. Fairchild and C.M. Valdez (eds), *Bilingual Education: Issues and Strategies*, 60–74. Newbury Park: Sage.

Spears, A.K. and C.M. Berotte Joseph (eds) (2010). *The Haitian Creole Language: History, Structure, Use, and Education*. Lanham, MD: Lexington.

Speidel, G.E. (1987). Conversation and language learning in the classroom. In K.E. Nelson and A. van Kleek (eds), *Children's Language (Vol. 6)*, 99–135. Hillsdale, NJ: Erlbaum.

Tamura, E.H. (1996). Power, status, and Hawaii Creole English: An example of linguistic intolerance in American history. *Pacific Historical Review* 65: 431–454.

Thomas, W.P. and V.P. Collier (2002). *A National Study of School Effectiveness for Language Minority Students' Long-term Academic Achievement*. Santa Cruz: Center for Research on Education, Diversity and Excellence.

Trouillot-Lévy, J. (2010). Creole in education in Haiti: A case study. In A.K. Spears and C.M. Berotte Joseph (eds), *The Haitian Creole Language: History, Structure, Use, and Education*, 217–228. Lanham, MD: Lexington.

UNESCO (1968). The use of vernacular languages in education: The report of the UNESCO meeting of specialists, 1951. In J.A. Fishman (ed.), *Readings in the Sociology of Language*, 688–716. The Hague: Mouton.

Wiley, T.G. (1996). *Literacy and Language Diversity in the United States*. Washington, DC and McHenry, IL: Center for Applied Linguistics and Delta Systems.

Winer, L. (1990). Orthographic standardization for Trinidad and Tobago: Linguistic and sociopolitical considerations. *Language Problems and Language Planning* 14: 237–268.

Winer, L. (1993). Teaching speakers of Caribbean English Creoles in North American classrooms. In A.W. Glowka and D.M. Lance (eds), *Language Variation in North American English: Research and Teaching*, 191–198. New York: Modern Language Association of America.

Winer, L. (2006). Teaching English to Caribbean English Creole-speaking students in the Caribbean and North America. In S.J. Nero (ed.), *Dialects, Englishes, Creoles, and Education*, 105–136. Mahwah, NJ: Erlbaum.

Winford, D. (1994). Sociolinguistic approaches to language use in the Anglophone Caribbean. In M. Morgan (ed.), *The Social Construction of Identity in Creole Situations*, 43–62. Los Angeles: Center for Afro-American Studies, UCLA.

Wiruk, E. (2000). Report: Papua New Guinea. *Pidgins and Creoles in Education (PACE) Newsletter* 11: 1.

Wolfram, W. (1998). Dialect awareness and the study of language. In A. Egan-Robertson and D. Bloome (eds), *Students as researchers of Culture and Language in Their Own Communities*, 167–190. Cresskill, NJ: Hampton Press.

Wolfram, W. (2009). African American English and the public interest. In J.A. Kleifgen and G.C. Bond (eds), *The Languages of Africa and Diaspora: Educating for Awareness*, 249–269. Bristol: Multilingual Matters.

Wolfram, W. and Schilling-Estes, N. (1998). *American English: Dialects and Variation*. Malden, MA: Blackwell.

Zéphir, F. (1997). Haitian Creole language and bilingual education in the United States: Problem, right, or resource? *Journal of Multilingual and Multicultural Development* 18: 223–237.

ANDROULA YIAKOUMETTI

12 The Dangers of Dialects: Debunking (or Substantiating) the Myths

Introduction

Dialectal variation has been in the research spotlight for several decades. Researchers agree that dialectal diversity is natural and widespread. They argue in favour of linguistic equality and assert that nonstandard dialects are just as viable means of communication as standard varieties. However, research has also shown that, across the broader population, people do not judge nonstandard and standard varieties to be equal: most view dialects as inferior and, consequently, also view dialect speakers as somehow inferior to standard speakers. These views persist in spite of researchers' best efforts to demonstrate the structural regularity and invaluable sociolinguistic functions of dialects. Since many of the misinformed views that surround dialectal variation have been repeatedly addressed, it might seem trite to revisit the issue. However, the issue is a dynamic and perennial one in which new elements are constantly surfacing: dialectal variation affects us all and plays a significant role in the day-to-day interactions, educational attainment and professional advancement of many dialect speakers. It is for this reason that the debate on the role of dialects (with particular reference to the benefits and dangers associated with their use) shows no sign of abating.

Drawing on research carried out worldwide since the 1960s, the present chapter aims to debunk (or substantiate) the popular views that have formed as a consequence of concomitant use of dialect and standard in dialectally-diverse communities. The discussion focusses on regional and social dialects and explores some purported dangers of dialect as they are said to manifest themselves in formal education as well as in the workplace.

Background: standard–nonstandard dialect dichotomy

The culture and beliefs of mainstream societies are clearly reflected in the standard–nonstandard dialect dichotomy. The standard, the existence of which is a highly contested issue given the extent of linguistic diversity in today's world, has traditionally been assumed to be inherently better whereas the dialect has been associated with inherent deficit. Significantly, the ideal standard is a single variety (alluding to its almost unattainable uniqueness) whereas nonstandard dialects are numerous. Lanehart (1998) notes that the former is intentionally singular and the latter plural because this distinction denotes that there is only one right way to speak. The standard is seen as the correct variety against which other varieties are judged as sub-standard (Haig and Oliver, 2003). Nonstandard dialects have even been referred to as bastardized forms of the standard (Baugh, 1983). Linguists generally agree that linguistic difference is not a deficit and, as such, no deficits can be attributed to speakers of nonstandard dialects. Like many others (e.g. Wolfram et al., 1999), I assert that the standard and its assumed superiority is merely a mythical illusion: one simply has to look at multidialectal and multilingual societies in which speakers, for reasons of solidarity, are accustomed to codeswitching between various varieties to understand the falsehood of allegations of superiority of the standard (Le Page and Tabouret-Keller, 1985; Milroy, 1987). In addition, as Trudgill (1975) asserts, because dialects occur in continua, it is often impossible to draw boundaries between them. Indeed, language is in constant flux and, even among prototypical standard speakers, there is evidence of variation (Smakman, 2006; Grondelaers and van Hout, 2010).

Standard varieties gain their ascendancy as a result of particular historical, political, economic and social reasons (Toohey, 1986). Stubbs

(1980) describes the selection of a variety to serve as the standard as an 'accident'. Nevertheless, the existence and supremacy of the standard has been accepted as real by many lay persons and educational policy makers who associate nonstandard dialects with negative stereotypes, educational difficulty and socioeconomic stagnation (Ohama et al., 2000). Indeed, discussion of the standard–nonstandard dialect dichotomy has, at times, approached polemical proportions (Clarkson, 1977). Although the inferiority of dialect is a myth that is unsupported by any linguistic basis, this myth is so powerful and deeply entrenched in our society that it can often cause harm. Wolfram et al. (1999) and Siegel (2006) make the case that education itself continuously perpetuates the perceived superiority of the standard and inferiority of nonstandard dialects. Sterzuk (2008) warns us of the devastating effects that misconceptions regarding linguistic equality can bring about in relation to the academic performance and social inclusion of speakers of nonstandard dialects. Indeed, many researchers around the globe have discussed such effects. In Australia, Beresford and Gray (2006) explain that, for decades, Australian Aboriginal youth has actively and/or passively resisted participation in educational processes. In the United States, it has regularly been assumed that students who speak African American English have inherent language problems which has often meant that they have been misdirected into special-education classrooms or even referred to language pathologists (Adger et al., 1993). James (1996) has gone as far as using the term 'self-revulsion' to describe the devastating effects that could develop in Bruneian children if their home dialect of Brunei Malay is not treated with respect in class. Roof (1984) has described dialect students' writing experience as traumatic because they are made to feel that their language is inadequate for writing.

The frequent imposition of the standard variety on dialect speakers in many educational systems is not in keeping with equal rights for all. It is no surprise then that this imposition has been characterized as linguistically oppressive and discriminatory (Heit and Blair, 1993, St Denis and Schick, 2003). To avoid institutional racism, educational stakeholders need to re-think the way in which dialectal diversity in education is approached (Sterzuk, 2008). Indeed, forty years ago, Labov (1973) showed that dialectal students' educational underperformance does not lie with the students but with the failure of educational institutions to recognize and build on their existing verbal abilities, linguistic systems and cultures. Goodman and Buck (1997) also assigned great responsibility for dialect students' underachievement to educational systems. They view the rejection of students' dialects and educators' propensity to confuse linguistic difference with linguistic deficiency as key factors which undermine the academic experience of dialect students. It is therefore not dialect *per se* which should be blamed.

The purported dangers addressed here are the outcomes of the standard ideology which dictates that (i) standard speakers are superior to non-standard-dialect speakers, (ii) standard speakers do better in school whereas dialect speakers are associated with low levels of academic attainment, (iii) banning the dialect from the classroom will ensure that the standard will be learned and produced without any interference from the dialect, (iv) dialects are not good enough for formal education, and (v) standard speakers are more employable.

Myth: dialect speakers are inferior to standard speakers
Status: debunked

Since the 1960s, research has demonstrated that dialect speakers themselves assign more unfavourable characteristics to other dialect speakers than to standard speakers. Tucker and Lambert (1967), using a matched-guise technique to investigate the attitudes of college students from the southern states of the US towards various American English dialects, discovered that southern black students had more favourable impressions of people who spoke in the standard educated northern variety than in their own southern black dialect of English. Extending Tucker and Lambert's (1967) study, Hewett (1971) set out to determine the attitudes held by pre-service teachers towards standard and nonstandard varieties of American English. She discovered that teachers consistently rated standard speakers highly and nonstandard speakers poorly on education, intelligence, upbringing and speaking ability. Independently of the merits and disadvantages of the matched-guise technique which have often been debated (Giles and Coupland, 1991), it is obvious from such early studies that students and teachers hold negative views towards dialect speakers. In a more recent study, Koch et al. (2001) demonstrated that participants in their study rated standard American English more favourably than Black English. Moving away from the US to Italy, research indicated that southern Italians rated standard Italian speaking adults more positively than dialect speakers from the south on such factors as democratic values, external appearance, cultural refinement and spirituality and creativity (Marcato et al., 1974). Similar findings were recorded in students: Cremona and Bates (1977), for example, note that dialect-speaking students in a primary school setting in which use of dialects was strongly discouraged described their dialects as 'hick', 'bad' and 'abnormal'. Similar findings relating to the pejorative view that some teachers hold towards dialect speakers and their academic abilities were recorded in Wales. Garrett et al. (1999) discovered that teachers felt greater affinities towards students who strove for the standard Received Pronunciation rather than with those (such as the Valleys speakers) who were not stereotypically associated with successful employment of the standard.

However, and crucially, research has also indicated that the assumed superiority of standard speakers collapses when people are unaware of the social status of different accents and dialects. An experiment conducted by Giles and Trudgill (cited in Andersson and Trudgill, 1990) cleverly demonstrates that it is not the linguistic value of dialects that matters to people but rather the social status of the varieties. Participants in the UK and the US were asked to rank British English accents based on desirability. The findings revealed that, in the UK, the accents were easily identified and ranked by prestige. However, in the US, subjects who were unaware of the social status of the accents ranked them differently. Research such as this provides ample evidence in support of the fact that standard superiority – and consequentially standard-speaker superiority – is only a myth. In the case of the varieties involved in the specific experiment, lack of awareness of the social attitudes associated with British English accents meant that the mythical illusion of the superiority of certain accents over others was lost.

Myth: dialect-speaking students struggle to exclude dialectal
features in their standard production
Status: substantiated (under certain circumstances)

It has been argued that students who speak a dialect cannot help but
include elements of their dialect into their standard production. This
dialectal interference has been associated with underachievement and the
blame for dialect students' underachievement has been attributed to the
fact that students are dialectal. However, as Giesbers et al. (1988) note,
dialect speaking is not an educational disadvantage *per se*. The authors
came to this conclusion when they tested dialect-speaking and standard-
speaking students in the municipality of Gennep in the Netherlands
and found that dialect speakers did well in some measures and standard
speakers did well in others. There were even cases in which there was no
difference between standard and dialect speakers: for instance, similar
levels of spelling mistakes, which were the most important source of writing errors, were recorded.

Having taken the blame for underachievement away from dialect
speaking, it still must be noted that dialect-speaking students face difficulties in the classroom when compared with their standard-speaking peers
because they are mostly unaware of the exact differences between their
dialects and the standard (Edwards, 1983; Valdés, 1995, 2001). Numerous
studies (some of which will be briefly explored below) have demonstrated
this lack of awareness which results in dialectal interference, albeit with
varying prevalence.

Upon investigating the influence of nonstandard dialects such as the
Tyneside dialect on pupils' ability to write in Standard English in the UK,
Williamson (1990) concluded that there was interference (even though this
interference was judged to be minor compared to difficulties in master-
ing aspects of the writing system itself). In a later study, Williamson and
Hardman (1997) demonstrated that students used nonstandard dialect
forms in their speech and writing (with more identified in oral production). Abd-Kadir et al. (2003) drew similar conclusions when investigating

Dominican students' writing in Standard Dominican English. The authors agreed that interference from nonstandard Creole dialect occurred even though they argued that it was less frequent than grammatical and orthographic errors (which were not attributed to the dialect). Winch and Gingell (1994) warned that researchers should not confound developmental errors with dialectal interference errors factors that influence children's performance. Other studies (carried out in Cyprus) have demonstrated that dialectal interference is a daily reality in classrooms even though exclusive use of the standard is advocated (Yiakoumetti et al., 2007; Ioannidou, 2009).

As can be seen from the abovementioned studies, dialectal interference does take place. However, caution is necessary such that the dialect is not blamed for dialect students' underachievement. It must also be emphasized that, when dialects are formally introduced into education and are systematically contrasted with the standard, dialectal interference is significantly reduced. (This issue is addressed under the myth 'dialects are unfit for formal education'.) It is for this reason that the view that dialect-speaking students cannot avoid dialectal interference is only partially true.

Myth: it pays to exorcise dialects from formal education
Status: debunked

Traditionally, it has been the norm for many language policies to explicitly ban dialects in education and to promote the standard variety. It has been advocated that, since linguistic prejudice can inhibit people's advancement, students had better talk and write like people with power (Sledd, 1969). Such policies are based on the premise that exorcising dialects from the classroom will inevitably lead to dialect speakers ceasing to use their home varieties as they successfully acquire the one 'correct' variety. Such an acquisition has been viewed as a currency of purported payment in achievement terms. In addition, it has been argued by believers in the supremacy of the standard that exclusive education in the standard will develop greater cognitive and logical abilities. Orr (1987), for example, argued that, for speakers of African American English (AAE), language is a barrier to success in mathematics and science. She believed that AAE was inferior to standard American English and thus incapable of conveying the abstract and logical functions that are conveyed in the standard. She thus concluded that AAE speakers perform poorly in maths and science.

However, research has shown that, contrary to common belief, when dialect-speaking students are taught in the standard variety alone, they do not perform as well as students who are taught bidialectally. Taking the case of Cyprus as illustrative of the potential pedagogical harm of banning a nonstandard dialect, research has shown that students (i) include more dialectal interference in their written and oral production of the standard (Yiakoumetti, 2006), (ii) hold negative views towards their dialects (Yiakoumetti et al., 2005), and (iii) underperform in a foreign language (Yiakoumetti and Mina, 2011). It is clear from this recent research that dialectal interference is more prominent when students are not explicitly taught about the linguistic and sociolinguistic differences between the varieties used in their settings. It is also evident that schools and language policies have not been entirely successful in their efforts to eradicate dialects.

The persistence of dialectal variation in education (despite common efforts to eradicate it) reflects the irreplaceable functions that dialects serve. As Trudgill (1983) maintains, dialects represent membership of a particular culture, class or geographical group. The imposed use of other varieties thus represents attempted violations of loyalties to one's group. The prominent presence of dialectal variation in education also reflects the reality of dialect speakers' lives: dialects survive (and, in many cases, thrive) because there is a population of speakers who use them in their daily lives. The presence of dialects in education is indicative of the fact that dialect speakers have refused to be silenced.

Myth: dialects are unfit for formal education
Status: debunked

The notion of dialect is frequently present in discussions about educational failure. Unfortunately, the role of dialects in formal education is associated with unjustified stereotypes. The fear shared by parents, teachers and language-policy makers is that children who are not taught exclusively in the standard but are, instead, also exposed to dialects will not become sufficiently proficient in the standard (which is the variety associated with power and prestige). Indeed, a number of studies has demonstrated that many dialect-speaking (as well as standard-speaking) students, teachers and parents view dialect as a liability and as inappropriate for formal education (Hoover, 1978; Sciriha, 1996; Hoover et al., 1997; Shameen, 2004). It is perhaps surprising to some that even dialect speakers themselves have such views. In an early study, Labov (1972) recorded this contradictory tendency: speakers with highly stigmatized speech features demonstrated the greatest tendency to stigmatize others for their use of these features. As Lippi-Green (1997) states, nonstandard speakers who are stigmatized ultimately consent to the standard ideology and come to denigrate their own variety even while they continue to use it.

Research carried out in various linguistic settings has clearly indicated that, far from harming students, introducing dialectal diversity into education often leads to academic advancement. In the US, dialect awareness programmes which address the linguistic differences between African American English and Standard American English led to improved student language performance (Harris-Wright, 1999). In Canada, it has recently been shown that Standard English as a Second Dialect programmes led to improvement in Aboriginal students' reading skills (Battisti et al., 2009). In Australia, the implementation of a two-way bidialectal education led to students' repertoire building (Malcolm and Truscott, this volume). Cognitive development and acquisition of the standard language was repeatedly recorded in a number of geographical and linguistic settings where expanded pidgins or creoles were used in formal education (Siegel, this volume). In Europe, various studies conducted in settings in which regional dialects are used indicated that, when children are exposed to dialects as well as the standard in the classroom, they demonstrate heightened academic performance (e.g. Sweden: Österberg, 1961; the Netherlands: Stijnen and Vallen, 1989; Norway: Bull, 1990; Cyprus: Yiakoumetti, 2007; Switzerland: Ender and Straßl, 2009).

The above studies unanimously point to the very positive outcomes that students can experience when their nonstandard varieties are utilized in education and thus refute the view that dialects are unfit for education.

Myth: exposing standard speakers to dialect is detrimental or of no benefit
Status: unresolved

The effect of dialect exposure on standard-speaking students is an area that has not yet received research attention. This is not surprising. Traditionally, standard-speaking students have had the good fortune of being educated in their familiar variety and thus have been shown to outperform dialect-speaking students (Jencks and Phillips, 1998, Connor and Craig, 2006). However, when devising language policies or pedagogical approaches, all students in dialectally-diverse communities should be taken into account.

As this is not a topic associated with empirical findings, the discussion is necessarily characterized by my own hypotheses which are largely based on principles associated with bilingualism and multilingualism. However, I thought it useful to address this topic as I have repeatedly been asked by standard speakers how dialects can be of benefit to them.

Extensive research on bilingualism/multilingualism and education has pointed to the various benefits speakers of multiple varieties enjoy when compared to their monolingual counterparts (Cummins, 1996; Bialystok, 2001). The same may well hold true for speakers in dialectally-diverse communities. Depending on the degree and type of nonstandard dialect exposure, monodialectal (standard-speaking) students could become passive or even active bidialectals/multidialectals. Linguistically speaking, exposing standard-speaking students to other dialects would be likely to enrich their vocabulary and to make them more aware of the differences and similarities between their varieties and those of their classmates. Societally speaking, standard-speaking students would widen their cultural horizons. Such students would come to question why people speak differently and this could be the staging point for discussions on the history of the development and standardization of linguistic varieties. All students would thus have the opportunity to understand how complex, diverse and intricate a language is. Educationally speaking, standard-speaking students may start to think about how their speech and writing is perceived by their dialectal peers. If appropriate, such thinking could even lead to accommodation of their peers' needs such that their standard discourse is more appreciated or better understood by dialect-speaking students. Sociolinguistically speaking, standard-speaking students may benefit from heightened awareness of the functions of the different varieties employed in their communities. Preliminary statistical findings show that, in the bidialectal community of Cyprus, monodialectal students have significantly lower sociolinguistic awareness of the expected functions of each variety compared to their bidialectal peers (Constantinou and Yiakoumetti, unpublished). Even though this research is on-going and qualitative analyses point to an alternative sociolinguistic awareness among monodialectal students, the results may be indicative of the benefits of speaking more than one dialectal variety.

Allowing dialectal variation in the classroom would mean that speakers of different varieties (standard and nonstandard) can model and represent their varieties. All students could be proud of their backgrounds and languages and thus no one would be made to feel inferior. Classrooms could become forums where all children have the opportunity to succeed and all children could feel welcome and included. Indeed, it has been suggested that reducing the achievement gap between standard-speaking and nonstandard-speaking students would do more to reduce racial inequality (in the US context) than any other single strategy (Jencks and Phillips, 1998).

If the validity of all students' varieties is acknowledged and the different (or even shared) functions of varieties are explored in the classroom, students would become more accepting of diversity (irrespective of their mother tongues). Fostering ideologies of equality and affirmative action is no small feat. If such fostering could be aided through exposure to accurate sociolinguistic information, why should language policy makers refuse to allow it? Of course, one has to be realistic and accept that social prejudice is difficult to eradicate. Indeed, as May (2000) asserts, no matter how cautiously the language policies that advocate diversity are promoted, they will invariably invoke opposition, especially by those standard speakers who wish to remain monolingual/monodialectal. Great initial effort is thus necessary to achieve favourable attitudes towards nonstandard varieties. Attitudinal change should then be seen as a stepping stone for eventual success. If linguistic diversity is presented as normal and, indeed, desirable to young students, there is a greater chance for our education systems to produce generations who are less discriminatory.

Myth: dialect speakers are less employable
Status: partially debunked

Over the years, dialect speaking has been linked to (un)employability. Many believe that using the standard as opposed to a dialect would open up additional occupational options. In an early study, Atkins (1993) reported that employment recruiters discriminated on the basis of nonstandard social dialects. In her study, recruiters held negative views towards 93 per cent of Black English characteristics and 58 per cent of Appalachian English characteristics. Recent studies have also demonstrated similar findings. Employing the matched-guise technique, Rakić et al. (2011) discovered that subjects who spoke regional German varieties in a simulated job interview were perceived as having lower competence and hirability than Standard German speaking subjects. Such findings are in line with the policies of numerous employers which aim to minimize employees' dialectal variation in the belief that clients would be persuaded more easily by standard speech (Carlson and McHenry, 2006).

However, other studies portray a different, contradictory picture. Mai and Hoffmann's (2011) work on customer satisfaction in Germany shows that, in contrast to conventional wisdom, salespersons who spoke with regional German dialects were perceived more favourably by purchasers. In fact, buyers did not devalue salespersons with a dialect. Rather, the use of a regional dialect was associated with satisfaction which fostered an intention to purchase. The authors concluded that it would be beneficial for companies if they did not urge sales employees to conceal their dialect.

As one can see, a regional dialect is not a liability which necessarily leads to a devaluation of dialect-speaking employees and their employers. It therefore seems unjustified that many employers in bidialectal or multi-dialectal societies demand that employees do not employ their dialects during interactions with clients. Such insistence is especially unnecessary in settings where all citizens share the same nonstandard dialect and learn the standard only once they enter formal education.

Conclusion

Dialectal variation has received considerable research attention. In the 1990s, Wolfram (1995, 1998) asserted that linguists, sociolinguists and dialectologists had not achieved as much as they had wished for with respect to the public understanding of dialectal diversity. Sadly, this assertion still holds true today in many dialectally-diverse settings all over the world. We continue to hear misinformed views regarding the linguistic integrity of nonstandard dialects and speakers. There is still a wide discrepancy between the truths perceived through research findings and widespread public opinions.

This chapter addressed some of the mythical dangers associated with dialectal variation. Drawing on past research, the chapter has highlighted that

(i)   it is not the linguistic value of dialects that matters to people but rather the social status of the varieties,

(ii) dialectal exorcising in education does not work,

(iii) allowing dialectal variation into education can lead to students' heightened academic performance, and

(iv) dialect speech can play a positive role in interactions between employees and clients.

These are some of the burning issues facing language-policy makers in bidialectal and multidialectal communities. When research is consulted appropriately and unjustified attitudes towards dialectal variation are put aside, it is clear that promoting such variation can have only positive outcomes. The self-esteem, social inclusion and academic and professional advancement of dialectal speakers will be enhanced when dialects are not devalued. If all citizens are to enjoy equal opportunities, then their linguistic rights must be respected (Skutnabb-Kangas, 2001). It is thus time to rethink education: harnessing dialectal variation will almost always lead to better education.

References

Abd-Kadir, J., Hardman, F. and Blaize, J. (2003). Dialect Interference in the Writing of Primary School Children in the Commonwealth of Dominica, *L1 – Educational Studies in Language and Literature*, 3, 225–238.

Adger, C., Wolfram, W., Detwyler, J. and Harry, B. (1993). Confronting Dialect Minority Issues in Special Education: Reactive and Proactive Perspectives. Paper presented at the 3rd National Research Symposium on Limited English Proficient Student Issues: Focus on Middle and High School Issues, Washington, DC.

Andersson, L. and Trudgill, P. (1990). *Bad Language*. Oxford: Basil Blackwell.

Atkins, C.P. (1993). Do Employment Recruiters Discriminate on the Basis of Nonstandard Dialects?, *Journal of Employment Counseling*, 30 (3), 108–118.

Battisti, M., Friesen, J. and Krauth, B. (2009). Non-standard English at School: Can Targeted Funding Improve Student Achievement? Paper presented at the European Association of Labour Economists conference, 10–12 September, Estonia: Tallin.

Baugh, J. (1983). *Black Street Speech: Its History, Structure, and Survival*. Austin: University of Texas Press.

Beresford, Q. and Gray, J. (2006). Models of Policy Development in Aboriginal Education: Issues and Discourse, *Australian Journal of Education*, 50 (3).

Bialystok, E. (2001). *Bilingualism in Development: Language, Literacy, and Cognition*. Cambridge: Cambridge University Press.

Bull, T. (1990). Teaching School Beginners to Read and Write in the Vernacular. In E.H. Jahr and O. Lorentz (eds), *Tromsø Linguistics in the Eighties*, 69–84. Oslo: Novus Press.

Carlson, H.K. and McHenry, M.A. (2006). Effect of Accent and Dialect on Employability, *Journal of Employment Counseling*, 43 (2), 70–83.

Clarkson, W.M. (1977). The Vernacular vs. Standard Spanish in the Bilingual Classroom: Implications for Teacher Training Programs for Chicanos, *Hispania*, 60 (4), 965–967.

Connor, C.M. and Craig, H.K. (2006). African American Preschoolers' Language, Emergent Literacy Skills, and Use of African American English: A Complex Relation, *Journal of Speech, Language, and Hearing Research*, 49, 771–792.

Constantinou, F. and Yiakoumetti, A. (unpublished manuscript). Monodialectal and Bidialectal Pupils' Sociolinguistic Awareness of the Phenomenon of Bidialectism in Cyprus. University of Cambridge.

Cremona, C. and Bates, E. (1977). The Development of Attitudes Toward Dialect in Italian Children, *Journal of Psycholinguistic Research*, 6 (3), 223–232.

Cummins, J. (1996). *Negotiating Identities: Education for Empowerment in a Diverse Society*. Los Angeles, CA: Association for Bilingual Education.

Edwards, V. (1983). *Language in Multicultural Classrooms: Education in a Multicultural Society*. London: Batsford Academic and Educational.

Ender, A. and Straßl, K. (2009). The Acquisition and Use of German in a Dialect-Speaking Environment: Facets of Inclusion and Exclusion of Immigrant Children in Switzerland, *International Journal of Applied Linguistics*, 19 (2), 173–187.

Garrett, P., Coupland, N. and Williams, A. (1999). Evaluating Dialect in Discourse: Teachers' and Teenagers' Responses to Young English Speakers in Wales, *Language in Society*, 28, 321–354.

Giesbers, H., Kroon, S. and Liebrand, R. (1988). Bidialectalism and Primary School Achievement in a Dutch Dialect Area, *Language and Education*, 2 (2), 77–93.

Giles, H. and Coupland, N. (1991). *Language: Contexts and Consequences*. Buckingham: Open University Press.

Goodman, K.S. and Buck, C. (1997). Dialect Barriers to Reading Comprehension Revisited, *The Reading Teacher*, 50 (6), 454–459.

Grondelaers, S. and van Hout, R. (2010). Is Standard Dutch with a Regional Accent Standard or Not? Evidence from Native Speakers' Attitudes, *Language Variation and Change*, 22, 221–239.

Haig, Y. and Oliver, R. (2003). Language Variation and Education: Teachers' Perceptions, *Language and Education*, 17 (4), 266–280.

Harris-Wright, K. (1999). Enhancing Bidialectalism in Urban African American Students. In C.T. Adger, D. Christian and O. Taylor (eds), *Making the Connection: Language and Academic Achievement among African American Students*, 53–60. Washington, DC: Center for Applied Linguistics.

Heit, M. and Blair, H. (1993). Language Needs and Characteristics of Saskatchewan Indian and Metis Students: Implications for Educators. In S. Morris, K. McLeod and M. Danesi (eds), *Aboriginal Language and Education: the Canadian Experience*, 103–128. Oakville: Mosaic.

Hewett, N. (1971). Reactions of Prospective English Teachers toward Speakers of a Non-standard Dialect, *Language Learning*, 21 (2), 205–212.

Hoover, M.R. (1978). Community Attitudes toward Black English, *Language in Society*, 7, 65–87.

Hoover, M.R., McNair, F., Lewis, R.S.A. and Politzer, L.R. (1997). African American English Attitudes Measures for Teachers. In R. Jones (ed.), *Handbook of Test and Measurements for Black Populations*, 383–393. Hampton, VA: Cobb.

Ioannidou, E. (2009). Using the 'Improper' Language in the Classroom: The Conflict Between Language Use and Legitimate Varieties in Education. Evidence from a Greek Cypriot Classroom, *Language and Education*, 23 (3), 263–278.

James, C. (1996). Mother Tongue Use in Bilingual/Bidialectal Education: Implications for Bruneian Dwibahasa, *Journal of Multilingual and Multicultural Development*, 17 (2–4), 248–257.

Jencks, C. and Phillips, M. (1998). *The Black-White Test Score Gap*. Washington, DC: Brookings Institution.

Koch, L.M., Gross, A.M. and Kolts, R. (2001). Attitudes toward Black English and Code Switching, *Journal of Black Psychology*, 27, 29–42.

Labov, W. (1972). *Sociolinguistic Patterns*. Philadelphia: University of Philadelphia Press.

Labov, W. (1973). The Logic of Nonstandard English. In R.W. Baily and J.L. Robinson (eds), *Varieties of Present-Day English*, 319–354. New York: Macmillan.

Lambert, W. (1967). A Social Psychology of Bilingualism, *Journal of Social Issues*, 23 (2), 91–109.

Lanehart, S.L. (1998). African American Vernacular English and Education: the Dynamics of Pedagogy, Ideology, and Identity, *Journal of English Linguistics*, 26 (2), 122–136.

Le Page, R.B. and Tabouret-Keller, A. (1985). *Acts of Identity: Creole-Based Approaches to Language and Ethnicity*. Cambridge: Cambridge University Press.

Lippi-Green, L. (1997). *English with an Accent: Language, Ideology, and Discrimination in the United States*. New York: Routledge.

Mai, R. and Hoffmann, S. (2011). Four Positive Effects of a Salesperson's Regional Dialect in Services Selling, *Journal of Service Research*, DOI: 10.1177/1094670511414551.

Marcato, G., Ursini, F. and Politi, A. (1974). *Dialetto e Italiano*. Pisa: Pacini.

May, S. (2000). Accommodating and Resisting Minority Language Policy: The Case of Wales, *International Journal of Bilingual Education and Bilingualism*, 3 (2), 101–128.

Milroy, L. (1987). *Language and Social Networks*. Oxford: Basil Blackwell.

Ohama, M.L.F., Gotay, C.C., Pagano, I.S., Boles, L. and Craven, D.D. (2000). Evaluations of Hawaii Creole English and Standard English, *Journal of Language and Social Psychology*, 19, 357–377.

Orr, E.W. (1987). *Twice as Less*. New York: Norton.

Österberg, T. (1961). *Bilingualism and the First School Language: An Educational Problem Illustrated by Results from a Swedish Dialect Area*. Umea, Sweden: Västerbottens Tryckeri.

Rakić, T., Steffens, M.C. and Mummendey, A. (2011). When it Matters how you Pronounce it: the Influence of Regional Accents on Job Interview Outcome, *British Journal of Psychology*, DOI: 10.111/j.2044–8295.2011.02051.x.

Roof, M. (1984). Dialect Collision and Student Trauma, *Journal of Teaching Writing*, 3 (1), 63–77.

Sciriha, L. (1996). *A Question of Identity: Language Use in Cyprus*. Nicosia: Intercollege Press.

Shameen, N. (2004). Language Attitudes in Multilingual Primary School in Fiji, *Language, Culture and Curriculum*, 17 (2), 154–172.

Siegel, J. (2006). Language Ideologies and the Education of Speakers of Marginalized Language Varieties: Adopting a Critical Awareness Approach, *Linguistics and Education*, 17, 157–174.

Skutnabb-Kangas, T. (2001). The Globalisation of (Educational) Language Rights, *International Review of Education*, 47 (3/4), 201–219.

Sledd, J. (1969). Bi-dialectalism: the Linguistics of White Supremacy, *English Journal*, 58 (9), 1307–1315–1329.

Smakman, D. (2006). *Standard Dutch in the Netherlands: A Sociolinguistic and Phonetic Description*. Utrecht: LOT Publishers.

St Denis, V. and Schick, C. (2003). What Makes Anti-racist Pedagogy in Teacher Education Difficult? Three Popular Ideological Assumptions, *Alberta Journal of Educational Research*, 49 (1), 55–69.

Stubbs, M. (1980). *Language and Literacy: The Sociolinguistics of Reading and Writing*. London: Routledge and Kegan Paul.

Sterzuk, A. (2008). Whose English counts? Indigenous English in Saskatchewan schools, *McGill Journal of Education*, 43 (1), 9–19.

Stijnen, S. and Vallen, T. (1989). The Kerkrade Project: Background, Main Findings and an Evaluation. In J. Cheshire, V. Edwards, H. Münstermann and B. Weltens (eds), *Dialect and Education*, 139–153. Clevedon: Multilingual Matters.

Toohey, K. (1986). Minority Educational Failure: is Dialect a Factor?, *Curriculum Inquiry*, 16 (2), 127–145.

Trudgill, P. (1983). *On Dialect: Social and Geographical Perspectives*. Oxford: Basil Blackwell.

Tucker, R.G. and Lambert, W.E. (1967). White and Negro Listeners' Reactions to Various American-English Dialects, *Social Forces*, 47, 463–468.

Valdés, G. (1995). The Teaching of Minority Languages as Academic Subjects: Pedagogical and Theoretical Challenges, *Modern Language Journal*, 79, 299–328.

Valdés, G. (2001). Heritage Language Students: Profiles and Possibilities. In J.K. Peyton, D.A. Ranard and S. McGinnis (eds), *Heritage Languages in America: Preserving a National Resource*, 37–80. Arlington, VA: Center for Applied Linguistics.

Williamson, J. (1990). 'Divven't Write That, Man': The Influence of Tyneside Dialect Forms on Children's Free Writing, *Educational Studies*, 16 (3), 251–260.

Williamson, J. and Hardman, F. (1997). To Purify the Dialect of the Tribe: Children's Use of Non-standard Dialect Grammar in Writing, *Educational Studies*, 23 (2), 157–168.

Winch, C. and Gingell, J. (1994). Dialect Interference and Difficulties with Writing: An Investigation in St. Lucian Primary Schools, *Language and Education*, 8 (3), 157–182.

Wolfram, W. (1995). Reconsidering dialects in TESOL, *TESOL Matters*, 5 (2), 1–22.

Wolfram, W. (1998). Language Ideology and Dialect: Understanding the Oakland Ebonics Controversy, *Journal of English Linguistics*, 26, 108–121.

Wolfram, W., Adger, T.C. and Christian, D. (1999). *Dialects in Schools and Communities.* Mahweh, NJ: Lawrence Erlbaum.

Yiakoumetti, A. (2006). A Bidialectal Programme for the Learning of Standard Modern Greek in Cyprus, *Applied Linguistics*, 27 (2), 295–317.

Yiakoumetti, A. (2007). Choice of Classroom Language in Bidialectal Communities: To Include or to Exclude the Dialect?, *Cambridge Journal of Education*, 37 (1), 51–66.

Yiakoumetti, A. and Mina, M. (2011). The Influence of First-language Bidialectism on Foreign-language Classrooms: Observations from Cyprus, *Language, Culture and Curriculum.*

Yiakoumetti, A., Evans, M. and Esch, E. (2005). Language Awareness in a Bidialectal Setting: The Oral Performance and Language Attitudes of Urban and Rural Students in Cyprus, *Language Awareness*, 14 (4), 254–260.

Yiakoumetti, A., Papapavlou, A. and Pavlou, P. (2007). The Degree of Dialectal Transference by Cypriots in a Strict Standard Modern Greek Context. In E. Agathopoulou, M. Dimitrakopoulou and D. Papadopoulou (eds), *Selected Papers on Theoretical and Applied Linguistics Vol. 1*, 266–273. Thessaloniki: Aristotle University of Thessaloniki.

Notes on Contributors

JESSICA BALL is a developmental-clinical psychologist and specialist in international child and family health education and research. She is a professor in the School of Child and Youth Care at the University of Victoria, Canada. Through her programme of research, Early Childhood Development Intercultural Partnerships, <http://www.ecdip.org>, she is primarily engaged in collaborative studies with Indigenous organizations and communities in Canada and the majority world. She is also a member of the Father Involvement Research Alliance of Canada, <http://www.fira.ca>. She has published over 100 journal articles and book chapters and three books, including *Supporting Indigenous Children's Development: Community University Partnerships*.

BARBARA MAY HANFORD BERNHARDT has been a speech-language pathologist since 1972 and a professor of speech-language pathology at the University of British Columbia, Canada, since 1990. Her main foci in teaching, research and publication have been speech and language development, assessment and intervention. Her current research involves two major projects: (1) speech, language and hearing support for First Nations, Métis and Inuit people in Canada and (2) an international crosslinguistic investigation of speech development. She has received a UBC Killam Teaching Prize and Honours of the Association for the BC Association of Speech-Language Pathologists and Audiologists.

SURESH CANAGARAJAH is the Erle Sparks Professor and Director of the Migration Studies Project at Pennsylvania State University, USA. He teaches World Englishes, Second Language Writing and Postcolonial Studies in the departments of English and Applied Linguistics. He taught previously in the University of Jaffna, Sri Lanka, and the City University of New York (Baruch College and the Graduate Center). His book *Resisting*

Linguistic Imperialism in English Teaching (1999) won the Modern Language Association's Mina Shaughnessy Award. *Geopolitics of Academic Writing* (2002) won the Gary Olson Award for the best book in social and rhetorical theory.

JOSEP M. COTS earned his PhD in English Philology at the University of Barcelona, Spain, in 1991. He is a professor in the Department of English and Linguistics of the University of Lleida, Catalonia, Spain, where he teaches English language and applied linguistics. He has carried out most of his research in the field of applied linguistics, focusing on applied discourse analysis, foreign language teaching and learning, multilingualism and intercultural competence. He is the director of a research group on internationalization and multilingualism in higher education, including researchers from three different universities, and supervises several PhD dissertation projects.

NELSON FLORES is an adjunct lecturer at the City University of New York, USA, and is finishing his doctoral dissertation in the PhD programme in Urban Education at the CUNY Graduate Center, with a specialization in language/literacy education and policy. His research uses poststructural and postcolonial social theory to examine how current US language ideologies marginalize language-minoritized students.

OFELIA GARCÍA is a professor in the PhD programme of Urban Education and of Hispanic and Luso-Brazilian Literatures and Languages at the Graduate Center of the City University of New York, USA. She has been Professor of Bilingual Education at Columbia University's Teachers College and Dean of the School of Education at the Brooklyn Campus of Long Island University. Among her recent books are *Bilingual Education in the 21st century: A global perspective; Educating Emergent Bilinguals* (with J. Kleifgen); *Handbook of Language and Ethnic Identity* (with J. Fishman); *Negotiating Language Policies in Schools: Educators as Policymakers* (with K. Menken); *Imagining Multilingual Schools* (with T. Skutnabb-Kangas and M. Torres-Guzmán); and *A Reader in Bilingual Education* (with C. Baker). She is the Associate General Editor of the *International Journal of the*

Sociology of Language, and has been a Fulbright Scholar, and also a Spencer Fellow of the US National Academy of Education.

PETER GARRETT is Professor of Language and Communication at the Centre for Language and Communication Research at Cardiff University, Wales, UK. His teaching areas include sociolinguistics, language attitudes, persuasive communication and media communication. Much of his research has centred on attitudes to language and communication, and on language and globalization. He has published widely in international journals in these fields, and his recent books include *Investigating Language Attitudes* (co-authored by Nikolas Coupland and Angie Williams, 2003) and *Attitudes to Language* (2010). He was editor of the journal *Language Awareness* between 1993 and 2008.

MADHAV KAFLE is a doctoral candidate at Pennsylvania State University, USA. He has taught English at school and college level in Nepal and has worked with ESL students in the US. World Englishes, multilingual writing and critical approaches to literacy and pedagogy constitute his major research interests.

NKONKO M. KAMWANGAMALU is Professor of Linguistics and Director of Graduate Studies in the Department of English at Howard University, Washington, DC, USA. He holds an MA and a PhD in linguistics from the University of Illinois at Urbana-Champaign, and has also received a Fulbright Award and a Howard University Distinguished Faculty Research Award. He has taught at the National University of Singapore, the University of Swaziland and the University of Natal in Durban, South Africa, where he was Director of the Linguistics Program. His research interests include language policy and planning, codeswitching, New Englishes, language and identity, and African linguistics. He has published numerous articles in refereed journals and books and is the author of the monograph *The language planning situation in South Africa* (2001) and co-editor of *Language and Institution in Africa* (2000). He has also edited special issues on language in South Africa for the following journals: *Multilingua* 17 (1998), *International Journal of the Sociology of Language* 144 (2000), *World Englishes* 21(2002), and *Language Problems and Language Planning* 28(2004). He is Polity Editor for the journal *Current Issues in Language Planning*.

DAVID LASAGABASTER is an associate professor at the University of the Basque Country, Spain. He has published on second/third language acquisition, CLIL (Content and Language Integrated Learning), attitudes and motivation, and multilingualism. He has published widely in international journals, books and edited books. He co-edited *Multilingualism in European Bilingual Contexts: Language Use and Attitudes* (2007) and *CLIL in Spain: Implementation, Results and Teacher Training* (2010), and he is co-author of *Plurilingualism and Interculturality at School* (2010). Since 2008 he has been a member of the executive committee of the International Association for Language Awareness.

ENRIC LLURDA teaches English and Applied Linguistics at the Universitat de Lleida, Catalonia, Spain. His research interests are English as an international language, multilingualism, attitudes to languages, language policies related to the internationalisation of European universities, and most notably non-native language teachers. He has published several journal articles and book chapters on those areas, and has edited a widely-referenced volume on non-native teachers, *Non-Native Language Teachers: Perceptions, Challenges and Contributions to the Profession* (2005). He is a member of the editorial board of six international journals and has been invited as keynote speaker at conferences in Australia, Turkey, Colombia and Catalonia.

IAN G. MALCOLM is Emeritus Professor and Honorary Professor at Edith Cowan University, Australia, where he retired as Professor of Applied Linguistics in 2003. His research into Aboriginal English has involved cross-cultural and bi-dialectal research teams and has pursued linguistic, discourse, pragmatic, conceptual and diachronic dimensions of the dialect. In collaboration with the Education Department of Western Australia he has worked towards the development of two-way bidialectal education delivered by teams of Aboriginal and non-Aboriginal educators.

YUMI MATSUMOTO is a PhD candidate in Applied Linguistics at Pennsylvania State University, USA. She has taught English at secondary schools in Japan for five years and is currently working with ESL students at university level in the US. Her academic interests include World Englishes/ English as a *lingua franca*, Second Language Writing, Conversation Analysis, and multilingual identities.

STEPHEN MAY is Professor of Education in the School of Critical Studies in Education, Faculty of Education, University of Auckland, New Zealand. He is also an Honorary Research Fellow in the Centre for the Study of Ethnicity and Citizenship, University of Bristol, UK. He has written widely on language rights and language education. His key books include *Language and Minority Rights*, originally published in 2001 and reprinted in 2008. The reprinted edition was recognized as one of the American Library Association Choice's Outstanding Academic titles. He has since published a fully revised second edition of *Language and Minority Rights* (2012). He edited, with Nancy Hornberger, *Language Policy and Political Issues in Education*, Volume 1 of the ten-volume *Encyclopedia of Language and Education* (2nd edn, 2008); and with Christine Sleeter, *Critical Multiculturalism: Theory and praxis* (2010). He is a Founding Editor of the interdisciplinary journal *Ethnicities* and Associate Editor of *Language Policy*.

SANDRA LEE MCKAY is Professor Emeritus of San Francisco State University, USA. Presently she is an affiliate member of the Second Language Studies Department at the University of Hawaii. Her main areas of interest are sociolinguistics, globalization and the spread of English, particularly as these areas relate to second language learning and teaching. For most of her career she has been involved in second language teacher education, both in the US and abroad. She has received four Fulbright grants, as well as many academic specialists awards and distinguished lecturer invitations. Her books include *Sociolinguistics and Language Education* (edited with Nancy Hornberger, 2010), *International English in its Sociolinguistic Contexts: Towards a Socially Sensitive Pedagogy* (with Wendy Bokhorst-Heng, 2008) and *Teaching English as an International Language: Rethinking*

Goals and Approaches (2002). She served as *TESOL Quarterly* editor from 1994 to 1999.

JEFF SIEGEL is Adjunct Professor in Linguistics at the University of New England, Australia. His main areas of research concern the processes involved in the development of contact languages, and the use of such languages in formal education. He has worked specifically on Melanesian Pidgin, Hawai'i Creole, Pidgin Fijian and Pidgin Hindustani. His most recent books are *The Emergence of Pidgin and Creole Languages* (2008) and *Second Dialect Acquisition* (2010).

ADRIANO TRUSCOTT is a primary and English as an additional language/dialect (EAL/D) teacher and linguist. He has worked with the ABC of Two-Way Literacy and Learning project of the Western Australian Department of Education researching cultural cognitive linguistic aspects of Australian Aboriginal English. He has run numerous language revival projects, published books in Aboriginal languages, and been involved in language policy consultation committees and developing language courses. He has been a member of state and national consultation committees on languages and EAL/D. He is currently the Westralian Association of Teachers of English to Speakers of Other Languages (WATESOL) councillor for, and secretary of, the Australian Council of TESOL Associations, and committee member for the UK-based Foundation for Endangered Languages.

LINDA TSUNG is Chair of the Department of Chinese Studies in the Faculty of Arts and Social Sciences within the University of Sydney, Australia, an Honorary Associate Professor in the Faculty of Education within the University of Hong Kong and Vice President of the International Association of Bilingual Studies. She has a track record in research into multi-lingual and multi-cultural education. She is author of many publications including the recent book *Minority Languages, Education and Communities in China* (2009), and a co-editor (with Ken Cruickshank) of *Teaching and Learning Chinese in Global Contexts* (2010).

HEATHER HOMONOFF WOODLEY is completing her doctorate in Urban Education and is researching the identities and language development of recently-arrived Muslim immigrant youth in a newcomer high school. Her research includes arts education and popular culture. She is currently an adjunct lecturer in TESOL and Bilingual Education at the City College of New York, USA. In the past, she has taught Bilingual/ESL and English Language Arts in NYC and Washington, DC public schools.

ANDROULA YIAKOUMETTI is an applied linguist at Oxford Brookes University, UK. Her research focuses on regional and social variation within linguistic systems and, more specifically, on the implications of such variation for education. She is interested in sociolinguistic aspects of linguistic variation and works within the research fields of multidialectism and multilingualism, second-language acquisition and language-teacher development. Her publications span a variety of language issues including bidialectism, language attitudes, learning of English as a foreign language and language-teacher training.

Index

RETHINKING EDUCATION

Rethinking education has never been more important. While there are many examples of good, innovative practice in teaching and learning at all levels, the conventional education mindset has proved largely resistant to pedagogic or systemic change, remaining preoccupied with the delivery of standardised packages in a standardised fashion, relatively unresponsive to the diversity of learners' experiences and inclinations as well as to the personal perspectives of individual teachers. The challenge of our times in relation to education is to help transform that mindset.

This series takes up this challenge. It re-examines perennial major issues in education and opens up new ones. It includes, but is not confined to, pedagogies for transforming the learning experience, any-time-any-place learning, new collaborative technologies, fresh understandings of the roles of teachers, schools and other educational institutions, providing for different learning styles and for students with special needs, and adapting to changing needs in a changing environment.

This peer-reviewed series publishes monographs, doctoral dissertations, conference proceedings, edited books, and interdisciplinary studies. It welcomes writings from a variety of perspectives and a wide range of disciplines. Proposals should be sent to any or all of the series editors: Dr Marie Martin, mmartin@martech.org.uk; Dr Gerry Gaden, gerry.gaden@ucd.ie; and Dr Judith Harford, judith.harford@ucd.ie.

Vol. 3   Judith Harford and Claire Rush (eds): Have Women Made
a Difference? Women in Irish Universities, 1850–2010.
248 pages. 2010. ISBN 978-3-0343-0116-9

Vol. 4   Maura O'Connor: The Development of Infant Education in
Ireland, 1838–1948: Epochs and Eras.
325 pages. 2010. ISBN 978-3-0343-0142-8

Vol. 5   Androula Yiakoumetti (ed.): Harnessing Linguistic Variation
to Improve Education.
328 pages. 2012. ISBN 978-3-0343-0726-0

Vols 6-8   Forthcoming.

Vol. 9   Thomas G. Grenham and Patricia Kieran (eds): New
Educational Horizons in Contemporary Ireland: Trends and
Challenges.
399 pages. 2012. ISBN 978-3-0343-0274-6

Vol. 10 Anthony David Roberts: The Role of Metalinguistic
Awareness in the Effective Teaching of Foreign Languages.
433 pages. 2011. ISBN 978-3-0343-0280-7

Vol. 11 Forthcoming.

Vol. 12 Thomas Walsh: Primary Education in Ireland, 1897–1990:
Curriculum and Context.
488 pages. 2012. ISBN 978-3-0343-0751-2